Praise for

Deceptions and Doublecross: How the NHL Conquered Hockey

(with Joseph Nieforth)

"Morey Holzman and Joseph Nieforth have written a very important book that documents hockey's rough and tumble past... their book deserves widespread reading and debate."

Journal of Sports History

"It fills a void in the early history of pro hockey in Canada."

The Globe and Mail

"A well-researched historical challenge to the standard view of the NHL's birth...one of the best books of the year."

The Hockey News

"This refreshing history reminds us that the NHL resulted frtom a bitter power struggle that included courtroom battles, backroom dealing and personal grudges as brutal as anything seen today on the ice."

The New Brunswick Reader

The Odd Fellow's Heart

Morey Holzman

Hockey Research Association

 For information, address Hockey Research Association, 2434 Auto Park Way Ste 200, Escondido, Calif. 92026.

www.hrabooks.com

Designed by Rose Miller.

The Library of Congress Cataloguing-in-Publication Data
Library of Congress Control Number: 2020914446

Names: The Odd Fellow's Heart
Description: Escondido, CA: Hockey Research Association, 2020
Identifiers: LCCN 2020914446 | ISBN 978-1-63615-001-7 (hardcover)
Subjects: LCSH: Sports – History
Classification: LCC | DDC LC record available at https://lccn.loc.gov/2020914446

ISBN 978-1-63615-000-0 (ebook)

Our books may be purchased in bulk for promotional, educational, or business use. Please contact your local bookseller or the Hockey Research Association Premium Sales Department at 1-760-445-0534, or by email, HRAPremiumsales@hrabooks.com

23 22 21 20 19 1 2 3 4 5

Dedicated to those who serve faithfully, honestly and lovingly, without being asked, and with integrity, even if the truth is not always clean and easy. And to Bill Fitsell, a founder of the Society for International Hockey Research, who has spent a lifetime researching hockey's beginnings.

TABLE OF CONTENTS

INTRODUCTION

One of the great hockey historians, the late Paul Kitchen, wrote about the dangers of using newspapers as sources in his 2008 book *Win, Tie or Wrangle*, which told the story of Ottawa hockey from its inception until the original Ottawa Senators became the St. Louis Eagles.

Kitchen explained the differences in newspaper reporting on the March 7, 1892, game between the Montreal Amateur Hockey Association and Ottawa Hockey Club, with the winner being declared champion of Canada and eventual winner of the first Stanley Cup.

Kitchen wrote that both the *Ottawa Journal* and *Montreal Gazette* agreed on the lineups, that the Ottawa ice was in bad shape and that the game was rough. "Beyond those points, the two papers seemed to be covering two completely different contests," Kitchen wrote. To illustrate, he continued:

> The only goal of the match, by MAAA's [Montreal Amateur Athletic Association's Archie] Hodgson, was, in the eyes of the *Journal*, "a lucky lift." To the *Gazette* it was a "well directed shot." To the *Journal*, the stoppages in play during the first half, when one Montrealer was shaken up and another had his skate lace broken, were too long and gave the visitors an unfair chance to rest. The *Gazette* took little note. The *Journal* continued its theme of too much breathing time for MAAA, saying the halftime break lasted sixteen minutes. It was the standard ten-minute break, the *Gazette* said . . . Was the officiating good or bad?

> The *Journal*: "A referee is needed who has the courage and knowledge of the game to stop tripping." The *Gazette*: "Jack Arnton made an excellent referee."[1]

Paul Kitchen was correct.

However, there are important undeniable facts to be gleaned through reading both newspapers' accounts.

1. Montreal won 1–0.
2. Jack Arnton was the referee and was one of the four men who wrote the rules. Knowledge should not have been an issue, but he might have had a bad day, or a bad train trip from his home in Montreal, or a bad meal before the game. It is safe to say one side was unhappy with his officiating.
3. The break, which may have been extra long, benefitted both teams. The question of fairness is open to the reader's interpretation.
4. A "lucky lift" or a "well directed shot?" I guess the unprinted corollary is "lousy goaltending" or "unstoppable." A better question: Who cares? The game is not won by how, but by how many.

The study of history is enhanced when the perspectives of the actual people involved are included. President Donald Trump gave biased reporting a name—"fake news"—although in Trump's case, he included news that may have actually been true but didn't fit his narrative.

Fake news has been involved in hockey reporting as long as there was hockey, as evidenced by Kitchen's comments. While writing *Deceptions and Doublecross: How the NHL Conquered Hockey* during 2000 and 2001, I relied heavily on newspaper sources. Most chapters began with a published comment by Elmer Ferguson on the forming of the NHL—stories he told over and over after being the last survivor from those early years—and most chapters easily proved that Ferguson not only was reporting "fake news," but also he was blatantly lying.

It's true that *Deceptions and Doublecross* never made anybody's best-seller list. But to those who research hockey, and for those historians who need a better understanding, my previous book has proven to be invaluable. More than sixty books have quoted from it, in English and in French.

Now an admission: *Deceptions and Doublecross* is not 100 percent historically accurate. But at the time of its original publication, the NHL's own story of how the league was formed was only about 10 percent honest. And this point is also very important: at the time of publication the NHL did not intentionally lie about its origins. No one in the league office had ever had a reason to doubt the words of Ferguson, while no one alive actually knew what really transpired. Professional hockey spent its first eighty years just trying to find a way to survive. To get closer to what truly happened, another imperfect history book, John Chi-Kit Wong's 2005 *Lords of the Rinks*, should be read in conjunction with *Deceptions and Doublecross*.

The Odd Fellow's Heart is not 100 percent accurate either. There are gaps where a fictionalized retelling as a movie may better serve the subject. But in telling a story that literally has never before been told and with all of the participants long deceased, it's close. There are experiences unrecorded that, unfortunately, died with the participants.

Kitchen, in whose honor the Society for International Hockey Researchers gives an annual award for the best project, once wrote a story called "They Refused the Stanley Cup," which told in a superficial way the story of how the Montreal Hockey Club refused to accept Lord Stanley's gift from the Stanley Cup trustees. Kitchen wrote with detail a one-sided perspective of how fragile the Montreal players' egos must have been to refuse something that today is the most popular trophy in all of sports.

What Kitchen missed is what journalism is supposed to bring: the other side of the story. No spoiler alert here. You'll have to read chapters 14 and 16 in order to get a deeper understanding of the controversy. It's safe to say if Paul were still alive, he would agree with me that his story needs a rewrite, and the only place to get the "non-fake-news" evidence was from a newspaper-published *mea culpa* from one of the antagonists.

That being said, I wish I had access to the *Montreal Post.* Montreal had four English language dailies at the time, each paper with their own version of facts. The *Herald*, *Gazette* and *Daily Witness* have a good run of their newspapers digitized. The *Post* does not. The *Post* also had the largest circulation of the era. This historian and former journalist would like to believe that people read the *Post* more because it was more accurate and honest. None of those readers are alive to be asked that question.

And without trying to step into the Quebec language issue—of which I am neither an interested party nor intelligent enough to have an opinion worth listening to—it would be my hope that Quebec libraries would make it easier for English researchers trying to find English newspapers such as the *Post.* When my son and I were researching in the Montreal Public Library, I'm very appreciative my bilingual friend Jean-Patrice Martel was there to help translate the written instruction on how to use the microfilm machine. Keep in mind it was local English history—in an area where English was once the dominant language—where the library was located and needed because there was no other English-language source available.

I hope I didn't start a fight.

CHAPTER 1
A HOCKEY FIGHT

The Swedish people, and especially their hockey players, do not have a reputation for being fighters.

Tell that to the seven million hockey fans throughout North America who turned on the television to watch Game Five of the 2017 Stanley Cup Final, and another estimated twenty-two million who watched in China.[2]

The Pittsburgh Penguins led the Nashville Predators 6–0 with eight and a half minutes left in the third period. Pittsburgh defenseman Ron Hainsey dumped the puck into the Predator zone and then circled back to his bench for a line change. Nashville's P. K. Subban chased the dump-in behind his own net while the Penguins' Patric Hornqvist aggressively forechecked him. Hornqvist checked Subban in the back as the Predator defenseman skated behind the net after the loose puck. Subban was knocked off his stride for a moment, which freed the puck, but Roman Josi, Subban's defensive partner, stepped into Hornqvist.

The Pittsburgh forward took offense and softly slashed Josi on the elbow. Josi retaliated with a crosscheck in the back, and then Evgeni Malkin took over for Hornqvist, punching then tackling Josi onto the ice. Nashville's Viktor Arvidsson joined the fray with his elbow raised and skated into Carl Hagelin. Tempers flared due to the soft, but potentially dangerous—and completely unnecessary—hit in a 6–0 blowout. Arvidsson met Hagelin with a glove in the face, under Hagelin's eye shield. Hagelin managed to knock Arvidsson's helmet off, and the two danced around for about fifteen seconds with Arvidsson throwing three left-handed punches into Hagelin's jaw before the Pittsburgh forward turtled up and the fight stopped on its own.

This was the last fight in the Stanley Cup Final prior to publication, but what is startling are a few random notes:

There were definitely punches thrown, but Arvidsson and Hagelin received misconducts (although the play-by-play on nhl.com lists fighting). As of the beginning of the 2020–21 season, neither player had officially received a fighting major in his career.

Arvidsson, Hagelin and Hornqvist are all from Sweden, and Josi is from Switzerland. Neither nation nor its people are renown for fisticuffs and brawling.

And yet, here, in the heat of the battle of a 6–0 blowout chasing the hardest trophy to win in sports, these European men were dropping gloves and acting, well, American.

Although fighting is widely accepted as part of today's NHL, emotions and fisticuffs were much more restrained during hockey's gentlemanly beginnings.

One hundred and thirty years earlier the founders and gentlemanly organizers of the children's game of shinny would be incredulous if they could foresee what would transpire. They had enough trouble persuading someone to officiate their friendly little game, with the bickering between the clubs creating up to an hour delay.

There are several ways to start a hockey fight in Canada. An insult to one's parentage is the old standby.

But for more antagonistic fun, visit Windsor, Nova Scotia, or Deline in the Northwest Territories and tell the locals that hockey was not started there.[3] During the past twenty years, hockey historians have almost "dropped the gloves" in meetings intended to discuss this very subject.

The battle to discover the truth nearly 150 years after the fact is harder than playing double overtime in Game Seven. Hockey's origin is a difficult and emotional subject that often leads to one's interpretation of when the current evolution of hockey turned into the game we know, and how an unwanted Stanley Cup became so desirable that one Swiss and three Swedish players were willing to fight for it in a 6–0 game.

The game as played seriously started in Montreal, and as the city and culture with a head start in the sport, there are certain nuances that Canadians have toward their sport versus Americans and other cultures who have adapted and adopted hockey as their own.

One of the subtle differences between an American and Canadian view on hockey is that most Americans look at any game with a stick, an object you strike and a goal as some version of hockey. Canadians, due to their strong British heritage, look at the child's unorganized and unstructured play as something different than hockey. Commonly called *shinny*, the Canadian easily differentiates between the two. Many Americans do not.

The largely English Canadian argument of where and when hockey began all has to do with where one defines shinny and how it evolved into the sport watched and played by millions worldwide.

As Canada's national sport, there is no shortage of pride or tourism board money being spent on promoting one place or another as the birthplace of hockey. Places such as Déline and Windsor unabashedly claim birthplace without consideration of context. The truth is, however, that most Canadians now grudgingly admit hockey was never born; it evolved.[4] The ones who believe it was born have fallen for fake news.

Even in 1887, less than twelve years after the "first" Montreal game, the *Montreal Herald* wrote, "Hockey is not, strictly speaking, a Canadian game so far as its origin is concerned, for under the various non de plumes of 'shinny,' 'hurley,' 'ball and stick,' etc. it has been known and played for centuries alike by the muscular Saxon youth and the light-hearted and fleet-of-foot lads of Donegal and Derry."[5]

However, thirteen months earlier, four Montreal men met on a frigid December night and updated the rule book, organized a league, published, publicized and shared hockey's new rule book, and gave birth to the modern evolution of hockey—direct ascendant to the game being played today.

The best contemporaneous account of how hockey began was written by Beverley Bogert, a Canadian expat whose lengthy 1893 story appeared in *Outing*, then one of America's most popular periodicals:

> The sport-loving people of the United States and Canada are quick to appreciate and adopt any new game which demands skill and courage in its participants, and at the same time is attractive to spectators. Such games as football, baseball and lacrosse combine all of these features admirably, and to this fact must chiefly be attributed to their growing popularity. What the young men of today want is a game wherein such valuable manly qualities as pluck, strength, agility and good judgment can be shown to the best advantage; and what the spectators want is a game that has dash and excitement connected with it, is lively from start to finish, and does not necessitate a too great consumption of busy folks' time in the watching of it.
>
> Such a game is what may be termed the national winter game of Canada—ice hockey—and it is quite safe to say that if climactic conditions allowed, it would speedily be the leading winter pastime in New York.
>
> Hockey is a skating game, therefore few Americans, comparatively speaking, can indulge in it. Where mild winters prevail it cannot flourish, and except in the most northerly States of the Union, it could never attain such a popularity as it has already found in Canada. There every town of a size sufficient to maintain a skating rink now possesses at least one club, while the larger cities and towns can number several. Montreal,

> the center of the game, and where the championship of Canada—for that matter, the world as well—is now held, boasts the greatest number. The members comprise fine specimens of manhood as the athletic world can produce.
>
> The name "hockey" is not an unfamiliar one, having been applied in England for years to a game somewhat resembling "shinny," and to which the modern game can claim a resemblance only through the fact that sticks are made use of in propelling an object towards and through a given goal. [6]

For many hockey historians that last paragraph is the missing link between the sport of the present and the game of the past. Even in 1893 it was recognized that the sport of hockey was something . . . different. Foreign. Unique.

A literary equivalent is the classic poem *Beowulf.*

According to Dr. Anne Savage, humanities professor at McMaster University, *Beowulf* is both strange and familiar: it has some links with the classic poems of Homer; nineteenth-century ideas of it have been received and reworked in the twentieth century in academia, children's literature and popular culture; and yet it remains an ancient artifact of a culture whose world we can never share.[7]

And the epic poem involves Swedes fighting.

With sticks.

Against predators.

Two Swedish hockey researchers—Carl Gidén and Patrick Houda—joined up with Montreal native Jean-Patrice Martel to throw new voices into the long-running debate as to hockey's origins—a debate that is as old as the sport itself. The three uncovered long-forgotten newspaper articles in Europe and wandered into a culture we can never share—innocent children and young adults, keeping active in an isolated part of the world, and finding an activity to keep themselves occupied.

If one were to hop into a TARDIS a la Doctor Who and travel back to the first attempt at commercializing the game in 1875, one would not recognize hockey as was played then compared to how it is being played today. In 1875 there were too many bodies and a wooden puck on the ice, which led to a slower game with minimal skating that looked like a cross between golf and field hockey. However, if one would fast-forward just eleven years to 1886, there would be some striking similarities to today's game.

To be fair, even today the sport constantly evolves—although these tend to be slow-moving glacial shifts compared to the lava-spewing, landscape-changing volcanic eruptions of the 1870s and 1880s.

Various forces contributed to changes over the years. Some of the evolution was due to concession sales—that's why there are three periods instead of two halves. Some rule tweaks needed to be made because a clever player or coach—and occasionally a referee—saw a loophole in the rules and exploited it. Instead of automatically criticizing the offending inventor, the hockey community sometimes adopted the change. This is how *changing on the fly*—unique to hockey—and *forechecking* came into being. Also born this way was hockey's greatest gift to all sports—*sudden death overtime*.

Sometimes the hockey community is slow to change. The World Hockey Association first gave us a *shootout* to decide tie games in a 1972 exhibition game in Duluth, Minnesota. It was so hated by the players that it took more than thirty years for the National Hockey League to incorporate shootouts as a regular-season feature.[8]

Sometimes the hockey community drops the verbal gloves and argues. In the late 1910s, for instance, the eastern-based National Hockey League played six-man hockey, and its western equivalent, the Pacific Coast Hockey Association, still played with a rover. Eventually the East won the argument, but not before several Stanley Cup Final series were played with alternating rules for the individual games.

And sometimes the terminology sticks even though the original interpretation is forever lost. Certainly, most hockey fans have heard of *playing the point* or the *point on the power play*. This term originated in the game's early days when a team's strategy looked more like football's T formation as opposed to the three-forward, two-defense horizontal approach familiar for the last one hundred-plus years. The *point* was a defensive position between the cover-point and the goaltender. Rarely would the point join the rush on offense; usually the point stayed on his half of the ice. It would be unusual for a point to take a shot on goal, let alone score one. Jimmy Stewart, one of the modern game's architects, was a point for the Montreal Hockey Club and played ten years at the highest level of hockey in the world. He not only never scored a goal, but also we could not locate one instance where he even crossed center ice, let alone took a shot—in his career. The cover-point, the player directly in front, might be more apt to go for a skate.

Jimmy Stewart, captain of Montreal Hockey Club

But that's hockey, as a sport. The game played for fun in England differed.

Original field hockey rules brought to ice by James Creighton in 1875 were modified or rewritten several times so that by 1886 the game—like *Beowulf* in its original Old English—is unrecognizable.

Wrote Bogert, "It is to be hoped that the game that has become so popular in Canada may find admirers and participants across the line, and in the near future we will find American clubs and competitors for the hockey championship of the world."[9]

American clubs in places such as Nashville, Tennessee.

Played by professionals.

From Sweden.

Who fight!

For the Stanley Cup?

With thirty million people watching?

Two words: unintended consequences.

CHAPTER 2
BROCKVILLE AND THE ODD FELLOWS

It's a typical Thursday summer evening in Brockville, Ontario. To major-city dwellers the scene would be remarkable—a giant-screen television is set up in the town park. Dozens of families—several multi-generational—bring their lawn chairs and their blankets onto the park grass—slightly wet due to a twenty-minute rainstorm that happened in the late afternoon. The children run, laugh, play and wander freely and safely as they wait for darkness to come. Being midsummer, the wait will be awhile. The main event, a Disney movie, will be the kids' nighttime programming once darkness falls.

Local volunteers representing a couple of service organizations sell popcorn, sodas and sweets for a couple of dollars; meanwhile the teenagers congregate and walk away into the historic area of the city, which is lined for visiting tourists with photos of the way Brockville used to look and the way it does today.

The park borders Home Street. Less than fifty steps from the park, Home Street ends in the St. Lawrence River. Not *at* the river, but actually *in* the river. Home Street is a boat ramp, without the ramp, perfect for a duck boat. There is a slight incline, but nothing too strenuous for any of the townspeople to walk if they were so inclined. Even in the dusk the trees south of Morristown, New York, across the St. Lawrence, look close enough to identify. In the winter the river freezes over and skating is en vogue after the snow is cleared.

The picturesque village is about 122 miles downriver from Montreal. Travel south another 194 miles, through and around the 1,864 islands that make up the Thousand Islands as the St. Lawrence becomes Lake Ontario, and the megalopolis of Toronto takes over the geography. In 1864, though, Canada's largest city was Montreal, with Toronto being three times smaller, housing about fifty thousand inhabitants.

Brockville in the 1860s was growing as the hubbub of activity involving the railroad brought the promises of jobs. Most residents hoped for a bridge to Morristown, which they could only visit by ferry in the summer or by skating across the St. Lawrence in the winter. There were churches in town, but complaints about the kids ice skating on the Sabbath instead of being in church were registered in the local papers as far back as 1824.[10]

Indoor skating rinks began popping up in the 1850s in Quebec. The Brockville Skating Rink opened in November 1863, featuring a 132-foot-long by 60-foot-wide ice surface, located at the corner of James and Garden Streets.[11] The rink was underutilized, as the kids apparently preferred to skate on the river for free. The rink has long since been torn down.

The New World gave many immigrants an opportunity that only one hundred years earlier would have required—even for white men—indentured servitude. Hopes and dreams of a better life, of better opportunities, of freedom, drove many of the immigrants to this part of Canada. As Malcolm Gladwell alludes in his best-selling book *Outliers: The Story of Success*, timing is a good chunk of being at the right place at the right time. What Gladwell did not mention is the law of unintended consequences—sometimes life just doesn't work out as planned.

For society's most vulnerable and optimistic, sometimes hopes and dreams become cruelly crushed.

A Scottish émigré named Alexander Hardie was one such victim. Hardie had emigrated from Scotland, while his wife Harriet left England with her family to find a new life in Canada East. They met in Trois-Rivières, fell in love and married in 1808. In 1811 Harriet gave birth to John. William followed in 1815, and Thomas was born in 1820. In 1826, at the age of forty, Harriet Hardie died.[12] Five years later, her husband Alex also died. At the time of their father's death the boys became separated. John went to the southern United States but eventually wound his way to New York, and William remained in Montreal, while Thomas went initially to Kingston in Canada West, but subsequently to the United States.

The three boys still somehow found a way to communicate as Thomas introduced John to the ways of the International Order of Odd Fellows. John joined the New York lodge in 1842.

To the uninitiated the Odd Fellows had strange rituals and rules. The fraternal club's stated goals were to give mutual assistance in times of sickness and to help defray funeral expenses. The society—not the first nor original in nature—began in England and had made its way across the Atlantic in 1819.

The newly born United States had just survived the War of 1812 and maintained her independence from Great Britain. The new republic was gaining a worldwide reputation offering the best in shelter, homes and advantages to the oppressed and poor. The world was changing. Mexico gained its independence in 1821. Napoleon Bonaparte had ended his career of warfare and ambition in death. Under the smiling countenance of peace, civilization and good and free government extended their arms of refinement and protection to some of the older, and much of the newly acquired territory. At least for white people.

The tide of good feeling and the era of prosperity had blessed the nascent nation during the first term of James Monroe, granted that statesman four more years, and sealed for all time the popularity of his doctrine.

Providence smiled, and peace and content folded its wings and settled in most homes. Almost unconsciously to the surrounding world, American Odd Fellowship was born. Its birth was unsung and unhonored. Nursed in secrecy, performing its deeds of charity in the modest manner required by Divine law, its growth was unnoticed by those without the pale of membership.[13]

The three dispersed Canadian brothers—John, William and Thomas Hardie—did in adulthood what was ripped away from their youth. William, the son who stayed in Montreal, started a successful paints and oils business and asked John to return and help.

The oldest Hardie brother returned to Montreal and met George Matthews, a past Grand of the Brooklyn Odd Fellows chapter who had moved to Montreal to become an engraver and lithographer. The two men started the first Canadian chapter of the International Order of Odd Fellows in 1843. So successful were the two men that within the first week of starting the Prince of Wales Lodge, eighteen men joined.

Thomas, who had settled in Springfield, Illinois, being a past Grand of the Odd Fellows lodge there, returned home to help his brothers. Within a few months, a second lodge opened in Montreal.

By 1845, lodges had spread into Canada West, with the second lodge—and ninth in the territory—being granted to Brockville, the small picturesque town on the St. Lawrence River that was founded by American Tories loyal to England.[14]

The Odd Fellows remain non-political and non-sectarian—a fraternal order whose members seek to live a better life through love, friendship and honesty.

The initial success of the Odd Fellows reads like a Who's Who of pre-Confederation Canadian citizenry—no fewer than thirty-four leading statesmen, members of Parliament, prominent merchants and manufacturers joined in Montreal. The Odd Fellows became the largest social club in British North America's largest city.

Many of the Canadian lodges were seen as private social clubs by many of its members. Its early members generally belonged to the nation's wealthiest. Some of the original Odd Fellows included Hugh Allan, the founder of Allan Shipping Line and the Merchant's Bank of Montreal; John A. MacDonald, who would become the first prime minister of Canada; William Henry Draper, who was joint premier of Canada at the time and later Chief Justice of the Errors and Appeals Court of Onatario; and John Torrance, who incorporated the Champlain & St. Lawrence Railroad and in 1853 merged it into the Grand Trunk Railroad.[15]

By the time the train rolled into Brockville in the 1850s the Odd Fellows were down to six lodges operating in the province, and membership had dwindled from a high of 2,300 to 512 members. The Montreal chapters lost so many members that all its lodges closed, but Brock No. 9 thrived.

The very character of the membership of the Odd Fellow pioneers proved to be its downfall. The early Odd Fellows belonged to the wealthy classes of society and were mostly young men. "Odd-Fellowship was not with them a great practical system of mutual relief so much as a social institution. They were prepared to be charitable . . . (but) as the members grew older, and became more deeply interested in their private business and involved in public life, they lost interest in the Society, could find no time to devote to its affairs, and finally dropped out altogether.[16]

A resurgence by 1879 saw the number of Odd Fellow lodges in Ontario increase to 186, and the number of members jumped to more than twelve thousand.[17] Such was the status of Brock Lodge, that lodges across Canada West gathered on August 23, 1855, for the purpose of instituting "The Grand Lodge of Canada West."

Members of the Odd Fellows are instructed to be dedicated to recreation, to help make the world a better place, to improve and elevate the character of mankind and to promote goodwill and harmony amongst people. Its simplistic command is to visit the sick, relieve the distressed, bury the dead and educate the orphan.

The Odd Fellows fulfilled a role that government couldn't. Without a system of taxation, there were very few government services offered, and when tragedy struck a family, it was up to the victims to find a way to survive. Some churches fulfilled that role in some communities, but not universally.

The Odd Fellows also believe in athletic endeavors. Keeping the body sharp is as important as keeping the spirit of friendship, love and truth for fellow human beings. The triple link chain logo reminds members with the letters *F*, *L* and *T* inside. When the Odd Fellows buried the dead, its Protestant members honored its Jewish members as well as its Catholic members. When a widow needed housing, the religion in the household became secondary to the need for the widow to have housing. This particular humane belief was certainly considered odd for the times. The industrial revolution was in full bloom in the United States, and the British Isles were starting to catch up. In Ireland there were five hundred miles of railroad track.[18] The British Parliament authorized eight thousand miles for rail construction.[19] In 1850 British North America, by contrast, there were only sixty-six miles of track. Canada's Guarantee Act, passed in 1849, changed all that. Under the Act, railways that were longer than seventy-five miles were eligible to receive a government grant that guaranteed interest of up to 6 percent on half its bonds once half of the railway was completed. The Act established government assistance for railway building, and in the process, inspired a railway-building frenzy that led companies and government to overextend themselves financially.[20]

Centrally located, Brockville was selected as the southern terminus for both the Grand Trunk Railroad and the Brockville & Ottawa Railway.

The very first train rolled into Brockville, Ontario, on November 19, 1855, from Montreal. The origin station celebrated with a colorful parade to show off Canada's progressive new industries. One year after the train rolled into Brockville for the first time, the first Montreal to Toronto train was completed.

Rail construction affected every Canada West community, as wealthy citizens and municipalities invested into projects to build the railbed and stations. Suppliers sold wood and tools. And thousands of laborers, especially displaced Irish immigrants, found jobs.[21]

The culture of Brockville seems as innocent today as it was in the 1850s, when Irish immigrants flooded the town looking for a better life. Approximately one million Irish died in the potato famine, about the same number as the diaspora to the New World. But most of the Irish settled in Boston and New York at the other end of their ocean voyage. Relatively few settled into the interior.

But if one digs a little deeper, beyond the pleasantries, one finds an almost utopian sophisticated view of humanity. Kindness, trust, love, friendliness.

Respect.

Many of the Irish that emigrated into Canada did not leave their homeland because of the famine, according to historian Don H. Akenson. The Queen's University professor is widely acknowledged as the world's foremost expert in the history of worldwide Irish migration, and he noted the locals knew what was going on in the world, despite Brockville's apparent isolation.

"The Brockville Odd Fellows lodge, in voting [to provide] relief funds for the distressed overseas, showed, in addition to a sense of charity, a degree of sophistication about the Famine that even most modern historians would do well to note," Akenson wrote.

"They recognized what is too often forgotten, that the potato famine was not solely an Irish famine but a disaster affecting all potato-dependent regions in the British Isles."

Akenson pointed out that the Odd Fellows donated £107 (approximately $24,000 Canadian today in a town of less than five thousand people) for famine relief, £77 pounds went to the Irish and £30 was allocated to the Scottish highlanders.[22]

John and Mariah Stewart emigrated from Antrim, Northern Ireland, to Brockville around the time of the Great Famine, bringing their son Alex with them. But Antrim was as far removed from the Great Famine as any city in Ireland. The repercussions of the diseased potato crops did not affect the Protestant North—fewer than 5 percent were hungry, and Lord Antrim had set up soup kitchens for those who were. The town of Antrim and its approximately fifty-five hundred residents was itself an important industrial center and was prospering during the British Industrial Revolution.[23] Only 15 percent of the population left Antrim, compared to 30 percent or more throughout the rest of the country.[24]

The citizens of Antrim, including the Stewarts, were Protestants who were English loyalists. The Northern Irish had more in common with the English than they had with the Irish Catholics on the rest of the Emerald Isle. That war was brought to North America with the emigrants. Most of the Catholic Irish did not sail past New York City or Boston, but many Catholics and Protestants continued down the St. Lawrence River to Quebec City and points south. The new locality, named British North America, felt like home to the Irish, many of whom had fled the Great Famine. This part of the New World was agrarian.

Unlike many of the estimated one million Irish immigrants—mostly Catholic—who were fleeing starvation or death, the departure of the Stewarts from Antrim was a little bit odd, as they sailed down to the Irish Protestant community of Brockville, then a town of barely two thousand residents.

Success soon found its way to the Stewarts, however. A nineteen-year-old Irish immigrant could expect to make 90 cents per day for his labor, which was an improvement on 65 cents to 75 cents per day for agricultural work.[25]

Alex Stewart was one such hard-working immigrant. But the powers of capitalism and the hope of financial security also has a dark side—many immigrants were one disaster or accident away from being destitute. Immigrants like the Stewarts knew the possibility, but hope helped them push forward. In Brockville, it was the Odd Fellows who helped unite those families when tragedy struck. Alexander Stewart, who lived very close to Brock Lodge #9, became a member.

Stewart joined the Grand Trunk Railroad in 1856, soon after the first train rolled into the town. As a nineteen-year-old, Stewart was primed to join Canada West's exciting new industry. Even today, Brockville brags about hosting Canada's first train tunnel, having turned it into a four-block walkway, complete with sound effects and a laser show. The walkthrough is free.

International Order of Odd Fellows Brock Lodge, located on King Street West in Brockville until 2019.

From at least the 1890s (records of prior years are lost), the Odd Fellows met on the second floor of a three-story gray brick building on King Street in Brockville's historic Centre Ward, on the corner of Apple Street, and one short block away from Home Street, where a kid could strap on his skates in the winter time and skate clear across to New York and back.

Whether Alex Stewart met James Wilson prior to joining the organization or inside the building at an Odd Fellows meeting is lost in history, but what isn't lost is that soon after Canada's census counters moved on, Stewart's personal life would change. Soon after James's daughter Louisa turned eighteen, she became Mrs. Alexander Stewart. Their first son was named John after Alex's father and was born in 1862. Two years later followed another son, named James after Louisa's father. And in 1866, the growing family welcomed daughter Edith into the fold.

In Alexander Stewart's life story the timing proved to be both good and bad fortune.

The end of the decade was tough on the family. In 1869, Louisa's father, James, died. And a year later, on November 15, 1870, Louisa herself was just twenty-six when she, too, died. The Odd Fellows helped bury both, while Alex Stewart and his three children moved in with his mother-in-law, Catherine, who still had three children of her own living in her home. Alex's younger brother William also resided with them.

If Alex Stewart dwelled on his situation, he left no record behind. Instead he spent more time with the International Order of Odd Fellows. Alex plugged ahead in the wake of the tragedy. The laborer was asked to be a witness as Louisa's eighteen-year-old sister, Charlotte, married twenty-year-old English immigrant Emmanuel Auburn. Also witnessing the March 23, 1872, wedding was Louisa and Charlotte's thirty-year-old sister, Mary.

The two witnesses themselves were wed in Brockville on January 4, 1873.[26] Stewart's professional life with the Grand Trunk Railroad also began to blossom. He was promoted to engineer, thanks to his ability and strict attention to detail.

Alex Stewart fathered another daughter with Mary in 1875. They named the child Louisia, after Alex's first wife (and Mary's deceased sister).

One Odd Fellows ideal imparted from father to son was the need to be physically engaged as in sport. When Jimmy was eleven years old, Montreal's new Victoria Rink in Montreal gave opportunities for people to play hockey inside, without having to worry about drowning in the lakes or rivers because the ice hadn't completely frozen over. It is highly unlikely that young Jimmy Stewart knew about James Creighton's attempt to bring hockey indoors. Highly unlikely because the local Brockville newspapers did not report it, but since his father was a railroad driver who frequented Montreal often, it is possible, but unlikely, the *Montreal Gazette* story reached the Stewart household.

Regardless, the Odd Fellows preached athleticism, and Stewart was raised with the Old World British amateur ideal, an ideal best described by former professional golfer turned orthopedic surgeon turned Olympic historian Bill Mallon. "Amateurism really started when the people who were rowing boats on the Thames for a living started beating all the rich British aristocrats," Mallon told the *Atlantic*'s Patrick Hruby. "That wasn't right. So they started a concept of amateurism that didn't exist in ancient Greece, extending it more and more to the notion of being a gentleman, someone who didn't work for a living and only did sport as a hobby."[27]

Growing up in a household full of people, young Jimmy Stewart found his wintertime escape by skating on the St. Lawrence River. When the river froze, the locals didn't sit idly by, according to Lorna Johnston of the Brockville Historical Society. "People often walked across," Johnston said. "I remember my great grandfather telling me stories of how he used to park a car on the banks of the river, and then they would take bets to see when the ice would thaw."

And while the car was still decades away from being invented when Jimmy Stewart was a child growing up in Brockville, it is easy to see that ice thick enough at the banks to hold a vehicle would be thick and safe enough to skate on—once the snow was cleared. "Strangely, the children would often rather skate on the river than at the rink," Johnston said.

The distance from Brockville to Morristown is about a mile to a mile-and-a-half, depending on where one jumps onto the ice on the Brockville side. Jimmy Stewart could skate to the United States in about six minutes.

As Hruby specifically surmised, snooty British elites who enjoyed rowing, winning and keeping the unwashed day-laboring masses at arm's length tried to exclude competition. [28]

Those unwashed, unwanted immigrants like Alexander Stewart and his family would prove they had a lot to offer amateur sport and that they, too, could live with the concept of not getting paid to play. But since historians often focus their storytelling on the more glamorous exploits of the elite, the contributions of hard-working people such as the Stewarts often get overlooked and unreported.

CHAPTER 3
THE ORIGINS OF HOCKEY

In *Outliers*, Gladwell wrote that one reason people have success is that they are born or raised at the right time and right place. He illustrates Bill Gates as an example. The future Microsoft founder happened to have free computer time at the University of Washington at a period of time when those who needed to earn a living were slogging through punch cards and IBM mainframe computers. Gates learning a new system while on a high school work-study program was a unique opportunity at a unique location at a unique moment of time.

"I had a better exposure to software development at a young age than I think anyone did in that period of time, and all because of an incredibly lucky series of events," Gates told Gladwell.[29]

Bill Gates could not have foreseen how his life would develop as he was working on the University of Washington's new system, and one hundred years earlier a group of young men in Montreal had no idea what they were about to create as well, as hockey began its journey from a children's game to a serious sport and business that provides tens of thousands of people jobs, whether as professional players, coaches, officials, administrators, ticket takers or concessionaires.

One change that affected Canadian lifestyles in the 1870s and 1880s and therefore opened the door for the creation of hockey was the growth of the new middle class. And those Irish and

Scottish residents who immigrated into Canada just to suffer for years would be the beneficiaries of the changes. Canada became self-governing in 1867, through a series of discussions that included concerns about shipping goods from the port of Halifax to other colonies. Building a railroad would be a very convenient method. By 1871 there was little immigration to the new nation. In addition, the United States and its aggressive Manifest Destiny agenda created fears in Canada that its southern neighbor was going to poach the lands now known as the Canadian Prairies. In response Parliament passed the Dominion Lands Act in an attempt to have its citizens migrate to the west as opposed to emigrating to the United States. The act, highly controversial today, offered 160 acres of land free and clear to any man over the age eighteen or any woman heading a household for a small registration fee. The only condition: the new owner had to live on the plot and improve the land. Being of British extraction was not a condition. The controversy? The Canadian government was short on funds and didn't bother to provide compensation to the indigenous people whose land the government decided to give away. And despite the offer of a free homestead, Canada still suffered a net outflow of residents.

In 1870 the new nation acquired Rupert's Land from the Hudson Bay Company, an enormous tract of land that stretched north and west to British Columbia. In return, the government had to promise to build a transcontinental railroad within ten years.

Despite all of these mandates, the country was still mired in a worldwide financial recession. Laborers tired of the twelve-hour workdays and started what was termed the Nine Hour Movement in 1872. This largely failed. Prime Minister John MacDonald feared the growing labor movement and granted some concessions to newly formed labor unions. The resultant labor strikes in the 1880s combined with the other external factors above to create a new, powerful class of citizens, especially in Ontario and Quebec. And with the shorter workdays that came out of these concessions came more free time to organize and compete in sports, just like the royals and the wealthy.[30]

It's probably not too surprising, then, that the first advertised and reported upon scheduled hockey event occurred in Montreal just three short years after the Nine Hour Movement. This is undeniable fact. Where problems get sticky is in the analysis of an 1875 *Montreal Gazette* article which advertised the game in advance. The 115-word story summarizes the differences between what readers already knew and what spectators would most likely see.

The rubber ball used outside would be replaced by a "flat circular piece of wood" to prevent the danger of leaving the surface of the ice. "Some of the players are reported to be exceedingly expert at the game," and if this is exactly literal, then some players were beginners and others had played before. By no reasonable person's definition could this be the first game ever played if some players were already experts. However, "subscribers will be admitted on presentation of their tickets" means that this was a scheduled event and that admission was expected by the rink hosting the event, whether that was a season ticket used for skating or for admittance.[31]

Although there are several newspaper accounts of unorganized hockey-type games being played on the ice throughout England and North America before Halifax native James Creighton moved to Montreal, Creighton is credited by most historians with being the first to experiment with organizing the children's country game of shinny. Creighton found eighteen men to participate, arranged with the rink a time to play, and promoted the game in newspaper advertisements. Hockey sticks, which were certainly integral to the game, were imported from Nova Scotia. This certainly was the first attempt at monetizing the game.[32] The game played was basically field hockey on ice skates, with goals eight feet wide, and a block of wood replacing a rubber ball. And yet with all of the bodies of both teams on the rink and a wooden block being hit by part of a wooden tree (the object being hit wouldn't travel far) it's little wonder that the final score was 2–1.

From this single match there was little continuity. There was not an immediate demand for hockey games or ice time, or hockey players, or hockey fans.[33]

Michel Vigneault has studied the sport's history in both English and French Canadian media since the 1990s. His perplexity on the origins are documented in the essay, "Big Bang Theory, Missing Link, or What Is Hockey?" which appeared in the 2014–15 *Hockey Research Journal* published by the Society for International Hockey Research. Vigneault points out quite poignantly the discovered history of hockey and the various steps of the evolution of the game, but he did not examine external factors which may have played a role in the development of the sport.

Two other professors have recently done that.

Stephen Hardy is a retired kinesiology professor at the University of New Hampshire, and Andrew Holman is a history professor and the director of Canadian studies at Bridgewater State University in Massachusetts. Their 2018 book, *Hockey: A Global History*, describes sociologically how the sport developed, with economic demand creating the growth of the sport. It is a book that belongs within reach of every hockey historian.

But often forgotten in history is that retold history is usually the story as told by the victors, especially if the winners are wealthy. The narrative is usually drawn into the best possible light by those who won. Howard Zinn's 1980 bestseller, *A People's History of the United States*, tossed aside the official narrative of American history that American students learn—with its emphasis on great men in high places—and introduced the perspectives of women, Native Americans, African-Americans, immigrant laborers and the working poor.

Turning reality instead of perception or perspective into a history book is a daunting task. Separating fact from exaggeration or flat-out lying is best done contemporaneously. When it comes to discovering hockey's origins, the best researchers in the world have been perplexed for generations. Many historians point to the obscure (at the time) 1875 game's organizer, James Creighton, and label him the father of hockey. Instead, he was honored to be called the first captain of one of the sides.[34] Bill Fitsell is a journalist who has spent thousands of dollars—not to mention decades—trying to solve the mystery. He has written four books on the subject.[35] In the process, he discovered most of the how, what, when and where. Other researchers have published the why, but the who has been elusive.

And yet history should strive to tell the story of all involved. Any story is incomplete without understanding not just the organizers of the movement but the masses behind the movement. That's what Zinn was trying to teach—that there were stories besides those of the elites.

In the last quarter of the nineteenth century it was the unmarried children of the well-to-do who could afford not to work and to attend university. Those McGill College students and other elites were the initial organizers at the attempt to turn hockey into a sport. From 1875 through 1882 only a few hockey games were played at a high level the entire year—not per team or club, which were not formalized, but total. The game was not catching on. Knowledge of these games was so sparse that many of the participants believed they were pioneers. The concept is basically the same as biology's convergent evolution in species. An example of convergent evolution is the similar nature of flight and wings of insects, birds, pterosaurs and bats. All four serve the same function and are similar in structure, but each evolved independently. The same concept as applies to a sport's development is that others come up with the same idea at the same time but independently of each other. Thus most of the claims made and uncovered by hockey researchers are true to some varying degree, just incomplete.

The search for hockey's origins was debated, believe it or not, from the beginning. In 1934 former *Montreal Gazette* sports editor Duncan A. L. MacDonald tried to interview and report on as many of the old-timers he could find who were there in the beginning. Writing a series of columns called Turning Back Hockey's Pages, MacDonald's original intent was to provide filler material for slow news days, usually Tuesday and Thursday editions.

The columns became so popular that by the fall of 1934, MacDonald and the *Gazette* felt it important to let the world know that the copyright was reserved. No longer filler, the columns themselves drew reader interest.

More than eighty-six years later, the disputes are still unresolved.

Fred Gnaedinger played in an 1878 game against the Victoria Skating Club, a team that Gnaedinger claimed was the first hockey club, ignorant of the 1875 match that Creighton organized.

Gnaedinger was responding to MacDonald's *Montreal Gazette* column where McGill's Richard F. Smith was taking credit for crafting the game's rules in 1879. It took Gnaedinger only six years to write his letter to the editor, responding against Smith being credited as the "father of modern hockey."

"Dick Smith has always been a good sport, but when hockey was first started, he was still a boy in high school," Gnaedinger wrote.[36] Gnaedinger told how Philip Foster took a sample stick to Longueuil and had thirty produced for the event.[37]

But what rules were in place? Where was the continuity? And why did Creighton receive his hockey sticks from Halifax, when Longueuil was just across the St. Lawrence River and much more easily accessible?

Gnaedinger said the Victoria Club was comprised of football players, so football rules were adapted as much as possible. Both teams practiced the same way, and finally a friendly game was agreed upon along with a few rules. In other words: organized shinny.

But we can't just throw these matches into history's dustbin. Gnaedinger was listed in Canada's book of important men for his work in the fur trapping industry. Albert Low, who played in the game, was also a McGill student destined for greater events off the ice.

However, if we dig deeper into the newspapers—history's contemporaneous keeper of the times—we find that Gnaedinger isn't even the most important person to be involved in a structured game called hockey.

Before Gnaedinger played, that honor would go to Frederick Temple Hamilton-Temple-Blackwood, more famously known as the Earl of Dufferin, appointed by Queen Victoria as her third representative since Canada's confederation.

Unlike his two predecessors, this governor-general involved himself in Canada's politics as much as permissible and consciously set out to get to know ordinary Canadians as much as possible. He felt that involving himself with the people would strengthen constitutional links between England and its former colony.

On February 5, 1876, officials of the Victoria Rink convinced Lord Dufferin to act as an umpire (*goal judge* in modern terms) for a hockey game in Montreal between the Montreal Football Club and the Victoria Rink Club.[38] He was in Montreal to present the Governor-General Awards for championship skating of the Dominion, and even surprised the crowd by strapping on skates and cutting a few figures into the ice. Stating his disappointment that only four boys competed for the medals in the fifteen-and-under category, Lord Dufferin considered the race a failure.[39] That may be why he had a sudden change of heart and decided not to follow through with the hockey match.

The game was very different then—nine men per side—and the playing time was ninety minutes. The final score was 1–1, but Lord Dufferin left Montreal on the 9:00 a.m. train and definitely did not officiate.[40]

The first formalized hockey club in the world—that we can document—was the McGill Hockey Club in 1877, although it did not last. The Quebec Hockey Club was formed in 1879. Interestingly, several of the seven members of McGill's club went on to form other clubs or play in other less formal games. It should also be noted that all eight members of the club were raised in households with two or more servants, including Rankine Dawson, whose father, Sir William Dawson, was the principal at McGill. These were not commoners.[41]

McGill's club was not continuous. Serious discussions occurred on campus to make hockey more than an adult version of a child's game. McGill College finally formed a permanent club on November 11, 1881.[42]

Even then the school club was not as formal as we are used to today. To illustrate, note this comment from the university's student newspaper, written in 1883, acknowledging that the team only played in the Winter Carnival: "Our Hockey Club has been very successful this season. The matches have been few for the reason that many members of the team could not afford to lose the necessary time after playing through the foot-ball season."[43]

The students graduated and moved on with their careers. Some of the students left the child's games behind, while others, such as Low, Thomas Green and Creighton, took their hockey-playing experience with them and joined or formed clubs in their new locales. Low and Green graduated from McGill and moved to Ottawa. Befriending Jack Kerr and Halder Kirby, the four men started the Ottawa Hockey Club in 1884.[44] Creighton eventually moved to Ottawa and became involved with an intermediate level club, one that should be forgotten in history except that two of its players were the sons of the then governor-general. But by the time the Rideau Rebels became involved, hockey was already established in Canada's capital.

The nascent game had a small following in Quebec City, starting as early as 1878 and using the curling rink. Most of the players in Quebec were introduced to the winter game by lacrosse players.

The Quebec team had issued challenges to the various rinks in Montreal—primarily the Victoria Skating Rink—and sometimes the challenges were accepted, and sometimes they were not. Again, there was no regularity or continuity.

The first formalized games between two permanent clubs occurred two years earlier on January 22, 1881, when a team representing Montreal's Victoria Rink traveled to Quebec City to take on the Quebec Hockey Club, formed by members of the Quebec Skating Club.

The teams played a scoreless first half, but Harcourt Smith scored the first goal, and Percy Myles added an insurance marker as the home team spoiled the train trip for the Montreal players. As was customary for the time amongst proper athletic gentlemen, the host team treated the visitors to supper at a posh hotel, the one in Quebec City being the St. Louis. Plans were discussed for a return visit.[45]

How this generation was able to accomplish this much requires an amazing set of circumstances, which include hunger, opportunity, diligence and familial love. All of these characteristics are demanded in hockey culture today—at least among the successful teams. There are few teams in any league that dominate so thoroughly that hunger and desire are not a necessary and major component; opportunity comes through craftiness and sometimes a little luck with whom the playoff opponent is; diligence equals attention to detail and hard work; and anyone who has won the Stanley Cup in the last thirty years can talk about the bonds of teamwork that equate to familial love. All four components are necessary—playoff failings of favored teams point to at least one failure of the four characteristics listed above. Even today "hot goaltenders" can be overcome through diligence and effort.

Possible but never easy.

The hard work, or effort, is certainly a characteristic of the New World immigrant. When a group of English, Irish and Scottish people left the British Isles for the United States and British North America in the mid-1850s, the great diaspora from the Potato Famine in conjunction with new opportunities in building transportation were the desired attractions. The quantity of work that these brave souls performed created opportunities and new ways of thinking for their children.

Like Brockville's Alex Stewart, Philip Simpson Ross was one of those immigrants. His skillset and timing were perfect, although like almost everyone in history who benefitted or was hurt by timing, his dreams were more based on hope than any actual reality.

Philip Ross was the son of a Scottish soldier serving the British Army and stationed in Belfast. Educated in Glasgow, he was employed as a bookkeeper in Scotland before emigrating to Canada in 1851. He settled in Montreal and found work as an accountant for Montreal Marine Works, the shipyard of Augustin Cantin. His arrival came as Cantin became the first to run an entirely integrated operation and therefore was the first to be able to sell and service complete vessels—engine and hull.

By 1857, Cantin employed between 150 and 200 and was estimated to be worth £32,000 (approximately $5.1 million US in 2020). He held several pieces of real estate in the Griffintown section of Montreal. But within two years Cantin had financial problems.[46] Ross, seeing the writing on the wall, left the company and started his own accountancy in 1858.

Demand for accounting services was slight in the late 1850s, as most businesses were sole proprietorships or partnerships. Few were accountable to shareholders, and none were required to file income tax returns. Companies hired their own bookkeepers and kept their financial affairs private.

Ross struggled to stay afloat for seventeen years, when he received an indirect gift from the Canadian government—the Insolvency Act, which provided for official assignees to administer the assets of insolvent businesses.

The early 1880s also saw the formations of large joint-stock companies, and Ross had the opportunity to become the accountant for a few of them. Bell Telephone Company of Canada and Sun Mutual Life Insurance Company of Montreal were two of his clients, and in the early years, Ross completed the audits himself. But as those companies grew to be some of Canada's largest, so did Ross. He expanded his accountancy firm to bring in three of his five sons. The firm eventually grew to be one of Canada's largest, and it is now a part of the international accounting giant Deloitte.[47]

The elder Ross also believed his sons should be involved in athletic endeavors, and his son Willie was considered by many as the fastest skater in the country. Another son, Philip Dansken (called Phil by the family) was also a pretty good skater.

CHAPTER 4
AN IMMIGRANT'S DEATH

Noting that the city of Montreal would give his children more opportunities while the patriarch drove the train, Alex Stewart moved his family out of Brockville to the then-Montreal suburb of Pointe St. Charles.

Unbeknownst to himself at the time, when the Stewarts moved to Canada's then-largest city in 1882, increasing numbers of Montrealers found time on their hands as workweeks were being reduced due to public pressure. The growth of casual clubs—especially in the working-class wards of St. Anne, St. Henri and Pointe St. Charles—provided the synergy and determination needed to take recreation to a new level.[48]

There were two types of clubs in Canada's largest city: permanent clubs that included a clubhouse, grounds, nonplaying members and a strong social component; and those clubs that bore the name of the Grand Trunk Railway (GTR)—Stewart's employer. These GTR clubs were initiated by the clerical staff in the various offices and played in by clerks.[49]

Alex Stewart definitely believed in physical well-being, and kept Jimmy active. The blue-eyed, sandy-brown-haired young man grew to be five foot ten, tall in those days, and never weighed more than 158 pounds.[50] The timing for Jimmy Stewart's 126-mile move from small-town Brockville to Montreal couldn't be better.

In a marketing effort to show off the city of Montreal to the world, the first Winter Carnival made its glorious debut in 1883. Stewart's first introduction to the Montreal sporting scene was prior to the 1883 Carnival, where he entered in two distance skating races. He was an unknown, but he had a lot of practice skating over the St. Lawrence, which many Brockville residents did quite frequently in the years before border security became an issue. Stories in Brockville about locals skating the half mile across the river to Morristown, New York, to pick up mail or US military pension checks were common.

In the big city, Stewart finished first out of nine entries in the Flat Race, which was twelve laps around the Victoria Rink.[51] The official judges were Fred Henshaw, A. W. Stevenson and Charles Lamb. The unofficial judges were three thousand spectators. Two days later the new kid in town was skating on the river rink in the official Carnival race.

Sponsored by the railways as well as the hotels who would benefit from an extravaganza bringing tourists, the Montreal Carnival became an event unlike any other seen in the young country's history.

The center of the Carnival was Dominion Square, the city gathering spot which gleamed in the snow while being surrounded by the luxurious Windsor Hotel. In the middle of the square, where a monument dedicated to the Canadian men who died in the South African War now stands, an ice castle was built from tens of thousands of ice blocks carved from the St. Lawrence River.

Shooting for a gold medal, the nineteen-year-old finished first of the eleven contestants in the mile (four minutes, two seconds). The favorite, Willie Ross, finished second. Stewart then beat Ross in the two-mile event as well. He was literally the fastest ice skater in Canada.[52]

Being challenged a month later, Stewart raced around the Prince of Wales Rink in 3:41.05 for the mile and 7:13 in the two-mile race, easily winning both.[53] Skating judge Fred Henshaw was so impressed with Stewart that he recruited the young skater to help form and organize the Pointe St. Charles Snowshoe Club. The nineteen-year-old railroad clerk was named vice president and helped host his first tramp in mid-November 1883. His stated goal was 125 members for the 1884 Carnival. Henshaw was president.[54]

Although a niche activity today, snowshoeing as a sport evolved from an article of clothing designed for human survival. Looking for food in the winter, the Canadian indigenous tribes of the Huron and Algonquin showed Europeans how to hunt for animals in the winter. A boot or shoe was attached to ash timber frames and untanned cowhide webbing to allow traction in traversing across heavy snow. Some of the earliest snowshoes were more than seven feet long and although unwieldy, were helpful to navigate in deep, powdery snow. Snowshoers looked to the efficiency of animals and started to modify the snowshoes to match the paw prints left behind.

The popular *beavertail* style had a round nose with the ends coming together in a long tail. The *bearpaw* was short and wide with a round tail.[55]

Snowshoeing was the "in" sport heading into the Montreal Carnival of 1884. Snowshoeing was considered the one sport that was uniquely Canadian—one that would unite the English, the French and the First Nations people who provided the inspiration behind it:

> Snowshoeing was deemed to be an exceedingly useful accomplishment for the sportsmen who tracked his deer in the snow and ran it down with his dogs and hauled it to camp with his toboggan or Indian sleigh. The farmer sometimes used the snowshoe, but not often—especially the English farmer. When the shoes were first used by the British Canadian youth to cross country for exercise, our French Canadian friends were slow to take up the idea. They now fall into line quite gracefully and soon will be, as they ought to be, much more numerous than British snowshoers.
>
> The army, drawing upon inspiration from the deeds and traditions of the aborigines, recognized early in

> the period of British occupancy the necessity, not to speak of the convenience, which the snowshoe must be to a solider in a campaign in Canada during the snows of winter. Fancy a detachment of troops on the march along country roads snowed up in a drifting storm with an enemy on snowshoes in pursuit or harassing them. The utter helplessness of the detachment would soon be apparent. Skrimishers on snowshoes could comfortably assail ten times their number, remain out of reach of the bayonet, and in comparative safety from either artillery or infantry firing, while at the same time they could easily communicate with their base of supplies.
>
> A few men could thus tire out and exhaust an invading or retreating army.
>
> It was a source of great trial to Her Majesty's Household troops to go through their snowshoe drill when first initiated to its mysteries and mishaps. Those who saw the first efforts of the six-foot guardsmen or Scots Fusiliers will recollect on how they looked and laughed like to split their sides at the drill. The men did not require to be told to "fall in." They fell in naturally, and went head over heels; this performance generally bringing down two or three others, all floundering in the snow in the fashion of a football scramble or scrimmage, while the officers' smothered laughter would often break into a volley.[56]

Pointe St. Charles was the home of the newly built Montreal Driving Park. Designed for horse races, the facility became multipurpose in a hurry. Without the horses running on the track in the winter, the intrepid snowshoers took their place. The race starter was Stewart's friend, Joe Laing.

Sixty-one contestants competed in ten different races ranging in length from the Fat Man's Race of one hundred yards to two miles. It is not known if Stewart competed or just helped organize the club, but the day's events were considered a success.[57]

Stewart's snowshoeing career didn't last long, but his ice skating did. He wrote a private letter, partially published in the *Montreal Gazette*, criticizing his recorded times:

> I am ashamed to see my name appended to such slow records as one mile in four minutes, two seconds, and two miles in eight minutes, twelve seconds, for I know I could do much better. In those races the ice was very poor . . . Under more favorable conditions, I am confident that not only myself but several of my townsmen can cover those distances in under four minutes and eight minutes.[58]

The rest of the summer was not newsworthy, as records show that Jimmy was working as a stationary accounting clerk for the railroad—a job no doubt initiated by his father.

But life and history would change at five minutes past midnight on October 23, 1884—just two years after the Stewarts moved to Pointe St. Charles. Alex Stewart was driving the Grand Trunk Railway No. 6 from Montreal and headed westbound for Chicago. The train departed late and was trying to make up time. As October 22 turned into the 23rd, Stewart's train was reaching the Pointe-Claire station.

At the exact same moment, a GTR heavy freight train with twenty-three cars slowly headed east toward Montreal. The freight train's conductor, Harry Jefferson, had received orders to cross the express train at Pointe-Claire. Although GTR regulations required the train to travel at eight miles per hour, the freight train ignored regulations and traveled at ten miles per hour. Combined with the late departure of the Number 6 from Montreal, the small difference would prove to be fatal.

The freight train reached the station first, but there was little time to spare. The freight train's engineer, Donald McKenzie, in a brief space ran the train onto the siding, and the switchman at the west switch immediately displayed the signal that the line was clear.

Due to the increased speed, however, McKenzie was unable to control his train. He applied the brakes, but thanks to wet tracks from the drizzling rain, overlapped the east switch and landed on the main track.

Both McKenzie and Jefferson realized it was too late to avert the impending accident when they saw their engine and two front cars on the main line. The two jumped to their safety and escaped unhurt.

The Chicago Express train was traveling between twenty-five and thirty miles per hour and did not stop at way stations such as Pointe-Claire. By the time the driver of the express, Alex Stewart, saw the impending accident, it was too late. The locomotives came together with such force they became interlocked. Four of the freight cars tumbled over, and the estimated 120 sheep carried within were instantly killed.

The two locomotives were firmly welded together due to the impact of the crash, with the front of the freight locomotive having telescoped the express train.

The passenger train locomotive suffered the most, having lost its fore wheels, the smokestack and other parts, besides being badly smashed and bent. The freight train locomotive had its front smashed in and the cab lost, but the wheels were all right. Of the cars, the worst damaged was freight car 991. Half of its wheels were gone and the side badly smashed in. The baggage car also had one end smashed in where the tender[59] fell on it.[60]

The tenders of both locomotives were upturned and coal scattered in all directions. The driver of the express, Stewart, failed to escape. The forty-eight-year-old Irish immigrant was scalded by the escaping steam, and when the tenders upset he became buried beneath the burning coal. Three passengers and the train's fireman were injured, with the fireman fracturing his femur being the worst of the injuries.

Stewart was labeled a hero for saving hundreds of passengers, and at least one newspaper editorial wanted to see McKenzie arrested:

> The freight train driver gives no reason for his accelerated speed. When it is shown that, with reversed engines and four or five brakes on, he overran the siding and met a fast express train, people will naturally think that he hurried to get to his siding to escape a collision on the main line and overdid it. But even if he had been running at eight miles an hour, even if his brakes controlled the train, and even had the express train rattled easily past in triumph, this would have been cutting railway working too fine…
>
> But most singular is the action of the coroner's jury. The weight of evidence shows that the driver of the freight was running above his proper speed, that he did not signal for brakes soon enough, and that his semaphore[61] was down—thus deceiving the engineer of the fast train with an indication that the line was clear.
>
> Very likely if the company's regulations had been followed there would have been no need for coroner or jury either.[62]

Jimmy Stewart took his family to bury his father in Brockville. They traveled by train in a special car filled with family, friends and supporters.

"The casket was covered with wreaths, one of which was from the Odd Fellows, one from the Loyal Brotherhood of Engine Drivers, one from St. Matthew's Presbyterian Church and another from the conductor and the train hands of the train on which he was killed."[63]

Brockville vandals damaged the final resting place of Alex Stewart, who was credited with saving the lives of hundreds in the train accident that cost him his life.

CHAPTER 5
A SON HONORS HIS FATHER

Every new beginning comes from some other beginning's end.

—"Closing Time" by Semisonic

After the shock of his father's sudden death, Jimmy Stewart needed to readjust to his new life and livelihood. The nineteen-year-old faced sudden decisions that needed to be made. Unlike many of his athletic friends and competitors who were able to attend university, Stewart's formal education stopped at grade eleven. He was already working as a stationery clerk for the railroad, landing the job with the assistance of his father. He also lived at home with his stepmother and younger sisters. Does he abandon them to see out his own path? His father belonged to an organization that looked after widows. What about his sisters? And on a smaller scale, what about his athletic exploits? Should he quit? Work harder?

Like Bill Gates and the others above, there was no way Stewart could have known this at the time, but his timing to be a co-designer and central steward of Canada's National Game was absolutely perfect.

And like most first-time fathers, he wasn't prepared.

One item that Gladwell espouses but in which we disagree is famously known as the *ten thousand-hour rule*—that in order to rise to the top in something you must put in ten thousand hours of training. That might work for some established industries, but we believe that as long as the hours one invests is some percentage greater than the average number of hours that an average person puts in, success will be more likely.

And hockey, at this time a barely organized activity with different rules based upon location and year in which only a few matches were played in any given year, no one came close to the ten-thousand-hour mark. This is important because looking back at the situation James Alexander Stewart faced, historians see a different opportunity than the orphaned nineteen-year-old knew he had. Especially a nineteen-year-old who took it upon himself to make sure his stepmother and his younger sisters were provided for in a Victorian-era Canada, which wasn't necessarily friendly to lower-class widows. However, this was a core belief of the Odd Fellow fraternity in which his father and grandfather belonged and strongly believed.

The advantage Stewart had over the other athletes playing hockey was Stewart only played hockey, and specifically, ice skating from his youth on the St. Lawrence made him a fast and strong distance skater. The other hockey players partook in other sports during the other months, lacrosse being the main sport of choice.

For Montreal's 1883 and 1884 Winter Carnivals, the hockey tournament played a minor role. The nascent sport was included as a way to induce Americans to come visit, as a rudimentary form of the game was played for years in the United States, according to the programs and souvenir guides for sale.

Proving that hockey before this date was not the organized sport we see today was in a program from the Carnival:

> We know nothing an Irishman enjoys better than an afternoon spent in "hurling," and the Scot gives the same pastime the name of "shinty," the Englishman

> and Canadian calling it "hockey." The game might be called winter lacrosse for that matter as in playing it the principal features are the same, excepting that the ball is struck along the ice instead of thrown from the 'crosse.[64]

All prior claims to hockey being born in Montreal were made in the middle or late twentieth century. This is a contemporaneous publication that asserts there is no real differentiation between Canadian and European rudimentary forms of the game.

But in developing this new game, the elite who organized the Carnival couldn't even figure out what playing surface to use. They just knew they needed ice to skate on because it was a *winter* carnival.

The first hockey trophy, the Carnival Trophy from 1883. It should be noted that the tournament was started on the St. Lawrence River on a 400-foot by 200-foot surface. McGill University was given the trophy because it had scored the most goals in the tournament.

At the 1883 Winter Carnival, the hockey was played on a rink created on the St. Lawrence River. The playing surface: 400 feet by 200 feet. As field hockey is played on a surface of 300 feet by 180 feet, it is safe to assume that the idea was just to bring the British game as is, using ice skates and making the playing surface a little larger to account for the fact that players can travel faster skating than running. This was also not a continuance of the game credited to James Creighton, as it was played eight years after Creighton's first game in the Victoria Arena. Creighton's game may have been the first commercial attempt at hockey, but this is further proof that Creighton's game didn't stick.

After two matches, the river was so badly chopped up that the championship game—a 2–2 draw—was moved back inside to the Crystal Rink with a much smaller surface. McGill was given the trophy because it had scored the most goals in the tourney.

Hockey was supposed to be an afterthought to the 1884 Winter Carnival. By moving the games onto an outside man-made ice arena on the campus of McGill University, the second year of the Winter Carnival saw an improvement over playing on the St. Laurence River. A smaller playing surface than the river, the rink was still enormous at 250 feet long by 140 feet wide. But the McGill students and the Carnival festival organizers forgot about one thing: rain. Rain plagued this festival, and it turned the outdoor ice surface to slush.

How bad was the hockey? All seven played games were shutouts, and five were by the score 1–0. There were also three forfeits when some players stayed home due to the weather, but the festival organizers expected the players to show up and compete in slush.

The hockey tournament was a disaster. Even *Harper's Bazaar Weekly*, then an upstart magazine dedicated to women and fashion for the new middle class, mentioned every event in the Carnival except hockey.[65]

Creighton's game had the farce of eighteen men hitting a wood block with a wood stick inside a cramped playing surface using modified field hockey rules, and then the next series of games were played using lacrosse players and lacrosse rules, and then the Carnival had a series playing on the river with small armies hitting a ball before moving the championship game inside under different constraints, and the very next year the games were moved onto an outdoor uncovered rink.

There was no continuity. One would not be too far from the truth that if all four of these events were being watched consecutively, one would think it was like Winter Olympic skating events—four different sports.

In the 1893 *Outing* article, Bogert does his best to explain the game that has a direct lineage to today's game:

> Unlike its namesake, the Canadian game requires truly skillful players as its exponents, and when properly played combines science, fast skating and grace. No game is stronger in fixing the attention of the onlookers. The kaleidoscopic changes of formation and glancing of varied colors are very pleasing as the gayly costumed players pass and repass the "puck" from end to end of the rink with the speed and accuracy of a lacrosse ball.
>
> In Canada the championship matches are played, and clubs almost invariably practice in covered rinks.
>
> The rink consists of a sheet of ice 180 to 200 feet in length by 80 to 100 feet in width, no especial dimensions being stipulated in the rules of the Amateur Hockey Association of Canada.
>
> Seven players constitute a side—their endeavor being, with the aid of regulation hockey sticks, to pass the puck through their adversaries' goals.[66]

Bogert then describes the puck and sticks, which are basically the same as today—or at least until composites replaced wood for the sticks in the 1990s. He explains special hockey skates differ from figure skating so players can gain extra leverage on the ice:

> The rules are somewhat similar to those laid down in football, the principal one being that a player must always be "on side," i.e. never playing in advance of the puck; consequently he cannot take the puck on a pass from a player on his own side unless he be behind him when the pass was made; neither can he, in the same way, touch the puck when a "lift" or "shoot" has been made by a player on his own side.

> A player, if he happens to be out of play or offside, however, is put onside immediately upon a player of the opposing team touching the puck.
>
> The goal posts are placed six feet apart, at the ends of the rink, and are four feet high. They are held in position by being sunk in holes made in the ice.
>
> A wooden wall, generally two feet in height, borders the ice. From this the puck readily rebounds, and it becomes a material factor in the science of the game, as a skillful player, when closely checked, often baffles his opponents by driving the puck against the wall, and allowing for the rebound, securing possession at an unexpected point.
>
> The puck may be intercepted, but must not be carried or knocked forward by any part of the skate or person.[67]

Going back to that Game Five fight in Pittsburgh, the sequence started when the Penguins' Ron Hainsey dumped the puck across the blue line to head to the bench and change. The blue line, introduced in 1910, was yet another tweak to the always difficult-to-understand offsides rule. The puck went behind the goal net, still six feet by four feet, with modern latex posts inserted into sunk holes in the ice to keep the nets from freely being dislodged, at least without a little bit of force. (The posts used to be more solidly in place, but a serious back injury to Mark Howe in 1980 led to a safer invention, so the nets became more mobile to help prevent serious injury.) In chasing the puck in Game Five, Subban passed the puck along the dasher board to Filip Forsberg, yet another Swedish player, but by that moment the other players described above had come together and play was stopped.

Those two-foot boards are now ideally forty-two inches in height and further secured with dashers about six inches from the ice.

The Carnival was important because of the public's fascination with this game. But there was still progress that needed to be made, and that progress would come from brainstorming. A group of four men in their young twenties would each add their unique perspective to bring us the framework for today's hockey.

CHAPTER 6
The Rich Kid's Influence

It's important to note that in the English-speaking, or western side of the island of Montreal, the local newspapers heavily promoted special events like the Winter Carnival.

One of the first Montrealers to use the power of the press to financially lift his family from the masses was John Arnton. Arnton became involved in selling real estate at quite the opportune time—as more and more immigrants became Canadians, they wanted to purchase a home, and Arnton was the auctioneer many went to.

A native of Montreal who was born in 1832, Arnton worked his way up. Going into his own business in 1860, Arnton struggled initially but by 1863 found a lucrative business selling farm commodities in the city. He learned how to leverage the power of newspaper advertising—one 1863 auction for 277 barrels of pork was even advertised in the *Chicago Tribune*, as Arnton tried to capitalize with the United States in the middle of its Civil War.[68]

Arnton found all kinds of items to put up for auction, of course receiving a commission for his efforts. In 1864, Arnton auctioned off United States bonds and books and provided a catalog on request.[69] Arnton's reputation grew when he was named the Canadian government's official auctioneer in November 1868.[70]

By the time of Montreal's real estate boom of the 1870s, Arnton was one of the city's most important conduits between buyers and sellers. Arnton also managed to keep his name in the public eye through charity and benevolence. At various points in his career, Arnton was on the board of the Irish Protestant Benevolent Society. He once was elected to the Montreal City Council, but resigned before completing his term. Arnton invested successfully, even being a board member of the Bank of Montreal as well as the Canadian Bank of Commerce.[71]

Despite being one of Montreal's wealthiest citizens—although not to the same degree as the Molsons—Arnton's personal life was generously sprinkled with tragedy. Making money came with severe personal sacrifices. In 1858, Arnton's first child, daughter Ida, was born. As John was expanding his reputation, his family was expanding as well. Willie was born next in 1859, followed by John James Arnton Jr. on December 2, 1863. Nicknamed Jack, the youngest Arnton was three years old when Ida died. John and Margaret Arnton would have two more sons and two daughters.

The Arnton household was full, with four servants helping to take care of the eight Arntons plus Margaret's mother and younger sister.[72]

Being involved in society circles sometimes meant getting the children involved. And before the railroads sponsored the grand Winter Carnivals, designed to make the frigid winters of Montreal feel like a tourist destination, the city had smaller local skating carnivals.

The 1870s were a time for more social activity amongst all of the classes, and Montreal's Victoria Skating Rink was often the site of the events. The Victoria wasn't the first indoor skating rink in Canada's largest city, but it was the largest and hosted an unusually brilliant spectacle called the Children's Carnival. A display of bunting decorated the building, and the streamers hung profusely in all directions, while the sheen of gaslight on the ice for a

Jack Arnton as a youth, dressing up for a children's carnival.

time reflected the swaying forms of many scores of gaily dressed young lads and misses.

The star of the show was ten-year-old Frank Crispo. The future banker wore a broad-brimmed hat, blue jersey and white duck trousers and had a knife hanging by the white cord around his waist, while the tar on his duck pants on his loins and hips showed that a master hand had dressed him—all two-foot-nine—in his stockings.

Skating were two Little Red Riding Hoods, complete with grandmothers who were two feet nothing in height, but missing a wolf. Some of the boys were dressed as knights-in-arms with terrible fake mustaches. Sailors and soldiers and newspaper delivery boys skated with the last of the Mohicans and children dressed as squaws, and a couple of children wore blackface, while yet another went as a "Chinese wanderer." A French post boy was depicted. A couple boys mocked Turks, another was a Swiss peasant, and his brother, a Greek.

Sensitivity to nonwhite races and other cultures was sadly missing in 1870s society, but the spectacle of children in costume skating was a sight for the eyes to behold, the ears were treated to twelve compositions by the band, mixtures of quicksteps, polkas and waltzes.

Jack Arnton Jr. skated as a youngster and first performed in front of spectators in the 1878 Children's Carnival. A precursor to the winter festival that would put Montreal on the international map, the children's carnival featured boys and girls ages ten through sixteen dressed in a colorful spectacle that would put Disney On Ice to shame.

Twenty-two girls and forty-six boys dressed in costume and as characters. The Victoria Rink was gorgeously decorated with flags of several countries while the youngsters skated upon the surface.

Jack Arnton, fourteen, performed as a Venetian chasing his nine-year-old brother Sidney, who played a gnome.[73] Three months later they reversed the roles to an even larger crowd.[74]

This was Jack's first brush with performing in front of a crowd. But while he enjoyed skating, it was on the cricket grounds as a rugby player that John James Arnton Jr. made his mark.

Jack's contributions to two sports have been largely forgotten. A halfback rugby player, Jack was a strong leader of the Montreal Brittanicas, who were usually referred to as the Brits.

There were a lot of rugby players who also played hockey. On the Brits alone Jack's brother Tom, Fred McRobie, Bunny Lowe, and Andy Shearer competed in both. Jack Arnton made his competitive hockey debut just a few years later, playing for the Montreal Victorias in the 1883 Winter Carnival. The Vics were formed in 1880 by James Monk, George Gardner and Charles Lamothe. The first recorded game they played was a challenge at Quebec City, where the Victorias lost 2–0.[75] The club was based out of the elitist Victoria Rink, hence the name.

Arnton was a rugby great and was a pretty good baseball player, but his love was hockey. Arnton made his hockey debut in the first Winter Carnival game on the St. Lawrence River, a game that ended in a 0–0 draw. After a couple of hours to rest, Arnton played his second game. Against a heavier—and rested—McGill team, Arnton and the Victorias lost 1–0. Arnton kept playing hockey, becoming one of the stars and leaders of the Victorias.

CHAPTER 7
FORMING THE CRYSTALS

Joe Laing was a "peculiarly built fellow with a pleasing though not handsome face," wrote the *Boston Globe*.[76] The reason the Boston newspaper cared about the Montreal native was that he was also one of Canada's finest scullers.

Laing was a member of the Grand Trunk Railroad Boating Club and was considered the amateur champion of Montreal. In June 1880, Joe traveled to Providence, Rhode Island, to take on the best American amateurs. The heavy betting was on local favorite Frank Holmes, with three others, including Joe, alternating as the second choice.[77]

Laing finished third in the three-mile race, twenty-six seconds behind Holmes's time of twenty-two minutes, forty-four seconds, in front of an estimated fifty thousand spectators. His time would have easily won the professional race that followed the amateur.[78]

Quite proud of his accomplishment, Laing went back to training for an even bigger reward: the 1881 National Association of Amateur Rowing championships in Washington, DC.

Wearing white and the number 2, the 145-pound single sculler was the favorite, with $25 bet on him and $11 bet on the other competitors in his heat—combined.[79] The smart money was on the favorite as Joe won his heat with the fastest time of the day. Laing would get his rematch with Holmes.

Laing was the favorite heading into the finale, but steered wildly off course and finished third as Holmes became the world champion.[80] Laing blamed his defeat on his body's inability to deal with the Washington heat.[81]

For the 1882 championships, Joe was not going to take any chances. He destroyed all Canadian records in the mile-and-a-half single sculls race, becoming Canadian champion with a time of eight minutes, thirty-six seconds.[82]

Rain poured down in buckets for Laing's first heat, but soon stopped. After a thirty-minute delay, the race was on. Laing jumped to an early lead and easily coasted to victory on the Detroit River, although the rain started up again. After the victory, Laing carried his shell above his head, water dripping out of the canoe. Before long there was a varied assortment of boating apparel hanging on the clothesline.[83]

For the next day's championship, Laing would have to defeat his longtime nemesis Holmes as well as Henry Kirby of Providence, Rhode Island.

But if heat was Laing's downfall in DC, he would have to overcome the opposite in Detroit. With a northwest wind blaring down, one reporter stated it made a witness "envy the polar bear with its coat of fur; the walrus with his coating of blubber. It established telegraphic station up and down one's spinal column. It made a fellow look over his shoulder to see if an iceberg was drifting down on him unawares."[84]

It was cold, and that was before Laing's race started.

Holmes, who had the inside position, advanced to the lead. The others pulling toward him were soon in a triangle, with Holmes's boat forming the apex. Some complications arose from the nearness of the boats. There was danger in locking oars, and no one but Holmes had freedom of action. Laing protested against Kirby, and Kirby replied unintelligibly. Laing's oars just cleared Kirby's canoe, and both slacked up while Holmes maintained a long, powerful stroke and took the lead. Holmes, who was two lengths ahead when the nose of his boat reached the finish line, stopped rowing, and Laing caught up to within a half a boat's length. The judges ruled that since all three rowers were equally at fault to the fouling made at the start, there would be no change in the standings.[85] Said Holmes, "Laing is a rattler, both in speed and endurance. He is undoubtedly the best amateur last year that I ever met."[86]

Holmes retired after this race, and Laing would face new upstart challengers. But if Laing had any luck at all rowing, it was all bad. In June 1883, he competed on the Charles River in Boston in the Union Boat Club's annual regatta. He finished second by two seconds, but a protest was filed saying that Laing went the wrong away around a buoy. The protest was allowed, and Laing was disqualified.[87]

In Newark, New Jersey, on August 7, 1883, Laing finally put it all together. In his first heat Laing finished with a time of eight minutes, fifty-four seconds. The race was one and a half miles on the Passaic River.[88]

Later that day, Laing set a world record of eight minutes, forty-four seconds in the single scull race to become not only the champion of Canada, but of the United States as well. Joe won the race by ten seconds, easily.[89]

The whining from the wealthy was already beginning, and it was emanating from Toronto. Wrote the *Toronto Mail*:

> The point generally laid against Laing by those—and a very large proportion of amateur rowing men—who dispute his amateurship, is that he gives up most of the summer solely to training, leaving all occupations completely, and that while doing so his means of support must necessarily come from outside sources. It matters little in this case whether such means of support come from his friends, from those who simply admire his ability and wish to see him free to do his best, or from those who hope to make money by his success. In either alternative the fact remains that the spirit but not the letter of the amateur law is ignored.[90]

Not surprisingly, his hometown paper came to his defense.

Wrote the *Montreal Gazette*, "According to the ethics of the *Mail* no man can be a legitimate amateur who is not independent in fortune, and if this rule is to be applied, amateur sports will either disappear or degenerate into 'duffer' contests."[91]

Looking for some activity to keep in shape during the long winter months, the Laing brothers turned to the old game of hockey. The timing was right for the brothers as the owner of one of Montreal's indoor rinks was trying to grow the sport.

Sam Robertson managed the Crystal Rink built on the corner of Dorchester (now Boulevard Rene Levesque) and Guy Streets. Looking for ways to compete in the city with two other covered ice rinks, Robertson decided he was going to go all in on hockey and start a club. He called his first meeting for club members on November 20, 1882, but not enough people were interested. Robertson pledged his rink on different days and times during the week so the boys could practice and be one of the best teams in the city, if not the Dominion.[92] The next week he tried again, and Robertson announced that enough men had skated forward to take on the challenge. The Montreal Crystals—named after the facility they played in—were born.[93]

Except they weren't.

For reasons unexplained, the club never started. But the next winter after the excitement generated by the Carnival hockey being played on the St. Lawrence River, Joe and Bob Laing held a meeting in their cigar store at 70 St. Joseph.[94] Jimmy Stewart, whose stepmother worked in the recently opened cigar store, helped the brothers organize the club. There they decided to start the Crystal Hockey Club, with the idea that Sam Robertson's Crystal Rink would be the team's home. The other members of the club included Billy Virtue, Allan Cameron and Jack Findlay.[95] It was decided that the team would practice three nights per week for two hours a night and take on challengers after two weeks of practice. Jimmy Stewart did not yet know it, but the orphaned Irish Odd Fellow was going to grow up being the stable heart that hockey needed.

Hockey had proven to be a popular draw in the 1883 Carnival, but having an inability to have fresh ice on the St. Lawrence River forced the championship game indoors. For 1884 the Carnival organizers moved the games to an open-air rink on the campus of McGill College. But that proved unsatisfactory as players had to battle the glare from the sun as well as their opponents. The team with the sun to their back always had an unfair advantage.

Due to the popularity with spectators, the organizers wanted to bring in outside clubs. Quebec City, with the most established hockey club outside of the area, was the natural inclusion. Ottawa was invited as well. Bringing Quebec into the fold after the successful series with the local clubs meant a permanent change to the rules, however, as hockey practiced in the north featured seven men to a side.

For the players who were used to playing indoors, the move to the larger outdoor surface at McGill University, the McGill Club questioned why the games shouldn't be played with nine men to a side. "Last year should not be a precedent, for everyone knows it was only out of deference to Quebec (who came here with seven men) that the clubs here consented to reduce their teams by two men."[96]

The unintended consequence of opening up the tournament meant that teams comprised of the new middle class could be formed and compete against the bluebloods. And the unintended consequences of reducing the number of men on the ice resulted in skating speed having a more prominent role in the way the game is played. The Crystals, formed in working-class Pointe St. Charles and playing out of the Crystal Rink, became the first working-class team to answer the bell.

The white-and-light-blue-clad Crystals made their debut against the blueblood Victoria Rink club team, led by Jack Arnton. The Crystals' James McCabe scored the first goal of the game, but the Vics tied it up by speed-skating demon Fred Learmonth. Ed McCaffery scored to give the Crystals a 2–1 lead, but Joe Muir scored four consecutive goals, and Vics' captain Arnton added the last two as the Victorias beat the Crystals 7–2.[97]

Before the Carnival hockey tournament got underway, the Crystals played a friendly exhibition against a team called the Wanderers, made up of members of the Bank of Montreal. The game was not reported in detail, but the *Montreal Witness* recorded the score as 5–0 in favor of the Crystals.

More important than the debut of the Crystals were the final preparations for the Carnival. Wrote the *Witness*, "Even those people who have been watching the growth of the Ice Palace were startled last night with its magnificence when fully lit up with the electric light."

Stands were being built in Dorchester park to accommodate the many visitors traveling from several parts of the United States. If the merchants can be forgiven for not paying attention to the hockey match, they were busy making preparations for the influx of customers looking for toboggans. The *Witness* reported that 3,250 visitors had preregistered for lodging.[98]

With the friendly exhibitions out of the way, it was time for this Irish working-class squad to face off against the cultural and educational elite in the Carnival.

The Carnival was opened by the governor-general, Henry Petty-Fitzmaurice, more famously known as Lord Lansdowne. Lord Lansdowne was the great-grandson of Lord Shelburne, the Irish-born former prime minister of England who agreed to the Peace of Paris Treaty with Benjamin Franklin and allowed America its independence. In England the treaty was so unpopular that Lord Shelburne lost his political power. Lord Lansdowne, like his great-grandfather, would later be reviled in England for his letter calling for a premature end to the violence in World War I.

Lord Lansdowne addressed the crowd gathering for the big winter festival. "It seems to me that we may be quite mistaken if we regard these national sports and amusements which you have promoted with so much success as destined to provide amusement and attract visitors, and nothing more. They have their serious place in their national life as in our individual life. Neither the nation or the individual can exist without recreation," he said.[99]

A call for a national winter sport had begun, but there were several tweaks that still needed to be made for shinny to become that sport.

The open rink on the McGill College campus had unfavorable weather on the morning of the game, making the ice less than ideal. As the afternoon turned into evening, a slight drizzle of rain started just as the game did. Despite this, ten minutes in, James McCabe scored, and the Crystals beat the Wanderers 1–0. Bob Laing was captain and center of the squad, and the fast-skating Stewart was cast as the point. Attending the game was Canada's governor-general. Lord Lansdowne was enjoying his first look at hockey, albeit on a 250-by-150-foot surface subject to the elements. "I would like to take a hand in the game if I could be sure of my skating," he said.[100]

The Crystals were scheduled to play McGill on the second day of the tournament, but with record low temperatures and a blizzard to boot, the Crystals decided not to show. The McGill team did come, however, and the game was declared a forfeit. The afternoon game held the same result, as the banker-led Wanderers did not show up to face the Victorias.[101]

The Carnival organizers had egg on their face with the two games not being played because teams stayed home due to inconvenient weather. British-Canadian sports historically did not let bad weather stop them from playing, whether it was cricket, football or lacrosse.

Carnival tournament organizers had arranged for the Ottawa Hockey Club to come to Montreal to play the McGill team. The organizers even built hockey's first suite on the west side of the rink for the governor-general to watch. Even Mother Nature cooperated—the ice was reported as being in splendid condition. McGill's Shirley Ogilvie, the son of Canadian Senator Alexander Walker Ogilvie, scored the only goal of the game with about fifteen minutes remaining. Unfortunately for the Carnival organizers,

Lord Lansdowne failed to show, so they scheduled another game between Ottawa and the Victorias for the next day.[102]

Mother Nature was not so cooperative for this match. The 10:30 a.m. start was delayed for an hour because one-and-a-half inches of snow fell overnight and had to be shoveled off McGill's open-air ice surface, complicated because stands were built to the edge of the rink so where to relocate the snow became a bit of an issue.

Encouraged by the McGill supporters, Ottawa's Tom Green scored as Jack Arnton's Victorias attempted a strenuous comeback but failed. The 1–0 defeat meant that four teams had won one match that was played, and all but the Crystals had one loss apiece.[103]

A decision was made to have the four clubs play a semifinal championship round, although the Carnival was scheduled to conclude that same day with fireworks lighting up the winter Montreal sky during the closing ceremonies. The fireworks never went off.

Ottawa had defeated McGill 3–0 in a game that looked like it was being played in a snow globe. The special stands built for the governor-general went unused. He left for Ottawa before the closing ceremonies, leaving on the 4:30 train.[104]

For some unusual reason, the hockey committee decided to play a championship game three days after the close of the Carnival.

Joe Laing of the Crystals officiated, but the starting time was delayed as some of the Montreal Victoria players were late to arrive. Both teams, tired, failed to score in the sixty minutes, so another thirty-minute half was played.

About twenty minutes into the extra session, Montreal's Percy Myles scored, and the Victorias held on to defeat Ottawa 1–0 to win the tournament.[105]

The *Ottawa Citizen* reported that the team and players were not happy about the tournament layover, nor the apparent disorganization. "The Ottawa hockey club returned home last evening, and to say they are disgusted with the way things were managed in that place would be drawing it mild."[106]

CHAPTER 8

THE BIRTH OF THE MONTREAL A.A.A.

In the corner of the general reading room of the Montreal Amateur Athletic Association (MAAA) clubhouse, a bronze bust of a long-dead association president stood for decades. There is no memorial inscription on the base, nor did it bear a name. The formality was unnecessary. The figure was familiar to all of the club's members as one of its twelve founders, who was an untiring promoter of amateur sport who wanted to build the largest and most successful sporting club in the world.

Thomas Laird Paton could certainly back up his promotion by his participation. Paton was a lacrosse star when the MAAA was formed in 1881. He helped create history in 1883 when he toured with a Canadian team across Great Britain and competed in sixty matches—including one witnessed by Queen Victoria. Paton was also one of the regulars on the tramps staged by the Tuque Bleues snowshoeing club. After the debacle of the 1883 Winter Carnival hockey tournament, Paton decided to start a hockey club.[107]

Called the Montreal Hockey Club, the team's headquarters were located just blocks from where the Canadiens play their home games today.

Take a stroll in downtown Montreal with the proverbial hockey gods and all those Forum ghosts. Walk along Avenue des Canadiens-de-Montreal, which like the hockey team it is named after, seems to always be under construction during the summertime. Assuming no construction, the street changes its name after a couple of short blocks to Rue de la Gauchetiere. The cross street is Peel.

Turn left onto Peel. About three hundred feet on the right-hand side is a giant statue—one of at least sixty-three monuments in the city honoring people or their ideas. But even in Montreal the statue on the right is unique. The only equestrian statue in Montreal features a horse not mounted but restrained. One side of the statue is inscribed with the following, "In grateful recognition of the patriotism and public spirit shown by Lord Strathcona and Mount Royal in raising and equipping a regiment of horse for service in South Africa as evidence of his sympathy with the cause of imperial unity." On the opposite side, "To commemorate the heroic devotion of the Canadians who fell in the South African War and the valour of their comrades." It should be noted that the Boer War was very unpopular in Quebec society. About 280 Canadian soldiers died in the South African war along with an estimated three hundred thousand horses.[108]

The statue was unveiled in 1907. The spot it covers was the site of the great ice palaces built and was the highlight of the Winter Carnivals. The Dorchester Square statue also serves to mark two other spots of great historical interest to hockey fans. Across Metcalfe Street sits the Sun Life Building, which for decades was the head office of the National Hockey League, and across the square in the other direction is the former site of the Windsor Hotel. The original Windsor Hotel burned down in a 1957 fire, but the 1908 addition stayed intact. Rooms in the Windsor Hotel hosted meetings in which the National Hockey Association and later, the National Hockey League were created.

Dominion Square today

Ice Castle in Dominion Square, 1887
Source: J.T. Henderson, publisher/Library of Congress

Continue the walk northwest along Peel Street, past what's left of the Windsor Hotel, and across three more streets until an old red-brick building is found. The five-story building looks out of the place within the modern neighborhood skyrises. Looking straight up to the sky on the building façade is a winged wheel on a shield.[109]

This five-story building, still existing and operating, was a reward to the sporting organization who reached fame for its competitive teams. The most prolific was its affiliated hockey club.

The Montreal Amateur Athletic Association was formed in 1881 a couple of blocks east at the corner of Mansfield and Burnside[110] when three sporting organizations joined forces to form one club.

The founders decided that the badge of the association should be a "silver grey shield, similar in shape to the Dominion Coat of Arms, crossed diagonally from left to right by a blue and red stripe and surmounted in the centre with the 'winged wheel.'"[111]

Amongst the twelve incorporators of the MAAA,[112] William Whyte and McGill Stewart represented the Montreal Lacrosse Club. On April 1, 1881, the lacrosse club requested to be incorporated. The Montreal Snowshoe Club next followed. James Starke and Sam Baylis requested authorization to purchase the Montreal Gymnasium on April 28, and two weeks later asked the lacrosse players to buy in as partners. The shareholders of the gymnasium wanted to sell for the assumption of $12,000 in liabilities. Although a bargain, the two groups asked the Montreal Bicycle Club to join the new organization.

To start the funding, the three clubs issued $5,000 in bonds without interest, to be payable in ten years.

Tom Paton would be named Honorary Secretary of the upstart organization. Paton was a forward in lacrosse (then called *front*); he also competed with the Montreal Snowshoe Club, racing in the half-mile open race in 1880 and finishing fourth.

Born on September 30, 1855, in Montreal,[113] Paton was one of those, as Hruby wrote, British snooty elites who enjoyed rowing, winning and keeping the unwashed day-laboring masses at arm's length, except that Paton was quite affable, available and welcomed the unwashed with open arms, if they would help him win.

Paton excelled in school, graduating at the age of sixteen.

He first entered the firm of Robert Stephen & Co., and it was not long before he was induced to go on the road, where his successes followed him. Paton spent eight years traveling, and his opinion was eagerly sought after by businessmen all across the country.

Despite being a "British snooty elite," Paton may have been Montreal's most popular citizen. He was elected to the presidency of the Amateur Athletic Association of Canada, and the vice presidency of the Amateur Skating Association of Canada; he was president of the Montreal Amateur Athletic Association. He was a life member of the Caledonian Society, Royal St. Lawrence Yacht Club, and Board of Trade, and last but not least, he was a director of the Dominion Commercial Travellers' Association.[114]

There were few sports that Paton did not partake in, and he certainly was a huge proponent of the amateur ideal. But his first love was promoting the Amateur Athletic Association. One sport without Paton's involvement, until later in life, was skating and hockey. There were three main sports in the new country of Canada: lacrosse in the fall, snowshoeing in the winter, and bicycling in the spring and summer. Paton played them all, but it would be in the developing sport of hockey where he would really make his mark.

Tom Paton

After immediate success as a start-up, the Montreal Amateur Athletic Association began to stagnate after its first three years—its membership plateauing with very little excitement being generated. Minutes show as many members were resigning as were signing up. Serving on the rink committee for the 1884 Winter Carnival, Paton saw firsthand the excitement generated by the fans by this new version of the old game of hockey.

Paton watched the Carnival sport of hockey and thought perhaps the sports could combine with lacrosse so lacrosse players could stay active and in shape by playing a winter version of the game.

In late October 1884, the Montreal Lacrosse Club generated negative headlines when two of its players—John Paterson and William Cleghorn Jr.—were suspended from the club after a 3–1 loss in Toronto. It was Tom Paton who had created the problem, and little did Billie Cleghorn know, but he was paving the road for his yet-to-be-born son Sprague to be a Hockey Hall of Famer.

Before leaving for a game in Toronto, lacrosse captain Fred McIndoe showed on paper the team he chose to play, with David Paterson being chosen amongst the twelve. The Lacrosse Club held a committee meeting, and Paterson's name was listed as a reserve.

Cleghorn, the team's goaltender, was upset that the committee had left David Paterson off the starting team, refusing to travel to Toronto if Paterson did not play. McIndoe told Cleghorn not to worry, that Paterson was going to play because Paton was not traveling to Toronto. David's brother John Paterson, also a member of the team, agreed with Cleghorn. "Why he is better than eight of the men on this team, put him on in my place; I won't play. You can put me on reserve in his place."

Cleghorn said that McIndoe told the players not to worry and that David Paterson would play. With that information, Cleghorn telegraphed John Paterson, whose employer sent him to Alexandria, Ontario. "You are on the team. We go by Grand Trunk Railroad 8:00 p.m. Friday." David Paterson spoke with his employer, who gave him permission to miss work to play in the game. Cleghorn relayed the information to McIndoe, who voiced no objections. The club accountant confirmed to Cleghorn to make sure David Paterson was on board the train. Paterson approached McIndoe several times on the train ride to Toronto and asked what position he would be playing, but received an evasive answer. While dressing in the hotel, McIndoe told John Paterson, "Mr. Paton has changed his mind and is going to play."

Both Patersons were upset after confirming to David Paterson's employer that he was needed to skip work to play an amateur game only to sit on the bench. Both players declined to play, and Montreal lost 3–1.

McIndoe offered a different version of events, however. The captain denied that he could change the team and that David Paterson was on the team as a reserve. "I may have been a little too anxious to have David Paterson up with the team because I thought there was a chance of some member not being able to get off, but I in no way gave them to understand that David Paterson was on the team, or would play."

The Lacrosse Club's management committee decided to punish Cleghorn and the Paterson brothers by requiring them to apologize to their teammates and to reimburse the club the $11 spent on travel. The players offered the apology, although they felt deceived. But they refused to pay the $11 because they felt it amounted to a fine. "We were told by [McIndoe], whom we consider a competent authority, that [David Paterson] would play, and were thus brought to Toronto under false pretenses, and therefore, do not consider ourselves liable."

The next day, club secretary Horace Tibbs replied that the apology was not good enough and if the travel money was not returned the club would start expulsion procedures. Both players sent two more letters, with a stronger apology in the first and a request for the committee to reconsider payment as they did not go to Toronto for a holiday. Tibbs responded that once the two men repaid the club, the club would reconsider the investigation.

Both men took their version of the story to the *Montreal Gazette* instead.[115]

The Lacrosse Club held a special meeting to consider the expulsion of Paterson and Cleghorn. A heated discussion ensued, and a motion was made and seconded for expulsion. Before that could be voted on, however, an amendment was made accepting the two men's apology and granting them relief of repaying the $11 the committee demanded. This last amendment carried by a wide margin.[116]

Rebuked, Paton then asked the MAAA board for permission to call a meeting for the purpose of forming a hockey club, under the auspices of the association. Permission was granted.[117] On November 28, 1884, the Montreal Hockey Club was formed—not as an official organizational club, but as an affiliate that could use the MAAA name.

If the thirty-year-old Paton had a master plan for this new club, he certainly did not execute it well. The Montreal Hockey Club was thrown together much like a Super Bowl party is thrown together today. Invite a few friends over at a set time, drink a couple of adult beverages, and while everyone is still sober, a hockey team is formed.

The truth of the matter is once Paton saw the turnout, he knew he had a new team to manage. The discussion could not have been particularly long or lively because not only did the club form at this initial meeting "to gauge interest," but a constitution and bylaws were submitted and adopted. The team's colors were decided to be navy blue. The club made arrangements with Robertson's Crystal Rink for Monday and Thursday evening practices, and officers were elected. All in one evening meeting.

Thomas Fraser was elected president. Billy Aird was selected vice president. Robert Whyte was named the secretary-treasurer. And the management committee consisted of Jim Ross (brother of Phil and Willie), Fred Barlow, Billy Hodgson, Fred Learmonth, Archie MacNaughton and Paton.[118] Fraser, Aird, Learmonth and MacNaughton were teammates of Paton on the Montreal Lacrosse

Club. (Learmonth and Aird had played for the Victorias in hockey's first intercity battle against Quebec in 1881.[119])

Paton probably did not believe the sport would take off because of a couple of interesting clauses he inserted into the membership rules to join the hockey club.

The first was that a player had to be a member of the Montreal Amateur Athletic Association, which seemed redundant since most of the players were already members of the organization. A proposed member of the MAAA had to be recommended by at least two other current and active members, and the rest of the executives voted on whether to accept. Furthermore, any member of the Montreal AAA could join the hockey club if they paid the annual fee. However, a club member could not belong to any other hockey club. This made selection for a hockey team a little on the difficult side as the hockey club was not an official MAAA club, but someone who wanted to play for the hockey team had to have club membership to both. And yet, unlike with the Cleghorn and Paterson brouhaha, Paton would be able to maintain control of the roster.

The Montreal Hockey Club also put this definition of *amateurism* in its constitution:

> An amateur is one who has never competed for a money prize or staked bet, or with or against a professional for any prize, or who has never taught, pursued or assisted in the practice of athletic exercise as a means of obtaining a livelihood, or has never entered any competition under a name other than his own.[120]

Despite exhaustive research since James Creighton first tried to organize hockey in 1875, no record shows Paton ever playing a hockey game. At the age of thirty Paton was old by any standard for starting out in any sport. And in the developing game of hockey, being thirty made you more of a chaperone than a peer. That's true today, but especially true in the 1880s.

Maybe the decision was a nod to his age, or perhaps made out of spite for Cleghorn, but despite being a high-scoring forward in lacrosse, Paton became a goaltender in hockey.

And the first captain of the Montreal Hockey Club.

CHAPTER 9

THE CARNIVAL YEARS

After the weather debacle of the previous year, the Winter Carnival was moved indoors with the games being played in the Crystal Rink. The game was now standardized with seven men a side, with the addition of a rover compared to how the game is played today.

The Carnival organizers found how powerful of a draw hockey could be on opening night. Carnival goers battling a biting cold could sit inside the relative warmth of an arena, protected from the elements, to watch athletes skate and chase an object—the inside venue makes the players appear to skate faster. The sounds that ricochet off the structure's insides brought the game to life more. The close confines brought a certain intimacy to the action. And this was the only competition that was exclusive to the carnival. Snowshoers had their tramps. Fancy skaters had other costume balls. Toboggan slides could be done at any time. What drew Carnival visitors was the uniqueness of the events, such as storming the Ice Castle, which seemed fake and orchestrated although visually stunning, and the fireworks opening and closing the games.

Tom Binns moved to Canada from England in 1886 and shared his experiences with storming the Ice Castle as a member of the Tuque Bleue Snowshoe Club.

> In the evening I attended the MAAA gymnasium as this was to be the great event of the week—the storming of the ice castle on Dominion Square. After falling in about eight hundred strong, we marched out on the street, each fellow receiving a torch and a bundle of colored lights. These we had strict orders not to light until the signal was given.
>
> We marched up the mountain, headed by our band, and took up our position among the other snowshoe clubs.
>
> Presently the whole army of snowshoers, each headed by its band, commenced to move slowly down the mountainside carrying their lighted torches. After taking a circuitous route we marched down Peel Street, passed in front of the Windsor (Hotel), and marched around the ice castle.
>
> The artillery had placed a gun on the Mountain and every few seconds it pealed forth a tremendous noise, frightening horses and timid people below. The streets were packed and Dominion Square did not seem to have an inch to spare.
>
> At a given signal, when the ice palace must have been surrounded by thousands clad in blanket suits, we commenced to discharge our supply of Roman candles, etc. The defending garrison suitably responded. During the attack a bomb exploded in the palace and a lady among the crowd in Dominion Square was struck by a piece receiving such injuries that she later died from the effects. After a considerable display of fireworks the castle garrison capitulated and we marched again.[121]

The hockey players had only the Carnival championship to compete for. Add in the weather, and this was an unscheduled recipe for success.

The *Montreal Gazette* noted, "One of the principal features of the carnival is hockey. Before the arrangement of these winter festivals it was very little thought of."[122] It should be noted that organization can only do so much. A little luck doesn't hurt, and the best form of the luck came on the opening morning of the Carnival when Ottawa faced off against Jack Arnton's Victorias. The cold weather brought a number of American visitors indoors, and Ottawa's Tom Gallagher scored first, about six minutes in. James Muir tied it up for the locals just a few minutes before halftime. The second half featured up-and-down skating and back-and-forth shooting and blocking, with the players trying so hard with their strap-on skates that many times they tumbled to the ice, giving the crowd a good chuckle as the players took it in good humor. With just five minutes left, Ottawa's Halder Kirby scored to give the visitors a 2–1 lead. He added an insurance marker a couple of moments later to secure the match for Ottawa. The governor-general heard the result and announced he would attend the next day's match between the Montreal Football and Hockey Clubs.[123]

Lord and Lady Lansdowne enjoyed the fancy skating competition at the Victoria Rink in the morning before heading over to the Crystal to watch the Montreal Football and Hockey Clubs battle. Mother Nature decided the host city needed a blizzard, so hockey played indoors was automatically going to center stage. In the previous two Carnivals, organizers tried to keep hockey as an outdoor sport, and the competitions could not be completed properly as the players and fans—and viceroy—did not know whether or not there would be a game.

At the Crystal Rink there would be no such obstacles.

This would be hockey's first showdown between rival goalkeepers. The Montreal Hockey Club started Tom Paton in net, and the Montreal Football Club started Billie Cleghorn. The two lacrosse teammates were playing for different honors. For some unknown reason the Football Club was short a player, and without a substitute played six against seven—hockey's first power play.

The lacrosse ball they used as a puck danced near the goal flags (goal nets would not be invented until 1895) of both teams for the game's first five minutes, but both goalkeepers remained calm and cool and rejected their opponents' shots. Fred Barlow scored for the hockey club by skating around the two slower-footed footballers. The hockey players scored the touchdown, beating the footballers 6–0.[124]

Jimmy Stewart's Crystals lost to McGill 2–0 the next day, which then set up the showdown between Ottawa and the Montreal Hockey Club. Montreal scored first before Ottawa tied it up on a disputed goal. Without a goal net, goal judges called *umpires* determined goals. And when Ottawa scored, the Montreal players claimed the ball was shot at least six inches wide of the flags marking Tom Paton's goal, but the Montrealers lost the argument. The second half remained tied at 1–1 after both clubs tried valiantly to score but were unable. With no rule in place, the clubs agreed to play another half hour. The host city scored first in overtime, but in just a few minutes Ottawa once again tied, so the third half hour ended with the score 2–2. The clubs could not come to an agreement on how to conclude the contest that had started three hours earlier, but many of the Montreal players decided it was time to go to work, so they left the rink and let the Carnival organizers decide how to break the tie.

The committee decided that the two clubs would play a full sixty-minute game starting at 8:30 in the morning, and if the teams remained tied, there would be a third half hour. And if there was still a tie, then the first goal would win. And, if possible, the winners were to play McGill for the championship later that afternoon.[125]

The last day of January would provide enough excitement for the approximately sixty thousand visitors to Montreal. And with the choice of either attending the Saturday-morning game or reading about it on Monday—no Montreal newspaper published on Sundays in those years—a large crowd filled the Crystal Rink, and they were not to be disappointed. The first half came and went without a score; the second did as well. Twenty-five minutes into the third half and neither side had been able to sneak a shot past either Tom Paton or Ottawa's William O'Dell. Finally, Billy Aird broke free and took a lacrosse-like scoop shot and tallied for Montreal. Ottawa furiously fought to tie the game, but time ran out. It took nearly six half hours of hockey, but Montreal pulled out the victory.[126] The Montreal players now had time to grab some lunch and play for the championship, against some rested college kids!

If the older players from the Montreal Hockey Club were worn out after playing four and a half hours of hockey in little more than twenty-four hours, they didn't show it. Both sides battled back and forth, but neither could score. The championship would go to overtime. For Montreal, this would be their eleventh half of hockey in less than thirty hours—and this was in a time when every man played the entire game. With only a few minutes remaining in the third half, Aird slipped a shot past McGill goalie George Stephens. Montreal held on for the tournament championship, won not even three months after the organization was formed.[127]

Many historians consider this the start of the modern hockey era, but there still was a standardization missing from the rules. Not knowing how to decide ties, for example, or what to do if six players showed up against seven. In childbirth terms, a fair analogy is *false labor*. The game was close to being organized, but with this Carnival tournament lasting just five days from start to finish, there was no continuity. There was excitement, however.

And not just from the American spectators.

For the first time, the players did not want the party to end.

The players organized a tournament, and despite the fact that they played for the Carnival championship a few days before, a large crowd attended the game.

The Grand Hockey Tournament would be played at the Victoria Rink, and the first match was between Jack Arnton's Victorias and Tom Paton's Montreal Hockey Club. The Montreal Hockey Club sneaked past the Victorias 1–0, scoring late in the second half to take the game.[128]

Montreal was not the only place hockey had taken off. The Ottawa Hockey Club went back to the nation's capital and started playing a series of exhibitions. In St. John, New Brunswick, a hockey match was part of their winter exhibition series. Moving the game permanently indoors seemed to have speeded up the game for the fans and made the game less hostage to Mother Nature, with the various sounds reverberating off the rink's walls added to the excitement and environment.

The excitement even passed through to the players who first attempted to master the sport. The St. James and Metropolitan clubs arranged to play a rematch—they last played in 1880—featuring several players who played ten years earlier. Henry Joseph, Sir Edward Clouston and Fred Torrance, who played in the 1875 game, played for St. James. Also playing for St. James were Fred Henshaw and H. Montague Allan, whose lifelong affection for amateur hockey would later result in a trophy donated to the top senior hockey club in Canada—the Allan Cup is still competed for today.[129] And Clouston was one of the first Allan Cup trustees.[130] Allan's father, Hugh, was an Odd Fellow.

On March 16, 1885, Arnton's and Stewart's clubs agreed to play an exhibition. It certainly appeared both teams had practiced some new maneuvers. Stewart had learned how to lift the puck down the ice, and the Crystals' Alfred Ritchie was the beneficiary of the pass, scoring the only goal of the game as the Crystals beat the Victorias 1–0.

To say the athletes could not wait for hockey season to start is an understatement. The natural ice surfaces needed the weather to be consistently below freezing in order to open, which put opening day for the 1885–86 season on December 12. The arena was to open at 5:00 p.m. for the customary afternoon tea, and the very first event was not going to be for the skaters, but for the players of the Montreal Hockey Club and the Victorias to play their first game of the season. The game was a tight affair, with Tom Paton's Montreal Hockey Club edging Jack Arnton's Victorias 2–1, the game-winning goal being scored with about eighteen minutes left.[131]

If hockey, as a sport, was going to build upon its successes during the 1885 Carnival, it was going to have to build without the Carnival. Not because of anything done at the Carnival, but because a luckless Chicago couple coming home from a European honeymoon changed hockey forever.

Slightly more than six months after Alex Stewart died driving the same route and one month after the Carnival ended—February 28, 1885,—a young couple from Chicago was coming home from their European honeymoon via Grand Trunk Railroad. The wife became ill on the train. She had smallpox. The train car was not sanitized, and the man who cleaned the car became ill. His family became smallpox victims as well. The train made its way to Montreal, and both the porter and conductor were felled by the disease and were taken to Hotel-Dieu Hospital. [132]

The conductor, George Longley, initially arrived at Bonaventure Station feverish and covered with fiery eruptions on his hands, face, chest and arms. Since Longley was a Protestant he was rushed to Montreal General Hospital. There the resident physician diagnosed him with smallpox and refused to admit him.

Not knowing where to turn, Longley arrived at the gates of the Hotel-Dieu where a nun assisted him. "Why did you not go to the English hospital?" the nun asked. "I went there but was refused," Longley replied. "Then we are happy to have you here," the nun replied.

Longley recovered and survived, but his bedding infected Pelagie Robichaud, an Acadian girl who worked in the laundry. She died on April 1 and was soon followed by her sister Marie.

By mid-April it was clear smallpox was loose in the hospital and could not be contained. The health department then made a catastrophic mistake—they released all patients who did not appear sick. Many were in the stage of incubation, and they set the virus loose on the streets of Montreal. The incubation period between contraction and the first obvious symptoms was around twelve days. The initial obvious symptoms mirrored that of the flu, COVID-19, and the common cold—a fever as high as 101 degrees Fahrenheit, muscle pain, a malaise, headache and prostration. As the digestive tract was usually involved, nausea, vomiting and backache often occurred.

The porter and conductor were attended to by family and nursing staff—none of whom were inoculated—and the final results tallied 3,164 dead Montrealers, mostly children, thanks to the train.[133]

The real tragedy of the smallpox epidemic was that it was completely preventable. Edward Jenner of England developed a vaccine in 1796, and it was widely available, but French Canadians were the nineteenth century's anti-vaxxers. Many of the French-speaking Montrealers were Catholic and had large families, living in overcrowded tenement housing in some of the poorest quarters of the city.[134]

Dr. Louis Martel, a native of St. Hyacinthe, had practiced in Montreal before emigrating to Lewiston, Maine. Martel wrote, "I witnessed the smallpox epidemic in 1872. There was some opposition to vaccination, for two reasons. Firstly, because two reputable doctors, one of who was a university professor, were themselves opposed; also because the virus used was bad; so bad that in some cases arms had to be amputated."[135]

It would be easy to blame the ignorance and mistrust of the French Canadians as the epidemic grew, and many people in border states such as Maine did just that. But Anglo-French relations were particularly tense during the summer and fall of 1885. The Anglo authorities had just arrested Louis Riel in May and would execute him in November, prompting widespread protests. To the Metis of Manitoba, Riel was a hero, an eloquent spokesman for their aspirations. In the Canadian west in 1885, the majority of the settlers regarded him as a villain. French Canadians believe Riel was a victim of English religious and racial bigotry. Even today the two ethnic sides disagree.

In 1885 Montreal, the French Canadians were in no mood to have government-mandated vaccination imposed on them by the English.

This was the mindset of many of the French population when the English government of Quebec tried to protect its inhabitants against the spread of smallpox. But when logic didn't work because of mistrust, the Anglo leaders decided to use force.

The smallpox epidemic rarely touched the English citizens, most of whom were vaccinated. And the young wealthy men of Montreal, who made up all of the city hockey clubs except the Crystals and all of them English-speaking, still wanted to play.

The epidemic forced the cancellation of the Carnival, so two American cities jumped into the fray. St. Paul, Minnesota, hosted their first Winter Carnival—it still runs today—and the organizers hired Montreal's ice castle designer to build their castle. The other Carnival was closer to hockey's center. Burlington, Vermont, located a little less than one hundred miles from Montreal, offered to host a tournament on Lake Champlain. Despite problems during the first two Carnivals, hockey was going back outside.

The tournament was too short for the hockey players who still wanted to play, so they also decided to create a little city competition for themselves, smallpox epidemic be damned.

But to do that the four Montreal club leaders decided to update, formalize, publish, publicize and share hockey's rule book. This effort is the birth of the modern evolution of hockey—a direct ascendant to the game being played today.

CHAPTER 10

FINDING A CAUSE, REWRITING THE RULES

Thanks to playing the Winter Carnival on the Crystal Ice Rink, the roles of each player became defined—a necessity Bogert explained:

> The team is made up as follows: Four forwards—one on each wing and two center men—a cover-point, a point and goal-keeper. The three latter men take their positions from the forwards and maintain a distance of several yards apart, the cover-point behind the center-forward and the point in same relation to his cover man.
>
> It is the prime duty of the forwards to "keep on the puck"—in the lingo of the hockey fraternity—never allowing the opposing team to remain in undisputed possession for an instant. They must always move down the ice in a body, always ready to support one another by being in position to receive a pass, shoot at goal, or assist a fellow player who is overtaxed; working like bees to keep the puck near the opponents' territory, and eventually to score a game.[136]
>
> The position of cover-point is the most important on the ice and a difficult one to fill. The player is both on

> the offensive and defensive, and must be ready at any moment to check a player or return a puck, or when he comes in possession of it, and a favorable opportunity occurs, to dart through the line of opposing forwards in the hope of a shot at goal.
>
> The point should be a tower of strength in both checking and lifting. He is purely a defensive player, and must allow no man to pass him; while at lifting he should be an adept, always returning the puck, if possible, over the heads of players, thus preventing a clear shot at goal, or demoralizing an opponent's aim.
>
> The goal-keeper takes position a few inches in advance of the goal posts, and when the goal is being threatened brings his feet together in the shape of a wedge, covering as much ground as possible between the posts. He is not allowed to kneel on the ice. He must be exceedingly quick with his hands, nimble on his skates, and have a good eye; prepared to ward off the puck with his stick, catch it in his hands or intercept it with his skates. He must never leave his goal except under stress at the most urgent necessity.
>
> The captain should be a man chooser, through his experience as a player and for his quickness of judgment. He must have the team under perfect control and enjoy the complete confidence of his men to secure the best results. He must make it a point to attend all the practice games of his club, taking care that the men are practiced in the positions they are to occupy in the matches, coaching them, and noting any weak point, that it may be strengthened at once.[137]

It goes without argument that the sport of hockey has grown more complex as the years have rolled by with the captain's original job being delegated to several members of today's organization, most of whom have played professionally at some level if not in the National Hockey League.

But a coach today who lacks the confidence of his players won't last long, just as in 1893. And while the game switched to six men a side in the 1910s and the two defensive players started to line up horizontally instead of vertically around the same time, the roles are still summed up quite nicely.

Sam Robertson, owner of the Crystal Rink, was born twenty years too late to play hockey. The Montreal native was a carpenter by trade, but by 1878 the then thirty-four-year-old dedicated his life to building ice rinks in Montreal. He lacked the capital and prestige of the Victoria Rink, so Robertson economically competed on amusing the rising middle classes.

The Victoria Rink, managed by Alex Caldwell, was the go-to place for the elite classes. For one example, the Victoria Rink held a skating masquerade in honor of Princess Louise, and that's where the majority of skaters were in a late-winter cold spell. The Crystal also hosted a large group skating, while at a third rink, outdoors at St. Denis Street, a group skated along with the band while several bonfires illuminated the scene.[138]

Robertson's indoor facility even got off under an auspicious start as the rink was being prepared for opening. A Mrs. Prior (whose identity could not be confirmed via either the Montreal City Directory or the 1881 Canadian census) hired the law firm of Devlin & Devlin to file a claim against the city's water division for neglect. When Robertson flooded the new rink, water seeped from the building and accumulated on St. Catherine Street. According to Prior's claim, the water froze on the footpath and she slipped on the ice and received severe injuries which would keep her confined to her house for three months. The claim was filed against the city because the litigants claimed the city was responsible for the rink's neglect since the city approved and sold the water to be used for the flooding of the rink.[139] While the incident was reported in the newspaper, no record of a payment was located.

Despite the slow start, Robertson focused on marketing to attract the newly-emerging middle class through his own masquerade skates and spectator sports that were also fun to compete in—such as speed skating and, to a lesser extent, hockey.

Seeing a weakness in the scheduling in the 1885 Winter Carnival, Robertson offered to host the hockey games, and the games were a rousing success. Robertson was also credited with inventing the Canadian skate, which increased the speed of skaters.

The 1885 Carnival showcased what hockey could be: fast and exciting, with closely fought battles with skating, spills and exhausting excitement for both players and spectators. The smallpox epidemic ruined any hope for a repeat performance, but that wasn't going to stop the players, or the rink proprietors, who realized that having hockey and a band were great winter attractions that still shielded people from the climate.

But Robertson had seen some of the battles of normally friendly sportsmen refusing to play because of a lack of consistency in the rules. The game played indoors on a uniform surface was different than the game played on an outdoor ice surface limited only by geography or someone's whim.

With Montreal's 1886 Carnival put on hiatus, Robertson recruited Crystal Club captain Jimmy Stewart to formalize and publicize the rules, and to help foster a competition. Hockey is a game of evolution. The rules and styles of play get tweaked every few years. But these rules serve as a foundation for the game that is watched by millions and played by millions as well.

The four men who cobbled those rules together in January 1886 have largely been ignored. Jack Arnton Jr., famed rugby and baseball player who wanted the offsides rules included, and speed skater Jim Stewart were the true architects of modern hockey. The two captains of the Victoria and Crystal Rink teams were supported by committee members Charles Swabey, a recent civil law graduate at McGill University, and Montreal Lacrosse Club captain James W. Woods,[140] who helped organize the first league as well as write the rule book. The four young men borrowed a couple of rules from the experimental years and then relied upon their expertise as a fast skater (Stewart), the offsides rules of a rugby player (Arnton) and the action of lacrosse (Woods) to cultivate the version of hockey played the world over today.[141]

Unfortunately for the twenty-four-year-old Woods, his career as a traveling salesman took off and he moved before any games were played, watching from afar and reading the reports in the Ottawa area, which was his territory for the Montreal-based Hodgson, Sumner and Company. Woods was one of two salesmen for the company, which imported goods from England and looked for markets to sell the goods. When it came to selling, Woods was a natural. Swabey would move to Toronto and attend Osgoode Hall Law School, and be instrumental in forming the Toronto Victorias Hockey Club.

By January of 1886, the four men had completely rewritten the rules. One important modification was the ability to play behind the goal line. In the past, a play that went behind the goal was called dead, even if the puck was on the ice. The new rules kept play moving.[142]

This is what they came up with:

> Sec. 1. Hockey sticks may be any length to suit the player, but must not be more than three inches wide in any part.[143]

Nothing about this clause existed in the original rules, but it was tweaked in the 1920s. Rule 10 of the 2020–21 NHL Rulebook still states that the widest part, or the blade, shall not be more than three inches wide.[144]

> Sec. 2. The puck must be one inch thick and three inches in diameter, and of vulcanized rubber.

The puck was a ball nine years earlier, but Rule 13 of the 2020–21 Rule Book is verbatim.

> Sec. 3. The top of the goals must be six feet above the ice, including any top ornament, and six feet apart.

No mention in 1877, and within a couple of years the height was reduced to four feet. Rule 2.1 of the 2020–21 NHL Rule Book lists the goals as four feet above the ice and six feet apart.

> Sec. 4. The referee and umpires shall be selected by the captains. Referee shall have powers to settle all disputes on the ice, and his decision shall be final. One umpire shall be stationed at each goal; all questions as to games shall be settled by the umpires, and their decision must be final. Umpires must not change goals during a match.

This was a drastic change of events from nine years earlier, which gave more power to the umpires, or as a term most of us would recognize in the modern era, *goal judges*. *Games* in this context means "goals."

In the modern game this rule is barely recognizable. As technology has improved during the last twenty years, hockey at the professional level allows for instant replay to overrule referees, and linesmen to overrule referees on certain calls (such as too many men), and the goal judges have been replaced by overhead cameras in all NHL arenas. Even a referee's decision is no longer always final.

> Sec. 5. Seven players shall constitute a full team. They shall be bona fide members of the club they represent; no player will be allowed to play for more than one club during a season.

This was never addressed in the original rules.

In 1911 the NHA introduced six-man hockey, although NHL teams played a few seven-man hockey games when playing under western rules against the Pacific Coast Hockey Association during the NHL's first few years. But unless a player is traded or released, he is still bound to one organization.

> Sec. 6. The game shall be commenced and renewed by a bully on the center of the rink. Goals shall be changed after each game, unless otherwise agreed.

This was one of the few rules of 1877 that was adopted nine years later. The bully would be replaced by the faceoff in 1900, and goals were later changed at half-time or between periods, depending on the era and the league.

Depiction of a bully, or faceoff, on AHAC Trophy.
Source: Doug MacLellan/Hockey Hall of Fame

> Sec. 7. A match shall be decided by the team winning the greatest number of games during a given time, games must in all cases be won by putting the puck through the goals from the front side.

Rules were all over the map during the preceding nine years. Some matches were decided by the team that first scored a set number of goals; others by time. This rule is basically intact today.

> Sec. 8. The time of the matches shall be two half hours, with ten minutes rest in between. In case of a tie, play will continue until one side scores a goal.

NHL Rule 77 covers this, although the two halves were switched to three twenty-minute periods during the 1910s, and ties were considered an evil necessity when the ice would be so chopped up action could not continue. This was a regular feature in the pre-Zamboni era. Travel restrictions by both the US and Canadian governments during World War II meant games had to end before the trains carrying the visiting teams left the station, so for consistency reasons, overtime was eliminated during World War II. After the war, the NHL, for some inexplicable reason, saved overtime for the playoffs only until the absorption of four World Hockey Association clubs in 1979.

> Sec. 9. When the puck goes off the ice, behind the goals, it shall be taken by the referee to five yards at right angles from the goal line and there faced. When the puck goes off the ice at the sides, it shall be taken by the referee to five yards at right angles from the boundary line and there faced.

Replace five yards, or fifteen feet, with twenty feet, and you have today's NHL dimensions, even in Canadian and European matches, even though those countries have long-converted to the metric system. Again, this rule was radically different than what was proposed in 1877.

> Sec. 10. The boundary line shall be latterly the extreme edge of the ice on either side of the rink.

This has been replaced in the early 1900s with boards. Enclosed arenas necessitated surrounding the playing surface with boards to protected spectators from lifted pucks.

> Sec. 11. When a player hits a puck, any one of the same side, who at such moment of hitting is nearer the opponent's goal line is out of play, and may not touch the puck himself, or in any way whatever prevent any other player from doing so until it has been played, a player must always be on his own side of the puck.

This is the biggest fundamental change to the way hockey was played in the 1800s and how it is played today.

It took approximately thirty-five years of modification to the offsides rule, where now it is only the offensive blue line where the puck must be ahead of the attacking players.

> Sec. 12. The puck may be stopped, but not carried or knocked on by any part of the body; no player shall raise his stick above his shoulder; charging from behind, tripping, collaring, kicking or shoving shall not be allowed, and any player, after being twice warned by the referee, it shall become his duty to rule the player off the ice for the match.

This is one of the few rules carried forward from 1877.

Several of these rules are still enforced today, although game misconducts are a little extreme compared to two minutes in the penalty box, where, as Denis Lemieux says in the movie *Slap Shot*, "you feel shame."

> Sec. 13. The goal-keeper must not during play, lie, kneel or sit upon the ice, but must maintain a standing position.

No mention in the 1877 rules, but this rule actually existed until 1916 in the West and 1917 in the East.

> Sec. 14. On the infringement of any of the above rules, the puck shall be brought back and a bully shall take place.

Still applies; of course, the bully has been replaced by a face-off.

One could write several dissertations just on hockey's rule changes and the effects on the development of the game. What started off as nine rules in 1875 has morphed into eighty-seven main sections and several sub-sections today.

From 1875 until 1886, however, the pioneers of hockey experimented and changed the rules so frequently that even a game from 1875 would not be recognizable in 1886.

Those nine rules in 1875 became fifteen rules in 1886, with none in common. However, four of the fifteen rules from 1886 are still in place today. It should be noted that while it's true that Creighton recorded seven rules in the 1875 Montreal game, every single one of those rules was changed by 1886. (Although to be fair, two of the rules just changed the word *ball* for *puck.*) However, most of the 1886 rules lasted for decades, even longer. Rules 2 and 7 are still in effect for every professional league in the world. And Rules 8 and 9 are basically the same today.

But before we can examine the rules and rule changes from 1875 to 1886, one must look at one of the earliest discovered publication of rules.

The *Montreal Gazette* published the game's rules in its February 27, 1877, edition, summarized and explained as follows:

The game shall be commenced and renewed by a bully in the center of the ground. A bully pre-dated a faceoff. Each opposing center would tap his stick on the ice, and then tap his opponent's stick. After the third tap of the stick, the puck was free to take.

Goals shall be changed after each game. *Game* in this instance means "the scoring of a goal."

When a player hits the ball, any one of the same side who at such moment of hitting is nearer to the opponents' goal line is out of play, and may not touch the ball himself, or in any way whatever prevent any other player from doing so, until the ball has been played. A player must always be on his own side of the ball. The spelling is correct—there was no mention of the word *puck.*[145]

Compare this statement with what was published in *Outing* in 1893:

> The rules are somewhat similar to those laid down in football, the principal one being that a player must always be "on side," i.e. never playing in advance of the puck; consequently he cannot take the puck on a

> pass from a player on his own side unless he be behind him when the pass was made; neither can he, in the same way, touch the puck when a "lift" or "shoot" has been made by a player on his own side.
>
> A player, if he happens to be out of play or offside, however, is put onside immediately upon a player of the opposing team touching the puck. [146]

The *Gazette* noted:

> The ball may be stopped, but not carried or knocked on by any part of the body. No player shall raise his stick above his shoulder. Charging from behind, tripping, collaring, kicking or shinning shall not be allowed.
>
> When the ball is hit behind the goal line by the attacking side, it shall be brought out straight fifteen yards, and started again by a bully; but, if hit behind by any one of the side whose goal line it is, a player of the opposite side shall hit it out from within one yard of the nearest corner, no player of the attacking side at that time shall be within twenty yards of the goal line, and the defenders, with the exception of the goal-keeper, must be behind their goal line.
>
> When the ball goes off at the side, a player of the opposite side to that which hit it out shall roll it out from the point on the boundary line at which it went off at right angles with the boundary line, and it shall not be in play until it has touched the ice, and the player rolling it in shall not play it until it has been played by another player, every player being then behind the ball.

From *Outing:*

> A wooden wall, generally two feet in height, borders the ice. From this the puck readily rebounds, and it becomes a material factor in the science of the game, as a skillful player, when closely checked, often baffles

> his opponents by driving the puck against the wall, and allowing for the rebound, securing possession at an unexpected point.[147]

The *Gazette* pointed out that on any infringement of any of the rules, the ball shall be brought back and a bully shall take place. To cover any situations not thought about, it was decided that all disputes shall be settled by the Umpires, or in the event of their disagreement, by the Referee.[148]

Not even mentioned in the *Gazette* are the size of the goals.

> The goal posts are placed six feet apart, at the ends of the rink, and are four feet high. They are held in position by being sunk in holes made in the ice.
>
> The puck may be intercepted, but must not be carried or knocked forward by any part of the skate or person.[149]

Going back to that Game Five fight in Pittsburgh, the sequence started when the Penguins' Ron Hainsey dumped the puck across the blue line to head to the bench and change. The blue line, introduced in 1914, became the new offside rule. The puck went behind the goal net, still six feet by four feet, with modern latex posts inserted into sunken holes in the ice to keep the nets from moving without a little bit of force. The posts used to be more solidly in place, but a serious back injury to Mark Howe in 1980 led to a safer invention, so the nets became more mobile to help prevent serious injury. In chasing the puck in Game Five, Subban passed the puck along the dasher board to Filip Forsberg, yet another Swedish player, but by that moment the other players described above had come together and play was stopped.

Those two-foot boards are now ideally forty-two inches in height and further secured with dashers about six inches from the ice.

Bogert then describes the puck and sticks, which are basically the same as today—or at least until composites replaced wood for the sticks in the 1990s. He explains special hockey skates differ from figure skating so that players can gain extra leverage on the ice.

With rules agreed upon hockey fever started earlier than ever. By December 17, 1885, the Montreal Hockey Club and the Victoria met and arranged a game. The Quebec Hockey Club played an exhibition, and scratch teams in Ottawa had an exhibition as well. The Crystal Club was the only club with a delayed start, but a couple of days before Christmas, Bob Laing was re-elected captain, and the team of commoners was also ready to go.

CHAPTER 11
THE FIRST SEASON

At the corner of Rene Levesque and Guy streets in downtown Montreal are newly built condominiums, conveniently located across the street from Concordia University.

But in 1886 the site where those shiny new condos now stand was the site of the Crystal Skating Rink, a natural ice surface, in a covered building to help shield spectators and participants from winter's harsher moments.

The owner of the rink, Sam Robertson, called a meeting at his rink and invited the known hockey clubs to join. The historic meeting was held January 7, 1886.

After a day of cloudy skies, the evening temperatures were rising to 32 degrees and the clouds were dissipating into a dark night brimming with stars.

Presumably the meeting room was heated as it lasted long enough for truly organized hockey was born; the first hockey season with a set of rules and a full schedule was developed. Robertson offered to put up $40 and asked each of the four clubs to put up $10, to purchase a championship trophy. The rules were sufficiently changed that the players from 1875 would recognize the game was different. A schedule of games was drawn up, with the games being played at the Crystal Rink every Friday night at 7:45 p.m. The schedule was called a *tournament*. A hockey fan today might recognize the scheme as the playoffs without the regular season. The Crystals would play McGill in the first best-of-three series, followed by the Montreal Hockey Club against the Victorias. The winners of both series would then face each other for the city championship.

Since the Montreal Hockey Club had won the Carnival, they were considered the defending champions. Robertson had offered prizes to the winning team, and his main reason for doing so was to drum up hockey business for his rink, away from the Victoria. Meanwhile the manager of the Victoria Rink, Alex Caldwell, was making plans for his own hockey tournament, to include Ottawa and Quebec City.[150]

This Montreal championship tournament, without an official name, was:

- an organized league that was continuous—even if there were subsequent member and name changes,
- played with consistent rules and a series of games,
- to determine a champion within a given time frame,
- reset at the end of one season and starts anew at the beginning of a new season, and
- consistent from year-to-year with minimal changes.

Organized hockey was born as a sport, and a direct lineage can be found from the January 8, 1886, organizational meeting in Montreal to today.

When McGill played the Crystals in the first game of the winter-long tournament, hockey had a new beginning. A primitive version of what we watch today was played—albeit slower—but it would certainly be recognized as an early forerunner of today's NHL. The first league had no formal name—the winner would just be called the City Champion.

Called the Great Tournament for the Championship of Canada by the *Montreal Daily Herald*, this was the first attempt to organize a hockey league with a regular schedule, featuring games every Friday in the Crystal Rink with a scheduled start time of 7:45 p.m.

The clubs winning two out of three matches in the first draw would play for the final, and the club winning two out of three in the final would be declared winners of the tournament.

The schedule was drawn as follows:

Jan. 15	Crystals vs. McGill
Jan. 22	MAAA vs. Victorias
Jan. 29	Crystals vs. McGill
Feb. 5	MAAA vs. Victorias
Feb. 12	Crystals vs. McGill
Feb. 19	MAAA vs. Victorias
Feb. 26	Winners Game One
Mar. 5	Winners Game Two
Mar. 12	Winners Game Three

The new entity's first obstacle came in the very first game. Sixty minutes were played in the opening match between the Crystals and McGill College, but neither team had scored, and the rules had no provisions as to what to do in case of a tie.

Jimmy Stewart, captain of the Crystals, and George W. Stephens, captain of McGill agreed to continue play without interruption until one of the teams scored a goal, and the game became one of endurance. Sudden death overtime was born.[151]

And sudden death it nearly was. According to the game report in the *Montreal Daily Herald*, "The match lasted four hours, with a rest of only ten minutes, and was certainly one of the hottest and roughest games of hockey ever played in Montreal. At the end every man of the teams presented a sadly battered appearance."[152]

As was the custom of the days, independent referees did not exist. The arbiter role was filled by a hockey player who was in the building as an interested fan. More often than not, the games would start thirty to sixty minutes late as no one would step forward to officiate.

On January 22, 1886, Stewart found himself in exactly that position. The Montreal Hockey Club and the Victorias were facing each other in a tightly competitive game.

The Montreal Club featured Tom Paton, and the Victorias featured Jack Arnton. The tightly-played contest ended 1–0 when Arnton scored. The goal was scored when Montreal supporters yelled "offside," and the MAAA players stopped playing although no whistle blew; meanwhile Arnton continued until the puck was past Paton.

Instead of reporting on the game, however, the unnamed writer for the *Montreal Gazette* decided to criticize the rules, which were cowritten by Stewart and Arnton and in their second game of being used.

Wrote the *Gazette*:

> The referee gave a decision for which he was bused, whether fairly or not we do not know. So far as we can see he is the only one who was in a position to judge, and we were pleased to see that having given his veto, which we do him the credit of believing it was his honest conviction, he stuck to it like a man. To our eye he was astray, but we were not in a position to judge thoroughly and not having any unbiased source of information we refrain from condemning where we might possibly be wrong.
>
> The game only demonstrated the utter uselessness of the "offside" clause. Hockey cannot be played without a very frequent offside, and the referee did not enforce it half the times he ought have. It is a rule which must, if observed at all, be observed every time, and we believe that if the game is left with a vestige of interest this cannot be done. Do away with the "offside" rule and play hockey as lacrosse and there will be a better game. The only objection is that this might leave it open to roughness, but there is no necessity of this, and the element, we're glad to say, was almost absent Friday night.[153]

Stewart took the unusual step of replying with a letter to the editor to explain his decision, as well as a couple of innovations that night which were new to hockey on that date, but might be familiar to readers.

Stewart wrote:

> In the first place, it occurred to me that some improvement was required as to the method of stopping play when an "off side" or foul should take place, so after procuring a whistle, I explained to either captain that play was to continue until the whistle was blown; this was eagerly accepted as a means to put a stop to the annoyance caused by some of the spectators, who are to be found at every match amusing themselves by calling "off side" when they are so inclined.[154]

Any youth who has played organized hockey has heard a coach instruct on more than one occasion to play until the whistle is heard, and if in doubt, keep playing. Jimmy Stewart invented that strategy in the organized sport's second match.

Stewart continued:

> If I mistake not the cry of "off side" which caused the disagreement on Friday night originated with a few of these spectators, and the Montreal players instead of continuing the game until they heard the whistle, stopped playing, while the member of the Vics who had the puck quietly put it through the goal and claimed a game, which I had no hesitation in allowing.
>
> Referring to the "off-side" rule generally, you say "the referee did not enforce it half the times he ought"—I am quite aware that the rule was not enforced at every "off-side," for the reason that before the match began I explained to the captain of each team how usual it is for a player, under certain circumstances, to play "off-sides" purposely, whereby, if a bully took place, he would gain a considerable advantage, and it was arranged that I should not call any "off-side" unless it was claimed.
>
> I cannot say I concur in your opinion that the "off-side" rule should be dispensed with, but I think the

> enforcement of it should be left to the discretion of the referee, for very often an "off-side" occurring does not influence the match in the least and the referee should have power to call an "off-side" only when any perceptible advantage has been gained by the party committing it. [155]

An astute reader will note that Stewart solved the problem in 1886, and he solved the offsides review in 2021 as well, if the NHL administrators, coaches and general managers would listen.

Stewart wrote:

> You also take note of the groans and hisses, which emanated from a few of the spectators on my decision becoming known. Now I consider that display of ignorance proof above all others that the decision was just; it reminds one of a practice not unknown at lacrosse matches a few years back, where a gang of ignorant roughs would congregate to groan and hiss at the referee every time he gave a decision against the team in which they were interested.
>
> Your further remark that the referee should not be in any way interested in the tournament, with which I should agree were it possible to find a disinterested person who is thoroughly acquainted with the rules, for when I say that quite a few of the players on Friday night were entirely at fault as regards some of the ordinary rules, and that some spectators (the same as referred to above) were several times indignant because the match was not "run" as they thought it should have been, you will agree that to look for an outsider to fill the position would be a task not likely to be met with success . . .
>
> I shall sum up my case in a few words: The Montreal team claimed an "off-side," which I would not allow, they stopped play without waiting for the signal to do so, which Victoria scored a goal, thereby winning the match.[156]

Unlike sports in the twentieth and twenty-first century, nineteenth-century hockey was officiated by the players, and the day after Stewart issued his explanation, he led his Crystals into action against McGill.

The Crystals defeated McGill in two straight games, so the February 19 game was canceled and the schedule advanced a week.

The first game of the final series was the Allan Cameron show. The lacrosse star was all over the ice. Listed as center in the newspapers, his position would more aptly be called *cover-point*, a position in the T formation two spots in front of goaltender Billy Hutchison.

Cameron was all over the ice in the first half. Right from the beginning Cameron was on attack—offensively and defensively. The first foray into the Montreal zone saw Cameron skating along the right wing boards with the puck, eluding a check from Fred Learmonth, and from about ten yards from the Montreal net passed along the near boards. The puck was intercepted by Montreal's Billy Aird, who started a rush into the Crystal zone. The play went back and forth with a crowd of players on each team trying to advance the puck with very little room to skate. After a few minutes of both teams battling for a loose puck, the puck became loose, and Billy Barlow started a run for Montreal, but Cameron came back and took the puck away, and like an earlier-day version of Bobby Orr, skated up the ice. Duncan McIntyre tried to check Cameron, but the Crystal cover-point avoided the check and skated around him. Cameron then passed to Bob Laing, who in order to avoid Billy Hodgson, passed back to Cameron. Cameron feinted past Dick Smith and took a hard shot that Aird intercepted. Montreal came back down the ice and took a hard shot at the Crystal goalie Hutchison. Cameron took the puck from his goalie and started another rush up the ice. He skated around McIntyre, Barlow, Hodgson and Smith, only to be blocked by Aird. Cameron still managed to get a shot off, but it was wide of Paton in the Montreal nets. The action sped up even more, with each team making four runs up and down the ice with little to show for it but snow on their blades.

Montreal's Smith broke free for the Crystal goal, but Cameron sent him tumbling to the ice with a ferocious body check—and for good measure, took the puck. Cameron worked his way back into the Montreal zone, but Aird knocked him down.

The Winged Wheelers almost scored the first goal when Crystal forward Bob Laing passed blindly in front of his own goal. The errant pass was picked up by McIntyre, but Hutchison saved the attempt. Cameron attempted another rush into the Montreal zone, but then he was stopped by Learmonth, who quickly passed the puck to Smith on the left side of the ice. Cameron chased Smith down, hacking and chopping at him all the way down the ice as if he were still playing lacrosse, finally stealing the puck when the Montreal forward had a clear shot to score.

The action settled back into the Montreal zone when Jack Findlay and Joe McGoldrick started a rush for the Crystals. Cameron took the puck from his teammates. The Montreal players forgot about the puck and tried to hit Cameron. McIntyre checked Cameron, but not hard enough, and the Montreal forward was sent rolling onto the ice. Cameron then knocked Barlow's stick out of his hands. Hodgson tried to check Cameron, but Cameron eluded the Montrealer, who slipped into the boards and hit the ice with a nasty bang.

More back-and-forth action followed with the forwards on both teams doing all of the work. On a Montreal shot saved by Hutchison, the Crystals' Laing flipped the puck down the ice. The lifted shot was blocked by Aird, but Laing had rushed the ice after he shot, and took the puck away after the Montreal point tried to shoot the puck down the ice. Laing swooped in and, eluding the Montreal defenders, shot toward the middle of the Montreal flags. Montreal goalie Tom Paton stopped Laing's shot with his feet, but the force of the shot was so hard it knocked the Montreal goalie onto the ice. The Crystal forwards attacked while Paton scrambled to recover to his feet. Paton stopped several shots in succession before another shot by Laing and another save by Paton knocked one of the flags out of the ice. This did not stop the Crystals, however, and Jack Findlay recovered the loose puck and set the puck between the flags, out of Paton's reach. Time had almost expired in the first half, but Montreal probably felt lucky they were losing by only a single goal. Paton's goaltending neutralized Cameron's outstanding play.

What happened next was the first time in organized hockey's history but is a familiar story to every fan or player whose team has been in a tough battle. The Montrealers attacked with fury to start the second half. For several minutes the Crystals protected their impenetrable fortress before a Montreal mistake occurred. Aird had attempted to clear the puck to the side, but Billy Virtue and Laing got ahold of the loose rubber. Virtue avoided McIntyre and Barlow by making a short pass to Laing, who then, being met by Smith, passed between his legs back across to Virtue. Virtue then dodged Hodgson and Learmonth and fired a hard shot to the right of Paton and through the flags for a 2–0 lead.

Montreal gamely tried to compete, but the players lacked the discipline to continue a team approach, and the Crystals easily stopped their individual rushes. As the watch showed fifteen minutes remaining, the Winged Wheelers played with a sense of urgency.

Cameron charged Smith viciously, but while he knocked the Montreal player down, he left the puck behind him. It was recovered by Barlow, who avoided Virtue and fired what looked like a sure goal, but Hutchison made the save. Cameron recovered and led the rush in the other direction. The Crystal player sent McIntyre flying and then shot past Aird and Hodgson, but Hodgson slipped on the ice and fell. Barlow tried to get at Cameron, but as he swiped the ice with his stick, the puck found its way to Laing. Laing avoided Aird and passed the puck across to Cameron, who was charged by Learmonth. Cameron calmly passed back to Laing, whose deke faked Paton and gave the Crystals a third tally, just a few minutes before time was called.[157]

The series' concluding match would be decided after hockey made its official United States debut in Burlington, Vermont's, Winter Carnival. Burlington officials saw an opportunity with the smallpox epidemic raging in parts of Montreal.

Imagine the Stanley Cup Final being interrupted after Game Three so the teams could compete in another tournament to help spread the game. That is what happened in February 1886.

Both the Montreal Hockey Club and Crystal Rink club left the city to face off on Lake Champlain at 9:00 a.m. The indoor championship would have to give way to a makeshift rink on the lake.

Only three teams competed in Burlington's Carnival: The Montreal Hockey Club, the Crystals, and the Van Ness House Hockey Club of Burlington. Despite being less than one hundred miles away from Montreal, hockey had never been played in Burlington prior to the morning match between the Crystals and the Winged Wheelers. The Van Ness club played ice polo, however.[158]

Both Montreal teams arrived the night before the match and participated in the Grand Procession. Similar to the opening ceremonies at the Olympics, the clubs and their athletes were represented by their colors and carrying torches. One of the clubs, the Argyle Snowshoe Club, even brought along two bagpipes and players. Fireworks ended the night's display, and the players would need to get their rest, for both Montreal teams would be continuing their hostilities at nine in the morning.[159]

What the Burlington organizers discovered is what the Montreal Carnival organizers learned a few years earlier: it's hard to commercialize a natural outdoor game of hockey due to unpredictable winter weather. Because the Carnival organizers had to fit three games onto one lake on one day, they limited the games to two 20-minute halves. Morning storms wiped out the start of the first game until noon. When the action started, the wind was ferocious, and most spectators stayed indoors. The local skating rink was not large enough to accommodate the game, so hockey matches, if they were to occur, had to be played on Lake Champlain. The games were played in the Central Vermont slip, and the *Burlington* (Vt.) *Free Press* stated the players were well shielded from the winds on the north and west sides.

Both Montreal teams were basically the same as had competed the previous week, but Aird was replaced by Frank Crispo, who was the two-foot-nine-inch star of the 1878 Children's Skating Carnival, now eighteen and presumably taller.

Naturally, neither the Winged Wheelers nor the Crystals could score in either half when their match started. A sudden death period of ten minutes was added. Smith needed only a few minutes, though, to score Montreal's first goal against the Crystals in nearly two hours of competition within a week. The one goal was enough, however, to win the game and the gold medals that came with eventually winning the tournament.

Before the Montreal Hockey Club could win the tournament, however, they had to defeat the local squad. The game was postponed to the evening due to the delayed start of the morning game. With the blustery wind blowing so hard it was hard to see from one dock to the other across the ice rink, the Montreal Hockey Club defeated Van Ness 3–0. Montreal was awarded the gold medals immediately after their victory.

The Crystals still had medals of their own to play for. With an even later starting time, night beginning to fall, and the Van Ness club tired from losing their first game, the clubs agreed to play two 10-minute halves. The Crystals won 1–0, with McGoldrick scoring. It only took twenty minutes of play for the Crystals to win the silver medal. Despite the wonky rules and the conditions, there were few openly spoken complaints.[160] Then again, there wasn't another Carnival in Burlington either.

With one championship won by the Winged Wheelers, they still hadn't scored a goal against the Crystals to win the longer city championship tournament. And the Montrealers were going to have to win without Paton, his position being taken by Robert Whyte.

Although the play lagged during the first twenty-five minutes of the game, Whyte was called on and made several stops on

McGoldrick as the play stayed around the Montreal goal for most of the half.

The Winged Wheelers caught a break when Aird flipped a puck down the ice and Jimmy Stewart flubbed it. The Crystals' point, who had missed the Burlington Carnival and the first game of the series, lost the puck to Hodgson, who avoided Cameron and potted the first goal for Montreal. Dick Smith fired a shot out of a collection of bodies that looked like a 2–0 lead, but Hutchison saved it, and play went the opposite direction. There was a crowd of white-clad Crystals in front of Whyte, and he appeared to be flustered as the puck got near him. Finally, Jack Findlay sent the puck spinning between the posts, and the match was tied at 1–1.[161]

About four minutes before the half, Smith scored to give the Winged Wheelers a 2–1 lead. Montreal's lead did not last long past the half. Three minutes after play had resumed, Joe McGoldrick tallied to tie the game at two apiece.

The action was furious and end-to-end. Seventeen minutes after the tieing goal, the fog-like drama came to a halt when Bob Laing broke his skate. A ten-minute delay followed until Laing emerged wearing someone else's skates. The game—and championship—looked like it was going to sudden death overtime with just three minutes remaining when McGoldrick scored to give the Crystals the lead. Montreal pressed the attack, but as time was running out McGoldrick tallied an insurance marker that gave the game, the championship and the trophy to the Crystals.[162]

This was the reworked, official schedule, with the results:

Jan 15	Montreal Crystals	1	McGill	0	Crystal Rink
Jan 22	MAAA	0	Montreal Victorias	1	Crystal Rink
Jan. 29	Montreal Crystals	4	McGill	1	Crystal Rink
Feb. 5	MAAA	3	Montreal Victorias	1	Crystal Rink
Feb. 12	MAAA	2	Montreal Victorias	1	Crystal Rink
Feb. 19	Montreal Crystals	3	MAAA	0	Crystal Rink
Mar 5	MAAA	2	Montreal Crystals	4	Crystal Rink

With the season over, the Crystals accepted a challenge from Quebec for the championship of Canada. The game lasted for twenty-eight minutes. The action was rough, and the Crystals took off to a 1–0 lead. But then Quebec's Art Scott became injured and could not continue. The rules allowed Quebec to substitute a player, but Quebec had not brought a substitute. Quebec asked the Crystals to drop a player, but the home team refused, remembering back to the first Montreal Carnival when the Montreal Football Club played six against seven. That was considered unacceptable to Quebec, so they skated off the ice. The game and championship of Canada were awarded to the Crystals.[163]

The Quebec team was already in town, so Jack Arnton hastily arranged a match at the Victoria Rink between his club and Quebec. Since Scott and his brother would both be unable to play, the Vics agreed to play four-on-four hockey. Quebec won the exhibition 4–1.

CHAPTER 12
BRANDING

The actions of the Crystals and Quebec in the season's final weekend would not exactly be encouraging for a growing sport or its integrity, so the group that organized the season decided to do a little more codifying, and the Amateur Hockey Association of Canada was born.

The scheduling arrangement of the previous season was not acceptable to two of the clubs, who felt that luck of the draw would dictate placement as opposed to skill. Although not listed, one suspects the two clubs bothered were the Victorias and McGill.

The Crystals never faced the Victorias, for instance, so the championships were not a true and equitable standing of the teams.

Instead the Montreal city tournament rebranded itself as the Amateur Hockey Association of Canada, and every scheduled game was declared a championship match. Each team that won a match was the defending champion, and the defending champion would play its next game at its home rink.

The Victoria Rink was locked out of the city tournament, but the arena hosted the meeting in which the first league was formed. The Victoria's Jack Arnton chaired the meeting. Arnton's vision was that hockey could be the winter's equivalent of lacrosse in the summer, noting the progression in popularity in the 1880s.[164]

James Monk, representing the Victorias, also supported Arnton's position, and was pleased when Ottawa made a commitment to join as well. The paradox the founders discovered is that while they all wanted to win every game, if a team from Montreal won every game, no one from outside Montreal would be interested in playing. Train travel, even for such a short distance as from Ottawa to Montreal, was still relatively expensive to do too frequently, and if players were going to go to the trouble and expense of travel for a challenge, they wanted a shot at winning. [165]

Monk said he would like to see the game prosper and approved of the idea of forming an association. Monk, a bank clerk, said the new organization should be placed on a firm basis and governed by certain rules. Forming an association would be an exceedingly wise thing to do, and to make hockey a recognized game, according to Monk. [166]

Ottawa's Tom Green, a McGill engineering graduate, stated his club was pleased with the association proposal and would join in doing what they could to further the project. With that proclamation, Arnton stepped aside and gave Green the presidency of the new organization. Arnton was named first vice president, while Bob Laing was named second vice president.[167] It bothered no one that Green was a Six Nations native and not white.

Unifying the rules and the structure of an organization was just the item needed to turn hockey into a full-fledged spectator sport. Visitors to the various carnivals had brought the game home as a souvenir. Whatever shinny rules were used locally were adapted to the concepts first shown indoors in Montreal, and the result was there were various forms of the same sport played, but tweaked with characteristics familiar to the local players. Lacrosse players played ice lacrosse, where lacrosse sticks were used to hoist the lacrosse ball while players skated after it. Ice polo was similar to hockey, but played primarily with one hand, a thicker stick and no offsides.

Where spectators hadn't brought the game, ambassadors such as the Montreal Hockey Club's Tom Paton did. Visiting Toronto as a member of the Montreal Amateur Athletic Association's lacrosse team, Paton introduced the sport to the Toronto Lacrosse

Club members as a method of winter training. The game wasn't completely foreign in Toronto. Shinny games were recorded as early as the 1840s but never were organized or structured until Paton's visit. An organized premature version was played regularly in Kingston starting in the 1880s.[168]

Wrote W. H. A. Kerr in *The Dominion Illustrated Monthly*:

> Its earliest stopping of importance (in Ontario) seems to have been at Kingston in '85–'86. The critical and enthusiastic audiences that now throng to see a good game and applaud a quick "lift," or a dodgy run would laugh could they see a reproduction of the first match in Kingston. It was played between the Royal Military College and Queen's University. Some of the cadets, recruits of the previous fall, had learned the game in Quebec schools and introduced it in '85 on the R. M. C. bay where "shinty" had been held, until then, a certain foothold . . . The game was satisfactorily arranged for and came off on the harbour on a fenced-in, and yet open, rink. There was a large circular band-stand in the middle of the ice, directly between the goals that quite prevented one end from being seen by the other. Out of this bandstand grew an electric light pole. But what did these trifles matter? It was agreed for mutual accommodation that the offside rule be waived.[169]

Amateur hockey was also being played at a high level in Ottawa and Quebec City, and both cities were invited to have a representative team. But transportation costs, namely train travel, were still too high to send a team of amateur athletes on a regular basis, so the challenge system was adopted.

One person who had no concerns about train travel costs was Tom Paton. The Montreal AAA founder and hockey club goalie had the good fortune to be born after his father entered commercial real estate in Montreal in the 1870s, just as Montreal's real estate market was taking off.

A lacrosse player as well, Paton ordered some hockey sticks from Montreal, along with some rule books, and had them shipped to Toronto. He introduced the new game of hockey to the lacrosse players in that city.

In 1887, Paton was visiting Toronto Lacrosse Club president John Massey at the Western Canada Loan & Savings vice president's office in Toronto, and casually mentioned to Massey and Charles McHenry—a clerk at the bank who also was an officer of the Toronto Lacrosse Club—that hockey was becoming the leading game in Montreal in the winter. Massey telegraphed for eighteen sticks, a couple of pucks and a few sets of rules and had them shipped by train the next day.[170]

Only two sticks were sold. Massey gave the other sticks away. But Massey was unconcerned—he fought the same battles when he introduced lacrosse to Toronto. Massey, his brother and Chris Henderson had bought lacrosse sticks from Montreal and had great difficulty finding customers. It worked out well.[171]

* * *

One player who was absent from the formation meeting but elected to the council was Jimmy Stewart. Stewart was elected to represent the Crystals, but unbeknownst to the rest of the hockey players, Tom Paton had a plan, and the timing was perfect.

Paton had recruited Stewart to join the prestigious Montreal Amateur Athletic Association, and jump to the affiliated Montreal Hockey Club in October. Stewart applied, and it took two meetings, but finally the MAAA board decided to grant membership to the 24-year-old who was providing for his sisters and step-mother.[172]

But Paton wasn't finished yet. Trying to build the best hockey club in the world, Paton and Stewart then recruited three Crystal teammates to join the MAAA. Allan Cameron was the next to jump the championship ship. The lacrosse cover-point joined the association the following week. Stripped of their defense, the

MAAA also persuaded forward Jack Findlay and goaltender Billy Hutchison to change colors.

The Montreal Crystals were still considered the reigning champion since they defeated Quebec—in a forfeit—the previous season. But with a decimated lineup, their reign as champions was not going to last long.

After beating McGill 3–1, the depleted Crystals battled Arnton's Victorias, who were also facing some personnel issues of their own—Arnton dropped back from point to goaltender. For the Crystals, Will Norris took over Stewart's point position, and James McDonnell was challenged with the unenviable task of replacing Allan Cameron. Laing tried to take on the role of tough guy for the Crystals, and it blew up as the patient Victorias shut out the Crystals 4–0 and took the championship title away.[173]

The following week the Vics had to defend their championship against the revamped Montreal AAA. Despite the Crystals' championship defense with Hutchison, Stewart and Cameron, it took just fifteen seconds for the Victorias to announce they intended to be champions all season long.

James Craven beat Hutchison on the initial rush to give the Vics a 1–0 lead. Arnton performed so well in the champions' net that the *Gazette* gave him the nickname "Stonewall"—the first time that the nickname was used in a hockey context. Arnton was applauded for his stops, and then Eddie Barlow and Dolly Swift gave him some breathing room when the former passed to the latter and the Vics went up 2–0. The pace was frenetic until the finish. Paton jumped in and replaced Findlay, but the Victorias outlasted the MAAA 5–2.[174]

And so it went for the rest of January and February for the Victorias, winning easily. Well, sort of. From February 4 through 24 the season-long tournament was shuttered in order for the Carnival to take center stage. The tournament games were scheduled to be played outdoors, but Mother Nature slyly canceled those plans. The Vics and the MAAA tried to play a game in the Victoria Rink, but players on both teams had to play through the decorations.

Decorations?

The Victoria Rink, being the center of the social elite, hosted Lord Lansdowne and his party. At the upper end of the rink a canopy was erected for the governor-general with a view called "entrancingly beautiful" by the *Montreal Gazette*. When looking out from the gallery, the governor-general would have seen a lighthouse about thirty feet in height, composed entirely of blocks of ice, and having at the summit a revolving light of various colors. At the base the rough lumps of ice were piled up to represent the rocks on which the lighthouse was built. The ice had the appearance of a tranquil sea from which arise the rough rocks. From the ceiling, flags of all nations were hung.

The Montreal A.A.A. Winged Wheelers attack the Victorias. Jack Arnton is the Victoria's defender in front of his goaltender, while Jimmy Stewart is at the other end of the ice with his stick rested at his waist, just in front of his goalie Tom Paton. The goalkeepers did not wear equipment in those days. Source: William Notman & Son/McCord Museum

Those are the decorations that Jack Arnton's Vics and Jimmy Stewart's Winged Wheelers had to play around. A lift shot might get caught in a flag, and if you think your favorite player hits hard, you haven't skated into a thirty-foot ice statue. The Vics scored two second-half goals while the MAAA couldn't figure out how to penetrate the ice-rock defense.[175]

One bad idea did not lead to a second, and so the Carnival hockey tournament was postponed—ironically—to after the Carnival. Both the Montreal AAA and the Victorias won their semifinal games. The four defectors of the Crystals led the MAAA to a 1–0 victory over their former team in the first semifinal game. The defensive troika of Jimmy Stewart, Allan Cameron and Will Hutchinson shut down the Crystals' offense while Hutchinson's replacement in the Crystal net, Will Norris, kept the game close by making several grand saves.[176] In the other semifinal, Jack Arnton's Victorias steamrolled McGill 8–0. This pitted Arnton's and Stewart's clubs in the finals. Before the finals the Victorias were testing the boundaries of human endurance, playing three matches in three days. After the 8–0 easy victory, the Vics played the Crystals in a challenge that was scheduled before the Carnival reworked the schedule. The Vics won the second of back-to-back-to-back games when Arnton kept the title with a lift shot from center ice five minutes into sudden death overtime.[177]

The next night the Vics were playing for Carnival diamond pins, but as a team they were wiped out. Arnton, the hero of the previous night, developed a cold and tried to play through it, as did Jack Campbell. The MAAA played a tough, physical game and blanked the Vics to win the pins.

The MAAA rested on their laurels for the season, but the Crystals decided to take one more shot at the Vics for the final championship match of the season. Joe Muir missed the game, and Arnton started at point for the Vics. Weakened, the Crystals jumped out to a 2–0 lead in the first half when Stewart McQuisten pumped in two goals. To start the second half, Arnton changed roles with forward Andy Shearer[178] and started attacking the Crystal goal. Dave Brown broke through for the Crystals to increase their lead to three, but Arnton scored twice quickly. The Vics scored a third goal that was disallowed and lodged a protest. For the time being the Crystals, who began the season with a depleted roster, finished as the league champions.[179] But only if the council concurred.

The council never met to discuss the protest.

Here was the schedule:

Jan 7	McGill College	1	Montreal Crystals	3	Crystal Rink
Jan 14	Montreal Victorias	4	Montreal Crystals	0	Crystal Rink
Jan 21	MAAA	2	Montreal Victorias	5	Victoria Rink
Jan 27	Ottawa	1	Montreal Victorias	5	Victoria Rink
Feb 4	Montreal Crystals	0	Montreal Victorias	3	Victoria Rink
Feb 24	Montreal Crystals	1	Montreal Victorias	2	Victoria Rink
Mar 11	Montreal Crystals	3	Montreal Victorias	2	Victoria Rink

CHAPTER 13

The Emergency Birth of the Playoffs

Racism was not shown on the ice, but league president (and Mohawk) Tom Green faced it at work. Despite being one of only eight McGill engineering students graduating in 1882, Green had a problem finding a permanent post.

His McGill hockey-playing friend, teammate and fellow graduate Albert Low had no such problem finding full-time work with the government, but the Six Nations-born Green could only gain temporary posts, and at half the rate of pay Low had received.[180]

One of Green's temporary posts resulted in an extended survey assignment in the Northwest Territories (now Alberta). Green, who had been elected president of the AHAC and pledged to do all he could, was a no-show for the first annual meeting, held November 9, 1887, in Montreal's Victoria Rink.

Jack Arnton took over the president's chair. The secretary-treasurer, William E. Stevenson, gave an encouraging report, noting that from five original clubs, junior teams had sprouted up and were looking for some organizational guidance. "I have also had correspondence with clubs from as west as Winnipeg, who were desirous of obtaining information on rules, etc., which I take it is an evidence of the growth of the game and of its increasing popularity," Stevenson said.[181]

Stevenson also noted that the championship of Canada was not false boasting. The directors of the Victoria Rink contributed $50 for the new trophy that eventually cost $75. Given the opportunity to contribute to the trophy, the Crystals' Robertson declined.

The Amateur Hockey Association of Canada agreed at its winter meeting that having a challenge system was unsatisfactory because it forced a team to play every seven days and possibly become stale.

The council agreed to a series schedule, where each team would face every other team twice. Ottawa and Quebec did not

AHAC Trophy
Credit: Doug MacLellan/
Hockey Hall of Fame

want to join due to concerns about the costs of travel and the amateur players both being stuck with the bill and also having to take time off work to participate. This left the league as a Montreal-only league. Meanwhile in other cities across Canada, hockey teams were forming their own organizations, albeit with limited success. With the new election, Arnton was voted president; Jimmy Stewart was voted first vice president.

One innovation unique to hockey was created: It was decided to let the winning club each year put a shield bearing their name on the base of the Amateur Hockey Association of Canada trophy.[182]

This will become important later.

In December Stewart took charge of the league meeting in Arnton's absence and oversaw the first series schedule in hockey history.[183]

The four Montreal teams played each other twice. The Victorias played at the rink after which they were named; the other three clubs played their home games at the Crystal. The season started January 13 when the MAAA faced the defending champions, the Crystals. Will Hutchinson had moved on, and Tom Paton returned to stand between the posts. The other three former Crystals—Finday, Cameron and Stewart—had seen their former team change several players from when they played just two years prior. Bob Laing stepped aside from hockey for the time being, but the defending champs were the defending champs, and they had no interest in letting the traitors win.

Ten minutes into the season debut, Sam Lee tallied the first goal of the season and gave the Crystals a 1–0 lead. Unfortunately for the defending champions, this would be their only lead of the season, except for their two games against McGill, which was outclassed and lost all six games, being outscored 40–4. The Crystals' lead lasted less than five minutes. The MAAA tallied the next four goals to take the game.

As the season unraveled it became clear that there were two really strong clubs and two really weak ones. The Crystals and Victorias were neck and neck all season long. Part of the lure for the lengthened schedule was the informal cancellation of the Winter Carnival. No one stepped up to organize it, and it was eventually acknowledged that the Winter Carnival just would not exist for the winter of 1888.

The lack of a Winter Carnival with visitors and visiting teams travelling to Montreal weakened the quality of play, and thus bored the crowds.

On February 3, the Victorias defeated the MAAA 3–1. Twelve days later, the Winged Wheelers returned the favor by the same score.

This left the remaining games on the schedule in the dull and uninteresting category. While the Quebec Hockey Club would not commit to traveling on a regular basis to Montreal, the team would consider playing a home-and-home series with one of the top-tier clubs.

Jack Arnton took the Quebecers up on their offer. The Quebec Hockey Club traveled to Montreal to face the Victorias in a friendly exhibition March 2, with the result being a tough 2–1 victory for the AHAC co-champions. The teams agreed to play a rematch in Quebec City on March 10, with the result being a 2–1 victory for Quebec. It was in this game that Arnton was injured above the right eye and had to be removed and treated on the train. Fred Ashe had been injured in the first friendly with Quebec, and he had missed the return trip as well as the Vics' last game against the Crystals.

Here was the schedule for AHAC:

Jan 13	MAAA	4	Montreal Crystals	1	Crystal Rink
Jan 18	Montreal Victorias	8	McGill College	1	Victoria Rink
Jan 23	MAAA	5	McGill College	0	Crystal Rink
Jan 27	Montreal Victorias	3	Montreal Crystals	1	Crystal Rink
Feb 3	Montreal Victorias	3	MAAA	1	Victoria Rink
Feb 10	Montreal Crystals	4	McGill College	1	Crystal Rink
Feb 15	MAAA	3	Montreal Crystals	1	Crystal Rink

Feb 22	Montreal Victorias	6	McGill College	2	Crystal Rink
Feb 27	MAAA	2	Montreal Victorias	1	Crystal Rink
Mar 2	MAAA	8	McGill College	0	Crystal Rink
Mar 7	Montreal Victorias	3	Montreal Crystals	2	Victoria Rink
Mar 12	Montreal Crystals	9	McGill College	0	Crystal Rink

The Montreal Amateur Athletic Association and the Victorias finished tied for first place with identical 5–1 records. League rules did not stipulate a tiebreaker, so a special meeting was held on March 13 to discuss a playoff.

Two options were discussed: to play the championship on March 15 at the Crystal Rink, which was the home of the MAAA, or on March 17 at the Victoria Rink, which was the home of the Victorias.

With Arnton and Ashe injured and not ready until the 17th, the AHAC secretary-treasurer, William Stevenson, suggested the latter date. Stevenson was also the Victorias' representative. A compromise was not feasible as the arenas had natural ice and were in danger of melting while the rinks' schedule of other events also had to be considered.

A vote was taken amongst the officers, resulting in a tie. The deciding vote went to the chairman, Jimmy Stewart, of the MAAA. Stewart voted for the earlier date at his own team's home rink.

This action generated considerable criticism in the press on both counts, with the most interesting coming from the *Montreal Gazette*, whose opinion expressed fear that professionalism and win-at-all-costs would ruin sportsmanship.

"There seems to be a delicate question in the background somewhere; it bears a striking resemblance to some well-known lacrosse matters; everyone is morally certain there is professionalism somewhere, but the difficulty is to prove it," wrote the *Gazette*.[184]

Stewart's desire to win was certainly greater than his sportsmanship as the game was held on March 15, 1888, with Arnton and Ashe both watching. And they were not the only ones watching. The Crystal Rink was sold out.

Despite the relatively uninteresting season, the fans got their money's worth in the championship playoff game. All of the scoring—but not all of the action—occurred in the first half. Archie Hodgson scored for the MAAA to open the scoring, but Jack Campbell evened the score for the Vics. Archie's brother Billy broke the tie on a play that was disputed by the Vics as being offside. The referee disagreed, and the goal was allowed to stand.

Still, the Victorias had thirty minutes to tie the game. Billy Hodgson went coast-to-coast on a solo attack, charging down the complete length of the rink with the puck dangling at the end of his stick while the Victoria defenders tried without success to stay his progress. While Hodgson did not score, the crowd literally cheered itself hoarse and marveled at the exhibition. At the other end of the ice, the defense of Allan Cameron, Jimmy Stewart and Tom Paton slammed the door shut as the MAAA survived the onslaught and won the championship.[185]

The Vics would have to be satisfied with capturing the junior championship over the Hawthorne Club of Montreal. The summer of contemplation would change the hockey world forever. None of the participants could predict how strongly the sport would emerge after a season in the doldrums.

And the good run started with a warning from a retiring board officer and the retirement of the college club whose members gave the idea and concept of hockey life thirteen years earlier.

Stevenson, who was retiring as the AHAC secretary-treasurer, cautioned that while the series system employed in 1888 was an unqualified success, there was a major disadvantage for clubs outside of Montreal. The costs of travel could not be covered by the current admission receipts.

After deliberation, it was decided at their November 16 planning meeting that the organization would return to the old challenge system. It was expected that Ottawa, Toronto and Quebec interests would sign up for challenges, but only Quebec did. One other casualty was the loss of McGill. The college boys, with an 0–6 record the previous year, decided to participate in just one friendly match. The university that planted the seed that grew into the star of the winter carnival and was about to reach international prestige had found itself without adequate representation. For now, the game had outgrown the college students.

CHAPTER 14

LORD AND LADY STANLEY ATTEND THE CARNIVAL

The last year of the 1880s had left the small-but-growing hockey community wondering what was happening. Some friendly matches were arranged, but no one wanted to challenge the powerhouse the Montreal AAA had become. Even the *Montreal Gazette* complained about it, noticing that the team hadn't even received a challenge to schedule through the first week of January.[186]

While no games were scheduled, the Victoria Rink had booked a practice for every night of the week, from 7:30 to 8:30 p.m. Finally a challenge came, but it was to be a friendly exhibition.

Jimmy Stewart, Jack Findlay and Allan Cameron's Winged Wheelers took on their old Crystal Club at the Crystal Rink. The game was a back-and-forth affair, with the defending champions eventually pulling out a 2–1 victory.[187]

Two weeks later the Crystals took on Jack Arnton's Victorias in a friendly exhibition. Despite playing just one half, the Vics easily defeated the Crystals 5–2. With the close game the Crystals played with the Montreal Hockey Club two weeks earlier, Arnton believed his team would be ready to claim the title.

But first, the Crystals challenged the Winged Wheelers, to see if they could claim the championship title. The start of the game was delayed nearly an hour because a referee could not be convinced to volunteer—leaving a large crowd of spectators near frozen and anxious. Stewart starred against his former club in the beginning, breaking up several plays. Eventually goalie Tom Paton lifted the puck off the ice and into the crowd near center ice—a two-minute delay-of-game penalty today but just a face-off in those times. The break didn't help much, as the Crystals' Sam Lee grabbed the puck after the face-off and passed to Dave Brown, who gave the Crystals a 1–0 lead. The Crystals had developed the strategy of passing the puck and were using it against the champions with great success. One drawback to the tactic, however, is that sometimes the players were drawn offsides because the players were receiving the pass ahead of the play instead of behind or laterally.[188] With five minutes to go in the first half, lacrosse players Archie MacNaughton and Archie Hodgson passed the puck as efficiently as they passed the lacrosse ball and after several passes between the two, Hodgson scored to tie the score at one. The game was far from innocent, the physical toll being absorbed by the defending champions. In the politically incorrect spirit of the times, the *Montreal Gazette* described the first-half injuries as such, "It appears the Montrealers had just returned from a fight with the Indians armed with tomahawks—MacNaughton had a big nose and a cut on his cheek. Cameron a black eye. Finlay [sic] a lame leg, and Stewart met with a nasty accident in a collision with Brown, by which his eye was badly cut, he was slightly stunned too." The Montreal Hockey Club played in desperate mode, but the Crystals fought them off until Lee scored to give the challengers a 2–1 lead. The Crystals went into a deliberate defensive mode, taking offsides whenever they could find a break. With less than two minutes left, MacNaughton picked up a loose puck in front of his goal and zig-zagged through the challenger's defense to tie the score at two apiece.

Hodgson and Fred Barlow each had a chance to win for the champions, but were thwarted by the stellar goaltending of Will Norris. Sudden death overtime gave the fans a thrill ride. Paton stopped two dangerous Crystal rushes, and Hodgson thought he had ended the game in victory for the champions, but Norris beautifully checked him and took the puck. Norris lifted the puck to center, but the Montrealers set up another offensive attack. Barlow got the puck and passed it to Finley, who was a touch offside. Finley passed to MacNaughton, who dodged two Crystal defensemen and Norris and scored. But the goal was disallowed due to offsides.

The Crystals were heavy on the stickwork, trying to stop the champions from keeping their crown. Cameron was slashed and tripped so hard by his former teammates that play was stopped for a few minutes so he could recover. MacNaughton was checked by three Crystals simultaneously and was laid out. He recovered and resumed. With the challengers barely on their own legs, it was the extraordinary goaltending of Tom Paton that kept Montreal in the game. Eventually the Crystals broke through the Montreal barrier and scored to win the game. There was a new champion, and just as the Carnival was set to begin.[189]

On February 4, 1889, the temperature in Montreal was twenty degrees below zero. Fahrenheit. If it felt like death to those loyal Canadians and curious Americans awaiting the new queen's representative to Canada to step off the train at the Bonaventure depot, it sure didn't look like it.

The air was as still as an Italian morning; the sun shone as bright as a summer's day. And fifty thousand pleasure-seekers gave a holiday appearance. Flags and bunting of several nations draped the houses on the governor-general's route, with the American Stars and Stripes sharing the honors with the Union Jack and the royal standard.

The governor-general, Lord Stanley, departed the train with his wife, children and aides-de-camp, and they entered their sleighs for the parade through Montreal to open up the Winter

Carnival. The route traversed down Notre Dame Street to McGill, then through the loving arch constructed out of ice, swarming with snowshoers in their blanket suits of every color. Victoria Square was packed with people who between cheers from their icicle-clogged throats, stamped their feet, clapped their hands and tried to stay warm.

The cavalcade mounted Beaver Hall Hill to Dorchester Street and passed along to the Windsor Hotel.

The great Carnival had opened auspiciously. Lord and Lady Stanley partook of five o'clock tea. Four hours later, the history of hockey would be permanently changed.[190]

A large crowd, numbering well into the several hundreds, bought a ticket for the opening of the Ice Palace. Citizens and strangers fraternized in a common misery: it was cold. A biting wind swept across the open spaces with an edge on it equal to the finest razor.

The mercury acted as if Jack Frost had no intention of rising until after the Carnival was over. At 8:20 p.m., the party was still indoors at the Windsor Hotel, when Lord and Lady Stanley walked down the grand staircase, crossed the square to the Ice Palace and officially opened the Carnival.

Joseph Hickson, the head of the Carnival committee, welcomed the new governor-general. "Your Excellency, I am charged by the Carnival committee to bid you a hearty welcome to our Carnival, and to express our gratitude to you for consenting to open our Ice Palace and attend the Carnival for the remainder of the week."

Canada's sixth governor-general replied, "I thank you sincerely for the kind welcome you have accorded Lady Stanley and myself, and I congratulate you on the entire success which appears to have attended your efforts. I trust the whole Carnival will prove the source of satisfaction which it deserves."

Lord Stanley declared the ice palace open, and then received three cheers from the large attending crowd. Three cheers then followed for Lady Stanley. Their Excellencies bowed in acknowledgment. Tea and chocolate were served by the Carnival committee to the vice-regal party, and Lord Stanley assigned Hickson the task of escorting Lady Stanley back to the Windsor Hotel.[191]

A display of fireworks then took place from the castle. While not extraordinarily different from years past, the darkness of the night enhanced the brilliancy of effect. The castle was illuminated with fifty-four electric lights; being judiciously placed gave a transparent, ethereal aspect to the structure.[192]

At the time the Carnival was officially being opened, the Victoria Rink two blocks away was filled beyond capacity. The hockey game was scheduled to start at 8:30 p.m., but as was a heavily criticized tradition in the day, the start was delayed by fifteen minutes until a referee could be located, attacked or persuaded, and suited up.

William Stevenson blew his whistle at 8:45 p.m., and Jimmy Stewart and Tom Paton's Montreal Hockey Club faced off against Jack Arnton and the Montreal Victorias. The Winged Wheelers would be without Allan Cameron, who had not recovered from his injury during the Crystals game three nights earlier.

The Carnival game was fast-paced from the outset, with the capacity crowd screaming and encouraging their side. The Victoria Hockey Club's Billy Barlow had a neat trick that he used to win bullies.[193] Barlow would place his stick between his own legs and pass the puck. The shots were flying fast and furious from all positions on the ice. Both goalkeepers—Paton for Montreal and Robert Jones for the Victorias—were more fortified than Montreal's Old Port. Nothing was going through. The fans thought that Archie MacNaughton and Jack Findlay combined to score for Montreal, but Jones denied.

Less than twenty minutes of the first half had passed when either alerted by his own curiosity or the noise, Lord Stanley decided to enter the Victoria Arena with his personal staff. The house band noticed when the queen's representative came in.

Stanley's arrival was heralded by trumpets while play in the first half continued. Play stopped immediately and Arnton gathered his men to the center of the ice. The Montrealers were still focused on scoring, and when Stewart had seen what Arnton had done, he gathered his teammates to the center of the rink while the band played "God Save the Queen." Arnton led the hockey players on both teams to call for three cheers to Stanley, and the spectators joined in. Then the players resumed hostilities. The play flashed back and forth down the ice, and several newspaper reports state that the men on both teams were playing flawlessly. The score remained tied at zero at the end of the first half. [194]

What Lord Stanley had seen was definitely very different from what he would know as hockey in England. He was an avid sportsman as well as a politician, and hockey was being organized and promoted in England at the same time as it was being developed in Montreal. Except what the English called hockey was different than what the Montrealers were calling hockey.

Since 1886 English hockey had its governing body—the Hockey Association—under the presidency of the historically-maligned Prince Albert Victor of Wales. The Hockey Association was formed by various clubs around London.

Writing in London's *Pall Mall Gazette*, an unidentified hockey player described the British version as safer than rugby or association football, and that it would be the most popular winter sport in England. The writer posits:

> In its broad features hockey closely resembles Association football. The main difference between the two is that instead of kicking a large and soft ball, you hit a small and hard one. The ball is an ordinary cricket ball, painted white to render it easily discernable . . . Probably many of the readers have played hockey on the ice, or have seen a band of roughs swooping about the frozen surface of one of the London waters, hitting a cork bung about with the accompaniment of a large amount of horseplay. To their minds hockey no doubt presents the remembrance

> of a confused melee in which the sole object was to obtain possession of the ball or bung, and retain it against all comers for as long as possible. This game is to hockey proper what stool ball is to cricket—the first rude outline from which the completed game has evolved.[195]

In North America, we tend to think of the development of ice hockey as evolved from British field hockey that was played on the ice with skates, while a contemporary article in London claimed that ice hockey was a primitive form of field hockey, and that field hockey was adapted from the ice version.

The British version is played on a much larger surface (300 feet long by 150 feet wide), with a goal that's 12 feet wide and 7 feet high (6 by 4 on ice), and played by eleven players to a side. There are no backhanded play, no charging and offside rules similar to Association football. In simpler terms, the beautiful game is soccer with sticks.

Bringing that game back to the ice-skating roots and placing it indoors captivated Lord Frederick Stanley of Preston, who may have regretted missing the first twenty minutes of action.

The second half was faster and cleaner than the first half. Only two whistles for offsides were called, and according to newspaper reports there was no rough play. With about fourteen minutes remaining in the match, the Victorias' Billy Barlow received a pass from Frank Scott and then passed across to D. A. Elliott. With Stewart fooled, Paton was left alone. Paton rushed Elliott, but the Vics' winger shot after Paton moved and scored the game's first goal.

Montreal came marching back, however, and in an era when goaltenders had the same equipment as the other six players, Archie MacNaughton took a high shot that only a lacrosse goalkeeper should have been able to stop. There was no record that Vics' goaltender Robert Jones spent his summers playing lacrosse, but he made the save by stopping the shot with his elevated stick and sent the puck to the side.

The clock ticked down to four minutes, and Scott added a second goal for the Vics. As time ran down, the Montrealers tried furiously to score, and Archie Hodgson managed to cut the lead in half. But there was not enough time left to complete the comeback, and the scoring was ended for the evening.

Lord Stanley was smitten, commenting to President Henshaw his great delight with the sport and that the expertness of the players,[196] which played indoors, with a puck, and rules, was something very different than what he had seen in England. Stanley then visited the players in the locker room before heading back to the Windsor.

Stewart and Arnton's rules, under their first major test, were a success. Wrote the *Montreal Witness*:

> Hockey, as played in the Victoria Skating Rink last evening, may be described as lacrosse on ice, played by men on skates, with hockey instead of lacrosse sticks, with a rubber puck, and under a special set of rules which combine the features of lacrosse and football. It demands from its players good skating powers, surefootedness, swiftness, courage, sharp sight and unbounded enthusiasm. Probably nowhere else in the world than in Montreal could be found fourteen young athletes who possessed all three characteristics in such an eminent degree.[197]

That Arnton's Victorias beat Stewart's MAAA 2–1 that night is of little relevance in the history books, but had Lord Stanley not heard the crowds, and had two other lesser teams been playing, or had the game not had been exciting, it is safe to say there would be no hockey as we know it today. The impression left on one British representative had a much longer lifespan than the actual Carnival. Despite its grand ceremony, the Carnival would not be claimed a financial success, showing a profit of $668.[198] This would prove to be Montreal's last Carnival. The Winter Carnival started out as a boast of civic pride managed by volunteers who proved that winter could be beautiful and active. After the one-year hiatus, the Carnival became maligned as a commercial venture on its reboot.

If hockey was going to survive, it was going to have to do so on its own merits.

CHAPTER 15
THE SAME, OLD, BORING CHAMPIONS

Although Lord Stanley was thrilled with the Carnival exhibition, Jimmy Stewart and the other hockey players had trouble growing their sport. With the series structure combined with the powerfulness of the Montreal Hockey Club, only four challenge games were played.

Unlike previous Carnivals where the hockey games would last a week, the Carnival hockey series lasted two weeks. With Stewart officiating, the Victorias and Crystals played each other for the Carnival championship. Although Lord Stanley had departed Montreal and returned to Ottawa, the story about the exciting game was reported in the capital's newspapers, albeit minus the details.

When Billy Virtue scored for the Crystals to tie the score at two apiece, the building was so loud the ice shook—a strange and unusual phenomenon at the time. The Victoria Rink cheers were so loud that they were clearly audible inside the Royal Caledonian Curling Club's rink on St. Catherine Street, a quarter-mile away. And Jack Arnton of the home rink club gave the crowd a little something extra to cheer after dodging several Crystals until he was alone against goalkeeper Will Norris. Arnton quietly lifted the puck over the keeper's skates amidst a deafening applause, which gave the Victorias the victory and the Carnival championship.[199]

Before the AHAC championship series could resume, a touring team from Halifax traveled to Montreal to challenge the world's best. The Chebucto Hockey Club was led by Charles Patterson, who was known as a one-to-three-mile distance skater, winning twelve medals in the previous three years. Of the eight members of the team, five had been playing together for the previous three years. The Chebuctos felt that experience would weigh in their favor.[200] Jimmy Stewart's Montreal Hockey Club was the visitors' first challenger. For the first half of the game, the teams played with Halifax rules: the goals were marked by curling stones and were placed at each end, parallel to the sides instead of at right angles. The idea was to prevent goals being scored by lifting the puck. There was no offsides as well, and the teams lined up as in lacrosse. Unfortunately for the Haligonians, the Montreal Hockey Club featured some of the best lacrosse players in the world—all but Stewart were lacrosse stars. The game was so one-sided that Montreal goalie Tom Paton spent more time in center ice than he did between the curling stones. The Nova Scotians were badly trounced 6–1, with the one goal being scored when Paton was outskated by one of the Chebuctos.[201] The Nova Scotians challenged the Carnival runner-ups two days later. Neither the Crystals nor Chebuctos scored in the first half under the simpler coastal rules, but the Crystals piled it on under the Montreal rules and won 4–1.[202] And to make the trip oh-for-three for the coastal visitors, Patterson lost in a special three-mile skating race to local Charles Gordon.

After the Atlantic Coast visitors returned home, the Montreal Hockey Club challenged the Crystals for a rematch of the city tournament title lost before the Carnival. With admission pegged at twenty-five cents, the fans who showed were treated to thwarted rush after thwarted rush. As the first half was closing, Montreal's Archie MacNaughton tallied to give the Winged Wheelers a 1–0 lead. The Crystals were outplayed in the second half as Montreal tallied three times to take back the championship.[203]

While the Winged Wheelers were reclaiming their title, the Chebuctos visited Quebec City and played two games there. Quebec won both games easily and felt they could challenge the Montreal clubs for supremacy. The Quebec Hockey Club issued a challenge and traveled to Montreal to play the Winged Wheelers in the first serious attempt to take the title out of the city.

The first half was extremely fast, and all fourteen hockey players were grateful for the ten-minute intermission to catch their breath. The visitors had scored the only first-half goal. About thirteen minutes into the second half, the hosts fired three shots in rapid succession at the visitors' goal, and three times the puck missed its destination by less than six inches. Archie Hodgson finally found the middle of the posts, and the Winged Wheelers tied the score. The next two goals came in quick succession as Quebec tallied to take the lead a minute later, only to see Montreal's Archie MacNaughton tie the score two minutes after losing the lead. Another two minutes later, the Winged Wheelers scored another. Then Jimmy Stewart's team tightened up defensively and the champions retained their title.

The last challenger for the season was the Carnival champion Victorias. A sold-out Crystal Rink was packed to the doors with latecomers seeing little of the game. Two strange fan behaviors were noticed—one was the large number of women in attendance, with many of them sporting either the blue and white of the champions or the red and maroon of Arnton's Victorias. The play in the first half was clean but ordinary. Any individual or team play out of the ordinary earned a loud cheer from the fans, but the first half closed without either team scoring. Eddie Barlow, playing on a fractured kneecap, scored the first goal of the game, and the Carnival champions appeared as if they would be the season's champions as well. For the next eight minutes the play was pretty even, but then the champions woke up, got mad and got even. The Winged Wheelers started playing more roughly and finally the

Vics cracked. Twelve minutes into the second half, Jack Findlay scored to tie the game, and two minutes later, he was followed first by MacNaughton and Hodgson. The Victorias, at that point, let their guard down, and the champions added three more goals to finish off Arnton's challengers. With the score 5–1, the Victorias' Jack Campbell, frustrated with his forwards, attempted a rush. Montreal's Allan Cameron was on him, however. Cameron failed to steal the puck away and knocked Campbell down. The two players started throwing punches. Players on both teams looked to grab another to square off, but spectators swarmed onto the ice and damage was averted. The two teams who had displayed true sportsmanship stopping midgame to pay homage to Lord Stanley when he entered the rink were now fighting at the end of a game already decided.[204]

Also decided was the final championship challenge of the winter: the Montreal Hockey Club captured their second straight title.

Here was the schedule:

Feb 2	MAAA	2	Montreal Crystals	3	Crystal Rink
Mar 1	Montreal Crystals	0	MAAA	4	Crystal Rink
Mar 7	Quebec	2	MAAA	3	Crystal Rink
Mar 12	Montreal Victorias	1	MAAA	6	Crystal Rink

By 1889 Arnton had stepped aside from managing hockey and Stewart was elected president of the league. Arnton was leaving the sport in good stead, as reported by new treasurer Jack Findlay (who also played for the Montreal Hockey Club along with Stewart and Paton). Findlay called the past season "the most successful season hockey has known in Canada; there was not one complaint made to the council in this year's play."[205] Political news spin occurred even in the late 1880s. Nice to see the organization could host four games during the season without a problem.

The defending champion, Montreal Hockey Club, decided to move their home games to the enlarged Dominion Rink, as the

Crystal Rink was being torn down and replaced. The Dominion Rink was used for skating races and masquerade skating—think Halloween at open skate night—but being expanded to 165 feet allowed hockey of the highest level to be played. As an affiliate of the Montreal Amateur Athletic Association, the Montreal Hockey Club was treated like a bastard stepchild—as long as the club didn't come begging for money and made the association look good, the club could hang around. Montreal Hockey Club president Tom Paton tried to pressure the MAAA to build their own arena, but was denied. One association dropout was Stewart's old club, the Montreal Crystals, who also decided to call the Dominion Rink their own and changed their name to coincide. The Laings had given up on hockey.

As fate would have it, especially being geared for the smaller surface, the MAAA won every single game in the challenger format and retained the league championship.

By offering Quebec the first date, it was hoped that the game would attract attention outside of Montreal as the calendar turned into 1890 and Jack Frost was settling in to visit for awhile. But few fans braved the clear but windy and cold night to attend the game. And thirty seconds in, the defending champions led 1–0. The next twenty-eight minutes was like an endless tennis match—both teams volleyed defensively, but neither team's offense could muster anything worth getting excited about. Quebec had a couple of opportunities, but Tom Paton stopped them all in front of the Montreal flags. One shot looked like the puck was going off his stick and between his legs, but Paton lifted his foot and directed the puck into the corner with his skate. Finally, with about a minute left in the first half, Art Scott tied the game up for Quebec. After the break, the Winged Wheelers came out on a mission. Archie MacNaughton scored three goals, and Quebec limped out with a 5–1 defeat.[206]

Since each match was basically for the championship, the Montreal Hockey Club became better and tougher as the season wore on.

The dilemma inside and outside of Montreal, especially with the domination of the Montreal AAA, can best be expressed by the *Montreal Gazette*: "Talk about hockey! Why they don't know how to play hockey outside of Montreal. Talk about a crowd! Well there was a crowd at the Dominion rink last night. Talk about enthusiasm! The ordinary substantive hardly gives an idea of the feelings of the audience."[207]

Unfortunately, when a team dominates the competition as well as the Winged Wheelers did, some sports become endangered. Dynasties are one thing; domination leads to boredom. And boredom was starting to envelop the Montreal hockey scene. The biggest threat to the Montreal Hockey Club was a 2–1 victory on February 18. Wrote the *Gazette*, "If the public could always depend on such a game as was seen last night, then indeed (hockey) would be as popular in winter as our national game of lacrosse is in summer. But maybe it takes a long time to learn and maybe the majority of the public are slow to understand."[208]

The following week the MAAA moved their games to the new Crystal Rink, erected one block southeast at the corner of Dorchester and Guy Streets. The MAAA squeaked out a 3–2 overtime win, but the game was far from exciting. With a leaking roof, moist and cold air left the arena with an unforgettable dank smell while the spectators' feet felt the cold. As the game progressed, puddles were formed on the ice, which left the decision to postpone the 2–2 game or play sudden-death overtime. The clubs agreed to overtime; the Montreal Hockey Club's Sam Lee scored within the first two minutes to win the game. Added the *Montreal Herald*: "Under anything but favorable conditions—in fact the dearest approach to describing them properly would be to say a shower bath."[209]

Just one week after encouraging the rest of Canada about how great hockey can be, the *Montreal Gazette* tempered the enthusiasm by expressing that having an adequate facility is also a necessity.

Both spectators and players were treated to the vapor bath and good hockey, the *Gazette* wrote:

> Yet, in spite of it . . . had it not been for a roof like a sieve, through which a continual spray bath poured, and the clouds of damp, cold, unpleasant vapor that arose from the ice . . . it would have been a really enjoyable match indeed. As it was it was simply cruelty to animals to allow anyone to suffer all the inconvenience and unmistakable discomfort that the people who attended the game had to put up with.[210]

Even in its toddler years hockey has certainly had its quirks and its dynasties. The Montreal AAA had won its third consecutive league title.

Here was the 1890 schedule:

Jan 7	Quebec	1	MAAA	5	Dominion Rink
Jan 17	Montreal Victorias	2	MAAA	4	Dominion Rink
Jan 31	Montreal Dominions	4	MAAA	6	Dominion Rink
Feb 11	Montreal Dominions	2	MAAA	6	Dominion Rink
Feb 18	Montreal Victorias	1	MAAA	2	Dominion Rink
Feb 25	Montreal Dominions	2	MAAA	3	Crystal Rink
Mar 4	Montreal Victorias	1	MAAA	2	Crystal Rink

Fearing that too many Montreal entrants would prevent other cities from joining the fray, the AHAC refused admission to the Shamrock Hockey Club for 1891. Instead, the organization granted membership to Ottawa and Quebec, with the hopes that both clubs would help grow the sport. Stewart was re-elected president, and on the same day the AHAC was hosting their meeting, the Ontario Hockey Association was hosting its own as well. But growing the sport meant someone other than the Montreal AAA would have to win a game, and with the challenge system, the Winged Wheelers kept getting stronger. The MAAA faced eight challenges; they won eight games to win their fourth consecutive title.

Here was the schedule:

Jan 7	Quebec	1	Montreal HC	5	Crystal Rink
Jan 17	Montreal Victorias	1	Montreal HC	4	Crystal Rink
Jan 28	Montreal Shamrocks	1	Montreal HC	4	Crystal Rink
Feb 4	Montreal Crescents	1	Montreal HC	2	Crystal Rink
Feb 12	Montreal Victorias	1	Montreal HC	2	Crystal Rink
Feb 21	Ottawa	0	Montreal HC	3	Crystal Rink
Feb 27	Montreal Shamrocks	1	Montreal HC	5	Crystal Rink
Mar 5	Montreal Crescents	2	Montreal HC	8	Crystal Rink

CHAPTER 16

THE NOT REALLY NEEDED STANLEY CUP

Life was good for Jimmy Stewart. He was captain of the best hockey club in the world. He was president of the best hockey league in the world. The rules he cowrote were being spread across the Dominion. The twenty-seven-year-old had sacrificed his own interests to help provide for his two sisters and stepmother, who finally had their own home that did not need to be shared with boarders. And on June 9, 1891, at St. Mathew's Presbyterian Church in Pointe St. Charles, Jimmy's sister Edith married the brother of his best friend, who also happened to be one of the most famous athletes in Canada.[211] Joe Laing was the six-time champion amateur sculler of Canada and even claimed the American title in 1885. Edith Stewart's new husband was Bob's brother, who cofounded the Crystals with Jimmy. Joe was also a member of the Odd Fellows, Wellington Lodge.

Popularity on the hockey front was giving Stewart new troubles. The MAAA was looking for their fifth straight title, and Ottawa was looking to be the first club to take the title of hockey's best team out of the city of Montreal.

The visitors from the capital defeated Montreal 4–3 in an upset of the season's opener at the Crystal Rink. Montreal cover-point Allan Cameron had missed the game due to other personal commitments, being replaced by John Barry. Stewart tried to help Barry stop the early Ottawa offensive onslaught, but in so doing left goalkeeper Tom Paton exposed. However, Montreal jumped out to an early lead when Bunny Lowe's shot hit Ottawa goaltender Albert Morel's skate and crossed the goal line. The visitors came back when Halder Kirby scored with five minutes left in the half. The goal was disputed by the Winged Wheelers, but to no avail. The best they could do was replace the goal judge, and so they did.

The defending champions scored within two minutes of the second half starting, but the lead was short-lived; Ottawa pumped in two goals quickly in succession to take a 3–2 lead five minutes into the half. Just before regulation time expired, Montreal tied the score, forcing sudden death overtime. Ottawa's Jack Kerr scored, and for the first time in history, hockey's champions were not from Montreal.[212] Montreal protested the decision, but the protest went nowhere. It was Stewart, after all, who had written in the rule that the referee's decision would be final.

As the 1892 series went through the winter, Ottawa looked as if it would be the league champions. The first five challenges Ottawa hosted in their cramped Dey's Arena were all victories for the home side. Twice Quebec made the long journey; the first time the northerners lost by a single goal, and the second they were shut out 2–0.

Taking full use of home-ice advantage, Ottawa blitzed through the other challenges at their Rideau Rink, outscoring their opponents 27–9, which included a 10–2 win over the Winged Wheelers two weeks after the upset. It should be noted, however, that Montreal sent its B squad to the game, knowing they would get one more rematch in to try to claim their sixth straight title.

The Montreal Victorias never challenged. The Shamrocks made one attempt and were easily beaten. This left it up to the Winged Wheelers. The Montreal Hockey Club had faced Ottawa four times, losing the first three times. The last attempt was on the last night good ice was to be had.

About two hundred Montreal hockey supporters took the Canada Atlantic railway to Ottawa to cheer on the Winged Wheelers in the final match of the hockey season—the one match that truly determines the league champion. Jack Arnton came along for the ride as well. He was appointed the game's referee.

The Ottawa team played as if it was skating uphill on the wet ice, as the majority of the play was in its end. For seventeen minutes, however, the game remained scoreless. Then Archie Hodgson received a pass from Archie MacNaughton. The puck went whizzing through a couple of puddles on the ice and between the flags[213] for the only score of the game. Ottawa pressed forward for the balance of the game but could not score. The Montrealers came up with several new tricks during the game, including a well-needed rest break when John Kingan broke a skate blade and the game was halted while the skate was replaced.

The Montrealers went wild with the victory, and the supporters were happy when they won their bets, as Ottawa bettors gave the Montreal faithful 10-to-8 odds. Reported the *Montreal Gazette*, "They returned home at eleven o'clock, one of the jolliest excursion parties that ever left the capital."[214]

That was the last hockey game Jack Arnton took part in. The wealthy young man who stopped the Carnival game and welcomed Lord Stanley to Canadian hockey and insisted on rugby's offsides rule had just finished officiating what would prove to be the first Stanley Cup hockey match. By summer he would seek greener pastures.

Arnton left Montreal for New York City in 1892 and joined the Masonic Temple. He lived the life of luxury in Manhattan, residing at 150 West Forty-Fourth Street, according to records of Arnton returning from a trip to Liverpool, England, in 1904.[215] He never married, nor resumed hockey or any other athletic endeavors publicly. He turned to business, traveling to England on several occasions. In 1910 he returned to Montreal to be hospitalized, and that is where he died on April 7.

Here was the 1892 schedule:

Jan 8	Ottawa	4	MAAA	3	Crystal Rink
Jan 15	Montreal Shamrocks	3	Ottawa	8	Rideau Rink
Jan 21	MAAA	2	Ottawa	10	Rideau Rink
Jan 28	Quebec HC	3	Ottawa	4	Rideau Rink
Feb 11	MAAA	1	Ottawa	3	Rideau Rink
Feb 18	Quebec	0	Ottawa	2	Rideau Rink
Mar 7	MAAA	1	Ottawa	0	Rideau Rink

Two months after the last game, the Ottawa Amateur Athletic Association decided to award the Ottawa Hockey Club and its players gold monogrammed lockets for holding onto the championship as long as they did.[216]

And two weeks later politics entered the fold.

Frederick Stanley, the governor-general of Canada, was disappointed that his local Ottawa squad were champions all winter long but lost the last game and lost everything. On one hand Lord Stanley sounded like a spoiled loser; on the other, he made a great point about a team recording one win all season and being declared league champion for the entire year.

Having his aide, Lord Kilcoursie, attend the Ottawa Hockey Club's season-ending banquet at the Russell House on March 18, Lord Stanley penned a note to be read at the dinner by Lord Kilcoursie:

> I am not quite certain that the general regulation governing the arrangement of matches gives entire satisfaction and it would be worth considering whether it could be arranged so that each team would play each once at home and once at the place where their opponents hail from.

It was a question that haunted the Montreal organizers of the sport. If there were too much travel, the pool of available players would be diminished because players would need to take time off of work, unpaid, and there were not enough quality players amongst the wealthy to perfect the sport.

But Stanley was willing to put his money where his mouth was:

> I have for some time been thinking that it would be a good thing if there were a challenge cup which should be held from year to year by the champion team of the Dominion. There does not seem to be any such outward and visible sign of championship at present, and considering the general interest which the matches now elicit, and the importance of having them played fairly under rules generally recognized, I am willing to give a cup which shall be held from year to year by the winning club.

When Lord Kilcoursie finished his boss's note, the Russell House broke out with loud cheers that lasted several hours. And Kilcoursie added one more shocker: Lord Stanley already authorized his secretary, Captain Charles Colville, to purchase a desirable cup when Colville returned to London.[217]

But the Amateur Hockey Association of Canada already held a trophy for its champion, one that was considered the best club in Canada. And the rules were clear. The team that was champion at the end of the season would earn the trophy as the best club in Canada. This was conveniently forgotten amidst the excitement.

Despite winning just one match, Stewart and the Montreal AAA won their fifth consecutive title. The summer off-season was shorter than most; hockey talk continued until May, and clubs were beginning to organize in early November. And not just in Montreal, Ottawa and Quebec, but in Toronto and Winnipeg.

Lord Stanley was not interested in managing his trophy – he had more important real issues to deal with. As fate would have it, those issues lacked the sustainability of his donation to hockey.

Stanley left Lord Kilcoursie the choice of whom to actually manage the trophy. Kilcoursie chose two highly respected Ottawa men with a passion for a game – Dr. John Sweetland, Ottawa's sheriff, and Montreal-born Philip Dansken Ross, the publisher of the *Ottawa Journal*, who also played with Lord Kilcoursie on the intermediate-level Rideau Rebels.

Phil Ross
Source: Courtesy Hockey Gods website

Ross, called Phil by his family, graduated with a civil and mechanical engineering degree from McGill University in 1878. A multisport athlete, Ross captained the McGill football team and was the provincial single sculling champion twice, as well as playing lacrosse.

Despite his civil engineering degree from McGill University, Phil declined to work for his father and instead chose to pursue journalism. By 1886, he and a partner purchased the near-bankrupt *Ottawa Journal*. Ross bought out his partner within five years.

The junior Ross's diaries in Canada's National Archives show how fond he was of playing hockey. During the winters well into the 1890s, he would think nothing of working for a few hours in the day and then going to the rink several times per week—sometimes to watch, sometimes to officiate, sometimes to practice, and sometimes to play.

It is not known how familiar Ross was with the 1875 game started by James Creighton, who by the late 1880s was a law clerk for the Canadian Senate. However, they did have a lot in common.

Phil Ross, the George Plimpton of publishers, loved playing the game so much he often neglected his editorial duties and fiscal responsibilities to play and support the restyled game.

After obtaining control of the *Ottawa Journal*, Ross was running short of money. He was appointed a Stanley Cup trustee, but instead of giving up those responsibilities to manage his business, he took a trip to Montreal to ask his parents for a loan to pay his staff Christmas bonuses. His father, Philip, founder of the accounting firm that became part of the Deloitte empire, wrote back, "My dear Phil. You are a good boy, but you don't know what you're doing . . . Better consult [brother] Billy, that boy's clever. He'll be a millionaire yet, but he skinned his old father. I never thought you would pull through."[218]

So Phil asked his mother.

She replied, "I think you have more money than brains . . . however I have one or two dividends falling this month and if you run short you can draw on me for a thousand as I have at last cut Willie off."[219]

At that time Phil was a Stanley Cup trustee for five years, and Billy (or Willie) was the Ross brother who lost that first Carnival skating race to Jimmy Stewart.

But Phil Ross never feared of taking a route less traveled. And he probably didn't think that the captain of the Montreal Hockey Club, who had just beaten Ottawa, was the same man who outraced his brother Willie in the 1883 Winter Carnival.

Perhaps Jimmy Stewart suspected something. At the Amateur Hockey Association of Canada's annual meeting on December 15, 1892. Stewart stepped down as organization president and relinquished the duties to Ottawa Hockey Club's Frank Jenkins.[220] The organization accepted Lord Stanley's suggestion and adopted a series system. Stewart still represented the Montreal Hockey Club, and he also helped compose the schedule.[221]

And Ross, for his part, was playing local supporter. In addition to his other duties, he helped form a city league in Ottawa and agreed to be an honorary vice-president. The league used the bylaws and constitution of the AHAC.[222]

The speed at which the game was growing competed with the speed of the game on the ice. Many of the older players and founders stepped to the sidelines to let the younger, faster generation take over. Tom Paton, the stellar goaltender since the Montreal Hockey Club's inception back in the Carnival days, announced at the annual Montreal Hockey Club meeting he was retiring due to business concerns. Jimmy Stewart was voted into and accepted the hockey club's presidency.[223] After guiding the AHAC for the previous four years, Stewart was now captaining hockey's most famous and powerful team. In modern terms it might sound like a demotion to go from president of the league to president of a club, but for Stewart it was recognition and a promotion.

Hockey may have been a growing organized sport just starting to sprout its wings, but the Montreal Amateur Athletic Association had more than two thousand members and was famed throughout all of North America. While the MAAA had a lot of champions, none of its clubs had put together the dominance that the hockey club had. And with hockey being a far more fascinating spectator sport than lacrosse or snowshoeing, being president made for a much more prestigious position within the Montreal community.

In just four years as AHAC president, Stewart saved the sport from being a Carnival casualty to a developed and growing sport that reached into Ottawa and Toronto to the south, Quebec City to the north, and Nova Scotia and New England to the east, to Winnipeg and points westward. The game was going places; the train helped the players, skates, equipment and rules get there, and the game was also heading to major United States cities such as New York and Detroit. The Detroit Hockey Club played its first game in February 1893 and was looking to take on challengers.[224] Although not all of his decisions were popular, Stewart gave the upstart sport the organization it needed to become and stay relevant.

The growing popularity of hockey, especially for the arena owners, made the next season very challenging. The sport's growth spread onto the prairies, made easier by train travel to get equipment. The long, cold winters of Winnipeg gave the local players a lot of opportunity to practice, and the western city put together an all-star team from its three clubs to travel to the east and see how they would fare against the best hockey clubs.

The Winnipeggers had played three exhibitions in Ontario, easily thumping the two upstarts in Toronto and escaping with a

4–3 victory over Queen's College in Kingston before heading off to the nation's capital to face the team that Lord Stanley thought should have been champion.

With Phil Ross officiating, the visitors impressed their hosts with their speed, although superior skating by the Ottawas resulted in a 4–1 victory for the home squad on February 13.[225]

Not discouraged, the travelers took a day's rest and took the three-hour train ride to Montreal. The Winnipeg hockey tourists traveled for an exhibition against the AHAC Champion Montreal Hockey Club. Although the game was merely an exhibition, the Winnipeg players introduced something to the game that surprised the fifteen hundred fans at the Victoria Rink.

Winnipeg goalie Art Stow wore cricket greaves,[226] and every player from the prairie wore cricket pads to protect their shins. The champions put on a clinic for the visitors, tallying four times in the first twenty-six minutes. After that the visitors calmed down and played an even game scoring four times to Montreal's total of seven. Montreal's young bloods took over. Billy Barlow, twenty-three, tallied three of the goals for the home team. Havi Routh, twenty-one, added two more. The other two goals were scored by veteran Bunny Lowe, who was twenty-seven. The speed of the Winnipeg team gave goalie Tom Paton, who came out of retirement, and point Jim Stewart a tough time. Paton was thirty-seven years old at the time, and Stewart was approaching thirty. And neither of the old-timers were wearing cricket pads.

As far as the season was concerned, the Montreal Hockey Club lost their opening game of the season when they traveled to Ottawa and left with a 4–2 loss. They won the remaining seven games to win the championship, but two of the games featured controversy.

A scheduling quirk left the Crystals and Winged Wheelers not facing each other until March, when they would play twice within a week.

The first shot across the bow was fired on March 3 when the Crystals and Montreal battled.[227] There was bad blood from the beginning. The Crystals' William Murray became the first bad boy of hockey, although it didn't seem like it at the beginning of the game. Murray was on the receiving end of a pass when he tapped it behind the Montreal goalie to give the underdog Crystals a 1–0 lead. Ten minutes later, Routh tied the game, and a few minutes later Routh scored another to give Montreal the lead. The Crystals tied the game just before the ten-minute intermission.

About eighteen minutes in the second half passed when Murray was ruled off the ice by Referee Gordon Lewis for lifting his stick over his shoulder after being warned. The Crystals played six against seven against the defending champions, and still managed to hold them at bay. To start sudden death overtime, the Crystals wanted to allow Murray back into the game, but the official would not allow it. The Crystals refused to continue, and Lewis awarded the game—and effectively the Stanley Cup championship—to Montreal. However, the Crystals immediately announced they would file a protest, which made Jimmy Stewart in the fairly uncomfortable position of defending his team regarding a title-clinching game at a hearing of the league he had just stepped down from as president.[228]

To be fair to Stewart, the popularity of hockey had skyrocketed under his watch, and while he imagined the sport as a gentlemanly game that the working class and upper classes could compete in, the competitive spirits of the men involved trampled that illusion.

"The possibility of protests had hardly been taken into consideration, and the result was that the rules were drawn up in a slipshod manner," wrote the *Montreal Gazette* in its March 13, 1893, edition. The *Gazette* pointed out that "interest in the game has grown so rapidly that every possible point is being taken advantage of. The point is to win the match any how—win, tie or wrangle."[229]

The *Gazette* also published verbatim the principal documents.

In the March 6 letter to the AHAC board, Crystal Hockey Club president Frank Willoughby wanted to declare the match off and appoint a time for a new match. "Otherwise it will create a precedent which will materially affect the existence of the game of hockey."[230]

Overdramatic? A bit.

In reply Stewart felt the need to defend his rules, his team and his integrity.

"In reply we beg to say that the hockey rules are so very clear and distinct in giving unlimited power to the referee that it appears superfluous to call your attention to them. In referring to the 'laws of hockey' you will notice that section 3 gives the referee power to settle all disputes and 'his decision shall be final.' This rule has always been recognized," Stewart wrote.

The spirit of friendly competition certainly had gotten lost somewhere along the way for Stewart to have offered this bit of trash talk, rarely seen in the late 1800s.

He concluded, "Gentlemen, we leave the matter entirely in your hands, and have only to regret that any club in your association should have considered itself justified in troubling you with a matter that is so completely covered by the rules of the game."[231]

So the protests and responses were filed with the league's governing board. Secretary Jack Findlay now had the task of addressing these items. Findlay played for Montreal.

Before the protest could be heard, though, the two clubs had their second game to play, and it was an important one, at least for the Montreal and Ottawa teams. Jimmy Stewart's Montreal Hockey Club needed the victory over the Crystals – the team he helped organize who became the Dominions but returned – to claim another championship. Meanwhile a loss coupled with an Ottawa victory against Quebec later in the week could set up a first-place tie, depending on the result of the protest.

And the two Montreal teams put on a clinic.

"The possibilities of hockey, the ideality of the game were never better illustrated than last night," wrote the *Montreal Gazette.* "It was the game of the season. For that matter, it was the game of the century, even if the ice was soft, and it was impossible to do any fine work with the puck.

"There was not a great deal of passing, for the teams were too evenly matched, and the pace was too fast. It was everybody for himself and Lucifer take the sandpaper."

The overexcited reporter for the *Montreal Gazette* managed to write one hundred eighty-seven words describing how "the whole match could be summed up in a very few words."

Like the match the week before, the Crystals tallied first. But the MAAA's Havi Routh tallied late in the second half to tie the score. Both teams had their chances in sudden death, but eventually Archie Hodgson scored the first Stanley Cup winning goal—and in overtime—to give Montreal the championship.[232]

But there were two items still pressing for the title to be official.

The first was dealing with the Crystals' protest for the game the week before.

At the March 14, 1893, meeting, Findlay acknowledged that the Crystals were disadvantaged but that his team was "there to take all advantage of the rules." The board, although sympathetic to the Crystals position, sided with the referee and stated his decision was final. Findlay then added that the Montreal Club had nothing to do with the unfairness of the referee. Alfred Ritchie, representing the Crystals, eventually caved in and agreed to drop the protest. The lengthy meeting was thus summed up by the reporter for the *Montreal Gazette* who attended: "Methinks the lady doth protest too much."[233]

For those unfamiliar with the *Hamlet* reference, let's just state that the more Ritchie talked, the bigger the hole he dug. And in the end it did not matter. The Montreal Hockey Club would be able to claim the victory and the Stanley Cup.

Now as the former league president and the championship club president, Stewart had the issue of the sport's shiny new trophy to deal with. Tom Paton had met with cup trustee Phil Ross on February 18, 1893, but the topic of discussion was not included in Ross's diary.[234]

Lord Stanley, so smitten with hockey at his first Carnival, had donated a silver bowl to be awarded to the best hockey club in the country. Lord Stanley called his gift—and had it engraved—the Dominion Hockey Challenge Cup, but trustee Phil Ross immediately asserted the chalice should be known as the Stanley Cup in honor of its donor. He confirmed that it would be presented in the first instance to the reigning champions of the Amateur Hockey Association of Canada (AHAC), with the idea that they would then defend it against the champions of the Ontario Hockey Association. Ross arranged for the Stanley Cup to be presented to the Montreal Amateur Athletic Association (MAAA) team as the reigning champions of the AHAC, and the cup should go to the next season's league champions before taking on challengers.

CHAPTER 17
THE POWER STRUGGLE

The attention being generated by hockey was beginning to get noticed south of the border. Bogert, in *Outing* magazine, explained to Americans how unlucky they were not to have such a sport and that by not braving the elements, the American sports fan was missing out.

Bogert wrote:

> To witness a championship match is to at once appreciate hockey. The speed attained by the players, the clever dodging, the grace with which they elude their antagonists, the sharp checking, the long "lifts," the lightning "shoots" and the combined and clever team-play must go straight to the heart of every onlooker, whose admiration can never fail to be excited by the great combination of skill, strength and daring . . .
>
> The players are purely amateur, and there is no instance of a charge of professionalism having been brought to the notice of the executive.[235]

Chicanery was not nonexistent. It just took other forms. And it was helped by both a gift and a blessing from Queen Victoria's representative to Canada. The pronouncement of the Stanley Cup — a people's trophy in its origin that in theory could be won by any Canadian—native born or immigrant, working class or the financial elite — eventually captured the young country's fancy. Where hockey was an afterthought just a decade before, now this new sport had captured the fascination of the literary and the poets.

Come, cross your blades upon the ice,
The air is keen, the watchers wait;
And eager as a cat for mice,
Around the puck the forwards skate,
Line up! In goal! The game is faced!
The puck's in play, the ice doth ring
Beneath the skates that seem to sing
We have no time to-night to waste!

Away! away! the roof doth ring,
Above the roar of party mirth;
From side to side supporters fling
Winged wit that mocks each other's worth,
And brown and blue eyes flash with pride,
And cheeks are red, and white teeth gleam,
And kerchiefs wave, and lassies scream
To see the forwards dash and glide!
—"A Hockey Song" by Charles Gordon Rogers[236]

Just a couple of months after this poem appeared in one of Canada's most successful literary magazines, the Montreal Athletic Association reported on May 8, 1893, the board had received a telegram from Lord Kilcoursie requesting a meeting to present the Stanley Cup for the first time. The board decided there should not be any special demonstration "in the event of any of His Excellency's household coming to present this cup in person."[237] None of this was discussed with the hockey club or its president, Jimmy Stewart.

The following week the MAAA board met again.

Stanley Cup trustee Phil Ross had sent a letter instructing the board that his colleague John Sweetland would be in Montreal at the annual meeting and had requested the players be present. James A. Taylor, president of the MAAA, stated that he had instructed

Stewart to show up for the presentation. But Stewart's issue was that the trophy should be presented to the hockey players first, not the organization. It was the players who practiced, paid and earned the trophy. Stewart also expressed concerns that the hockey club had not met all of the conditions of Lord Stanley's request. While Stewart did not publicly specify which of the five conditions the hockey club objected, it was probably the first that he and the hockey club had concerns about.

"The winners should give bond for the return of the cup in good order when required by the trustees for the purpose of being handed over to any other team who may in turn win," was the first of Lord Stanley's conditions.[238] The hockey players found objectionable that the MAAA was going to receive the trophy, and stick the bill without fanfare for the bond to the hockey club, which was an affiliated organization that had to fund its own rink and equipment while the other, less successful, MAAA clubs were directly funded. Stewart had also requested the MAAA board to forward his concerns to the Cup trustees, but they refused. In fact, the board said the MAAA president carried his duties and the board's desires.[239]

The hockey club had requested a loan from the MAAA before the season, and paid it back the week before the scheduled meeting. The MAAA had agreed to purchase trophies for the individual players, but before doing so, paid the sheriff the bond to make sure the cup would be taken care of and returned if warranted. Taylor had even written a check from the hockey club's account to ensure the bond. Yet when it came time for the glory, the MAAA board was front and center and making decisions for the hockey players.

An annual event—annual in all years the NHL does not lock out its players—had its origins on May 15, 1893. But instead of a multipurpose arena with nearly twenty thousand fans booing the presenter, about one hundred Montreal Amateur Athletic Association members sat in a board room on the corner of Mansfield and Burnside Streets as the sheriff of Ottawa made a presentation.

John Sweetland hand delivered the Hockey Challenge Trophy. The reader will know this as the Stanley Cup. Sheriff Sweetland made the presentation to MAAA president Taylor, due to the "unavoidable absence" of Jim Stewart.

The original Stanley Cup.
Credit: Doug MacLellan/Hockey Hall of Fame

Not only was Stewart missing, but not one single member of the hockey club was in attendance at the general meeting, including Tom Paton, one of the original fifteen founding members of the organization and the founder of the hockey club. If Stewart needed to be incensed any more, Taylor thanked Sweetland for his appearance and accepted the trophy "on behalf of the organization, and the above-named club."

After Sweetland explained that the governor-general had selected Phil Ross and himself as trustees, Sweetland's speech to the club would sound familiar to anyone who ever heard Gary Bettman present the trophy today, explaining how the champion team had won so nobly, ad nauseum. But if you notice when the NHL commissioner hands out the thirty-five-pound chalice, he awards it to the captain, not the owner or the coaches.

At the same meeting where the cup was first presented, Taylor resigned after writing the check to Sheriff Sweetland.[240]

Taylor was replaced by Tom Paton, the former goaltender, the man who had convinced Stewart to join the Montreal Hockey Club (and by extension, the AAA), and the man who had retired for the second time as goaltender for the Stanley Cup Champion Montreal Hockey Club.

Besides being thirty-seven years old, there was another reason Paton stopped trying to stop rubber pucks without padding: he was engaged to be married. Paton was charmed by the twenty-one-year-old Lilly Bowie, and on April 20, 1893, the two were wed in the Bowie family house.[241] One of the attendants of the wedding was Lilly's twelve-year-old brother, Russ, who would become one of the all-time great hockey players in the amateur era.

The Stanley Cup resided in the AAA clubhouse as spring turned into summer and summer into fall. Jim Stewart and his hockey teammates had still failed to pick up the trophy.

Taylor had contemplated returning the trophy to the trustees before his resignation, and wished to hear the organization's director's thoughts before returning the trophy. After some discussion it was agreed that returning the trophy would injure the reputation of the association in the eyes of the general public, and so a committee of Major Freeman, Tom Foster and Fred Learmonth was assigned to meet with the hockey board to see if the hockey players could give a positive reason for refusing the trophy.[242]

At the Montreal Hockey Club's board meeting, Harry Shaw and James Paterson secured the votes to name Alex Irving, Jimmy Stewart and Allan Cameron as a subcommittee to meet with the board and explain their actions.[243]

The initial response from the Montreal Hockey Club committee was they felt slighted that they were not communicated with directly by the governor-general's representatives. The entire team felt the Earl of Darby's representatives should make the presentation to the hockey club, as originally proposed.[244]

What offended the players was actually a favor that the cup trustees had provided. In the original terms of the trophy, the trustees stated that as a condition of His Excellency, "Each winning team to have at their own charge engraved on a silver ring fitted on the cup for the purpose the name of the team and the year won. (In the first instance the MAAA would find the cup already engraved for them.) And the trophy should "be held by the MAAA team until the championship of the association to which the team belongs, namely the Amateur Hockey Association of Canada, be decided next year, when the cup should go to the winning team."[245]

The hockey players already felt separated from the rest of the organization. The players had their own budget and covered their own expenses although the other clubs that made up the AAA had facilities and operations provided out of the organization's general budget. The hockey players wanted their own rink; the speedskaters were the ones who got the skating surface, leaving the hockey team in a position to negotiate with the Montreal arena owners for ice rental.

With the senior club being world champions and the intermediate team being solid in its own right, it was suggested at a board meeting that the Montreal Hockey Club bring in a junior team as well. Acquiring players would be relatively easy with the reputation the Montreal Hockey Club was garnering. What would be difficult was finding a place to play, so Stewart was asked to see whether the Victoria Rink could accommodate a third team.[246]

The Victoria Rink responded. The club could have the rink for Monday and Wednesday evenings, from 7:00 to 8:00 p.m., and for 50 percent of the ticket sales. The club also asked the MAAA for a loan of seventy-five dollars, to pay for the three members of the MAAA to travel on behalf of the club to the meeting in Quebec City, and for the players to purchase tickets for the practice and games at the Victoria Rink. The top players in the world still had to pay for their practice and game time at the rink.

Paton and the AAA board agreed to postpone action for a week and to request the hockey committee of Stewart, Cameron and Irving to poll the players and ask if the players confirmed their committee's position. At the same time, Stewart sent an application to the board requesting the loan. The loan would be paid back from receipts of the matches played by the Montreal Hockey Club's two teams. Major Freeman moved to not vote on the loan, and a decision was made to not make a decision.[247]

Stewart reported at the hockey club's December 7 meeting that he would not accept the trophy if the MAAA handed the trophy to the players. The MAAA then requested the Hockey Club to call a special meeting confirming the action of the club refusing to take the Stanley Cup. The players refused to address the question.[248]

The association read the note at their December 11 meeting, with Stewart, Cameron and Irving replying that a players' vote was not necessary and that the three of them had discussed the issue thoroughly. Forced with making a decision, Freeman suggested the Mansfield Street clubhouse hang onto to the Stanley Cup for the time being. A couple of AAA members were sympathetic to the players, and they requested another week to discuss the $75 loan. That suggestion only gained four of the ten members' approval, so the decision came down to whether or not the AAA committee was going to be petty and refuse the loan that was customarily done and never defaulted upon.

Freeman chose pettiness. And he had supporters. The loan was denied with seven of the ten committee members in agreement.

With the $75 thus saved, the AAA decided to allow the Montreal Tobogganing Club—a full-fledged and fully supported organization—to build a bandstand so a band could play during the skating season. Estimated cost: $50 to $75.[249]

With the exception of the blue-and-white uniforms with the winged wheel logo, the Stanley Cup champion was now completely independent. Without the loan in place to attend the league meetings in Quebec City, four members of the club traveled to Quebec City for the annual AHAC meeting. Tom Paton, Allan Cameron, Jack Findlay and Stewart attended as the team's representatives. Findlay was elected to be the league's treasurer.

And the first thing that Findlay asked for, since it was questionable as to whether the four representatives' travel costs were going to be covered by their own club, was to be reimbursed for his costs in traveling to Quebec City.

The request was granted.[250]

Archie Laurie, as president of the Quebec Hockey Club, also tried to restart the Winter Carnival in Quebec City. He requested the Montreal Hockey Club's appearance. Laurie had promised there would be trophies awarded to the winners, but the officers of the Montreal Club suggested that more information was needed, such as how long the tournament would last, how many days the players would be required to stay in Quebec, and on what dates the carnival would be played.

At the hockey club's next meeting, December 19, the players agreed to send a letter to trustee John Sweetland of Ottawa, stating they were aware of being awarded a cup from the governor-general, but would like to know how to apply to receive it.[251]

The players' complaint with the MAAA had more to do with the lack of recognition—the hockey club was completely independent of the organization, but the organization accepted its stature as its own. The hockey club which borrowed its winged wheel insignia and made as part of its bylaws that all players must belong to the organization was considered part of the organization for publicity sake, but not for support.

Without a commitment to the Quebec City Carnival, the 1894 AHAC season started. Neither side blinked as the season wore on. Paton had decided to stop playing, although he officiated a couple of AHAC matches as well as played goalie—in water polo. Stewart's season started off on a good note, with a 7–0 victory against Quebec. Herb Collins had jumped from the Crystals and replaced Paton in between the posts. Routh scored five goals to lead the Winged Wheelers in the rout.[252]

After the easy victory over Quebec, Stewart received a letter from Stanley Cup trustee Phil Ross. Ross wrote to Stewart and apologized if the trustees misunderstood the relationship between the Montreal Hockey Club and the Montreal Amateur Athletic Association. Ross requested some suggestions to aid in the proper execution of Lord Stanley's wishes to present the cup to the hockey champions of the Dominion. Stewart replied that the hockey club had not properly received the trophy and that the correspondence should be to the officers of the hockey club.[253]

Montreal won their second game in the last minutes of play, squeaking over the Victorias 4–3. A few days later, the Winged Wheelers took two goals by Billy Barlow and edged the Crystals 4–3. The team was now a perfect 3–0 on the season.

On January 29, 1894, an early season showdown between Montreal and Ottawa took place. It was the kind of game Lord Stanley had hoped for when he gave his trophy, but he had returned to England six months earlier after his brother had died.

As described by the *Montreal Gazette*:

> It was the biggest gate ever seen at a hockey match, and the excitement ran high. The solid citizen who during the day had gravely discussed the city's financial situation forgot for the time being that such a small affair as a city election was pending, and cheered himself hoarse when his favorites made a good play. For the time being King Hockey ruled supreme.[254]

For ten minutes, play went back and forth. The game was fast, with end-to-end action. On one Ottawa rush, Montreal point Stewart and cover-point Cameron did not see each other and collided with such force that both fell sprawling to the ice. This led to a delay.

About seven minutes later in a scrimmage in front of Montreal goalkeeper Collins, Chauncey Kirby scored to give the visitors a 1–0 lead. Three Ottawa players were whacking at the puck, and Stewart and Cameron couldn't clear either the players or the puck. Ottawa kept straight on the attack.

Kirby passed the puck to Joe McDougall who scored to make it 2–0 for Ottawa. On the play, Stewart fell on his shoulder again and was visibly hurt. After a delay of several minutes, he valiantly continued to play. The challengers took advantage of the injury and kept attacking Stewart and the Montreal goal. Somehow, Stewart, Cameron and Collins prevented the puck from going between the posts. As time was running out in the first half, Sam McDougall scored to give Ottawa a 3–0 lead.

When the second half started, Stewart had pulled himself out of the game, to be replaced by Henry James. The *Ottawa Journal* reported that the Montrealers believed Stewart's injury weakened them and was responsible for the loss.[255]

Montreal lost the game 4–1, which set up a tie for first place with Ottawa.

This was Jimmy Stewart's final game.[256] Hurt the next day was Cameron, who hurt his knee in a domestic accident and might not be able to skate the rest of the year. Suddenly, the defending Stanley Cup champions looked very vulnerable—on the ice and in the boardroom. Not in the treasury, however, as more than four thousand fans piled in to see the battle with Ottawa.

Cameron recovered in a couple of weeks and resumed playing, replacing Stewart as the point. And the vulnerable Winged Wheelers, champions of the Amateur Hockey Association of Canada for the past six seasons and seemingly indestructible three games into their seventh appeared to be former champions.

After Stewart's injury, the Winged Wheelers lost two games to even their record with three wins and three losses. On February 24, 1894, they traveled to Ottawa for a must-win game for both clubs. Unfortunately, Stewart's injury prevented him from going on the train. That would have been a good time to clear up the Stanley Cup trophy issue and for the cup trustees, whether or not Lord Stanley's gift would ever be seen again.

The Winged Wheelers came out on fire. With Cameron at point and James at cover-point, and the fast-skating kids up front, Montreal easily beat host Ottawa 5–1. One funny highlight occurred after Montreal's fourth goal. A Montreal fan had brought a loud horn to the game and let it blast after every blue-and-white-shirted goal. After the fourth goal an irate Ottawa fan objected to the music, and for a few moments the players had to dodge the horn, spinning on the ice.[257]

As for the unwanted Stanley Cup, Stewart received a letter from Ross on February 28 suggesting a compromise. Ross arranged for the transfer of the trophy to the hockey club, and he sent an order to MAAA secretary William S. Weldon to deliver the trophy without delay. Weldon, the manager of the posh Windsor Hotel, was not going to argue. By the time Weldon received the order, the scheduled hockey season had just one game left.[258]

Montreal defeated the hapless (and winless) Crystals 2–1 to conclude their season on March 2, but needed help from Quebec if they were going to capture their seventh straight league title and repeat as Stanley Cup champions.

On a slushy surface that gave players a bath every time they fell, Ottawa defeated Quebec 2–0 to make a three-way tie for first. That three-way tie became a four-way tie when the Victorias beat the Crystals in each of those team's two remaining games.

The drama in the boardroom continued, of course. Stewart could not play anymore with his bum shoulder, but it didn't stop him from writing. He wrote the association board that he would like possession of the Stanley Cup, as per Phil Ross's order, which he attached. The note was read at the association's March 5 meeting, and the snottiness continued when the association responded that any member of the Montreal Hockey Club, duly authorized, could come get the damned thing any time they wanted. The Hockey Club's secretary Harry Shaw was told to come by and take the trophy.[259]

On March 10, the Amateur Hockey Association held a meeting to decide how to arrange the playoffs. Further, they were under pressure from Phil Ross, who had accepted a challenge from the Ontario Hockey Association champion, the Osgoode Hall team in Toronto, to play the AHAC champions for the Stanley Cup, just as Lord Stanley had envisioned.

Lord Stanley never envisioned four-way ties.

The three-hour meeting seemed to have been settled when Archie Laurie, representing Quebec, said his team would just agree not to play. This left three teams to figure out a playoff format. It was agreed that the two Montreal teams—the Winged Wheelers and the Victorias—would face each other, with the winner playing Ottawa for the title. As a gesture of sportsmanship (and a free pass to the final) the Capital club would agree to play in Montreal. After much deliberation, it was agreed, but Findlay tendered his resignation from the league, citing his unavailability due to personal business obligations.[260]

At the March 15, 1894, meeting, Stewart wrote Ross to let the trustee know that the Montreal Hockey Club was in possession of the Stanley Cup. It was entirely possible that the Winged Wheelers would only hold onto the trophy for just a few hours. Montreal needed to play the Victorias in the first playoff game.

Ottawa point Weldy Young refereed the contest, which also gave him a good perch to scout the victors for his team the following week. Montreal came out pumped up at the start of the game, and less than a minute in, Billy Barlow scored to give the defending champions a 1–0 lead. The Victorias thought they had tied up the game soon after, but Sam McDougall was caught offside. The action was end to end, and the Vics went on the attack. Montreal goalie Herb Collins was pulled out of position, allowing for a sure goal by the Victorias' Shirley Davidson, but point Allan Cameron made a diving stop to save the score. The wall was breached, however, and Davidson later scored for the Vics to tie the game. The challengers kept up the pressure, but the outstanding work of Collins kept the scored tied at one when the half-time intermission came.

The maroon-clad rooters on the north side of the rink had great expectations for their Victorias to start the second half, but they were to be disappointed when their team came out flat. On the south end of the rink the blue-and-white-clad Montreal fans cheered mightily as the Winged Wheelers went on the attack. The Vics' defense held, and one of the great characteristics of hockey is in the transition game, which can take momentum away at any point.

McDougall picked up a loose puck at the north end of the rink and skated around and through the Montreal defenders, shooting the puck between the poles and giving the Vics their first lead of the night on the solo rush.

Montreal cover-point Henry James was then penalized, but the Winged Wheelers did not have to play shorthanded for long, as he was soon followed by the Victorias' Mike Grant. The luck was with the champions, however, as the Vics scored another goal, but it was ruled offsides. Just a few moments later Archie Hodgson scored a goal that appeared offside, but Referee Young allowed the shot to tie the game at two apiece.

The first playoff game for the Stanley Cup was going to sudden death overtime! The teams had their customary ten-minute break. Both teams had chances in the very early going, but three minutes into overtime Billy Barlow scored for the Winged Wheelers as Montreal won the first match to keep the trophy that most of the players had barely just seen.[261]

For five more days, anyway.

The Winged Wheelers still had to defeat Young's Ottawa Hockey Club to keep possession of the Stanley Cup. The previous two games between the two clubs presented victory to the visitors. The loss on January 27 was the game Jimmy Stewart was injured. Could the visitors win and bring the trophy back to Ottawa, which no doubt would have brought joy to the mourning Lord Stanley in London?

This was the first game in hockey history where a home-ice advantage could actually mean something. A capacity crowd packed the rink, many with tin horns that "might have cost all the way up to five cents originally" and some kind fans who "blew afterwards with the idea of getting square on the question of expenditure," wrote the *Montreal Gazette*.

The ice was soft due to the warmth of the season, and the game was a little rough, at least in the opinion of the *Gazette*.

"Nobody was ruled off, but [Montreal's Henry] James and [Ottawa's Harvey] Pulford ought to have been. Hockey is not necessarily synonymous with homicide."

The Winged Wheelers came out flying. For eight minutes, Montreal went on the attack, but Ottawa goalie Albert Morel stopped attack after attack. The striped-shirted visitors kept the home squad and their partisan fans at bay. Pulford and Chaucer Kirby got the puck out of danger for Ottawa. Kirby attacked the Montreal half of the ice, passed across to Joe McDougall, who then passed it back to Kirby, and the challengers took a 1–0 lead. Play went back and forth for the next ten minutes, although Montreal had the better of the chances. In a pileup of players and puck along the wing, Archie Hodgson pulled the puck out of the scrimmage, dodged in close and finally beat Morel to tie the game. Wrote the *Ottawa Journal*, "The cheering at this nearly raised the roof."

Ottawa had been playing on their heels for most of the first half, but they were still in the game. The next thirty minutes would decide Canada's champion!

Early in the period, however, Ottawa had a scare due to a freak injury to Sam McDougall. There was a stairway that projected over the ice in one corner, and McDougall skated right into it, getting knocked out. He recovered and resumed playing. The action was mostly in the Montreal end, but the Ottawa forwards could not penetrate through James and Cameron. Nine minutes after the half started, Billy Barlow scored when he was left uncovered in front of the Ottawa net. The puck had been fought in the corner, and during the scrimmage, the puck flew off the ice at the unattended Barlow, who batted it in. Desperate hockey by the Ottawas followed, while the blue-and-white-ribboned fans cheered their hometown heroes even more loudly. Nine minutes later Hodgson lifted the puck from the side wall and sneaked it between the posts, securing for Montreal back-to-back Stanley Cups and their seventh-straight league title. Weldy Young had played a tremendous game in defeat, and expended so much energy he fainted in the dressing room and needed to be revived.[262]

With the games and the Stanley Cup decided, all that needed closure were the sore feelings that the season had brought.

Findlay had let the hockey club committee know that he had resigned and that the team would not have a representative in the league. When Findlay's resignation was accepted by the league, AHAC President Watson Jack sent a letter to all of the clubs, asking for a contribution to give Findlay a mark of appreciation for his services to the association. Paton and Cameron suggested that a twenty-five dollar donation to the league could be used as a testimonial for the retiring secretary-treasurer.[263]

Jack Findlay

Jim Stewart did not record an objection; however, he could see the amateur ideal of playing sport for sport sake, like his father and the Odd Fellows preached, was ending.

The last two items of the April 2 meeting were a motion by Tom Paton, which was approved, requesting $190 dollars for souvenirs for the championship players, and a motion put by championship hero Billy Barlow to get the Stanley Cup engraved. These items should not have caused controversy, but this season was anything but easy.[264]

Jimmy Stewart thought he had a bum shoulder; he had a migraine.

CHAPTER 18
FIGHTING

Do you know what's worth fighting for?
When it's not worth dying for?
Does it take your breath away
And you feel yourself suffocating?
Does the pain weigh out the pride?
And you look for a place to hide?
Did someone break your heart inside?
You're in ruins.

The anti-war song "21 Guns" by Green Day, perhaps, but Billie Joe Armstrong's powerful lyrics resonate with anyone who has put a goal ahead of self-care or self-preservation.

Having claimed his seventh consecutive league championship, authored a rule book that the common folks of Canada could rally behind, organized the league to provide a champion that even got the aristocrats excited, taken the time to provide clarification to the fans and media if it helped promote the sport he had fallen in love with, and having done so with relative humility, one would think Jimmy Stewart should have been able to walk into any club in Montreal and be treated with the utmost in respect and courtesy.

Well, not the club on Montreal's Mansfield Street.

The last two items on the Montreal Hockey Club's agenda to close out the season were to order individual hockey trophies for the players as well as the engraving of the Stanley Cup. Of all the items that could be offensive, Jimmy would be hard-pressed to find two less offensive than this.

But with Tom Paton in the chair, the Montreal Amateur Athletic Association held a meeting on April 23. At the end of the meeting it might have been appropriate to try to mend the fence with what was becoming the most successful club wearing the Winged Wheel. Maybe even some congratulations to a fellow Montreal club national champion would have been in order.

Instead, the secretary read a letter from Richard Hemsley, who stated that he had been hired to make eleven gold watches by the Montreal Hockey Club. Before beginning to work, Hemsley requested permission to include the winged wheel insignia of the Montreal Amateur Athletic Association, as required by the Montreal Hockey Club committee.[265]

The person for the Montreal Hockey Club who made the motion to purchase the watches? Tom Paton.[266]

Naturally, a motion was made to cease the order. And it passed, but with some qualifications. The hockey club was instructed to provide a list of the individuals to receive the trophy, as they all were required to be members of the AAA. And because Paton was involved as well as Stewart, the request was issued to Harry Shaw, the secretary-treasurer. The AAA member who filed the motion? Gordon Kingan, brother of Alex Kingan, who had played four games for the hockey club.[267]

At the April 30 meeting of the AAA, the infighting and pettiness continued. Paton had asked on behalf of hockey club secretary Harry Shaw whether the hockey club's report should be included with the organization's report. The response? Absolutely not. When the hockey club said it was not connected with the organization, they were not in any way connected, and their report should not be entered.[268]

Finally, on May 19, 1894, the Montreal Hockey Club received a proper presentation of the Stanley Cup. AHAC president Watson Jack attended the meeting and made the presentation. With possession of the trophy, Stewart then went to make amends with the AAA. If Kingan's motion to establish a hockey connection was brought up, Stewart was to explain the history of the club and the association.

The players also received their watches. The celebratory players' cheers rocked the club. The hockey season and all the meetings were now over until the leaves started falling. Or so Stewart thought.[269]

Allan Cameron Jr., who had jumped with Stewart from the Crystals six years earlier, wrote a letter to the AAA board complaining that no one from either the organization or the hockey team ever intimated that the two were not connected. Cameron pointed out he had to be an MAAA member to play on the hockey team.

The AAA secretary was instructed to reply that the board stood by the report. Clearly time had not healed the wounds.[270] The secretary, William Weldon, was re-elected to another term at the May 28 Montreal Amateur Athletic Association meeting, and with all the concerns about amateurism, the person who turned down Stewart's request for a $75 loan six months earlier was awarded a salary of $116 per month.[271]

There was little talk about the Stanley Cup champions in the Mansfield Street clubhouse. Stewart's insistence on going it alone meant that instead of asking the association board for a loan, as had been the standard operating procedure in years past, the hockey club would be starting the year nearly $200 in the hole.[272]

James Stewart did not like the direction the Montreal Amateur Athletic Association, in general, and the Montreal Hockey Club, in particular, were headed. His interest started to decline beginning in November 1894, when capitalism started rearing its ugly head into the fortunes of the Stanley Cup champions, compounded by the league challenges his brother-in-law, Bob Laing, discovered when Laing wanted to get back into the AHAC.

Laing, who had stepped away from the Crystal team he had founded in 1884, had decided he wanted to run his team again. The

Shamrock Amateur Athletic Association had tried to get its hockey club into the AHAC, but a bylaw authored by Jimmy Stewart had prevented the predominantly Irish-Catholic club from joining. The AHAC, in trying to expand outside of Montreal, refused to allow membership to any club unless they won the intermediate league, which the Shamrocks had not. So the Shamrocks tried to merge with the Crystals, but that fell apart. Many of the Crystal players from 1894 left the club and joined the Shamrocks, with the idea that the Shamrocks would replace the Crystals.[273] The scheme even had the blessing of the Crystal Rink's owner, Sam Robertson, who was also instrumental in formalizing hockey.

When Bob Laing, William Drysdale and Frank Willoughby turned down the advances of the Shamrocks, they filled their roster the best they could.[274]

Stewart had his own club to worry about, however, along with the league mandate he helped create, which was to keep professionalism out of the sport. He was finding it harder and harder to keep the money out of sports, especially with the cunning of some business owners who wanted to profit from Stewart's team's success.

First, it was T. W. Boyd & Son, who had requested the Montreal Hockey Club write a letter stating the club was using Boyd's hockey sticks exclusively. Boyd was a longtime supplier of fishing gear, snowshoes, and hockey equipment as well as a gun manufacturer, and was looking to market the success of the amateur champions. The company offered free hockey sticks. Stewart and the board turned them down.

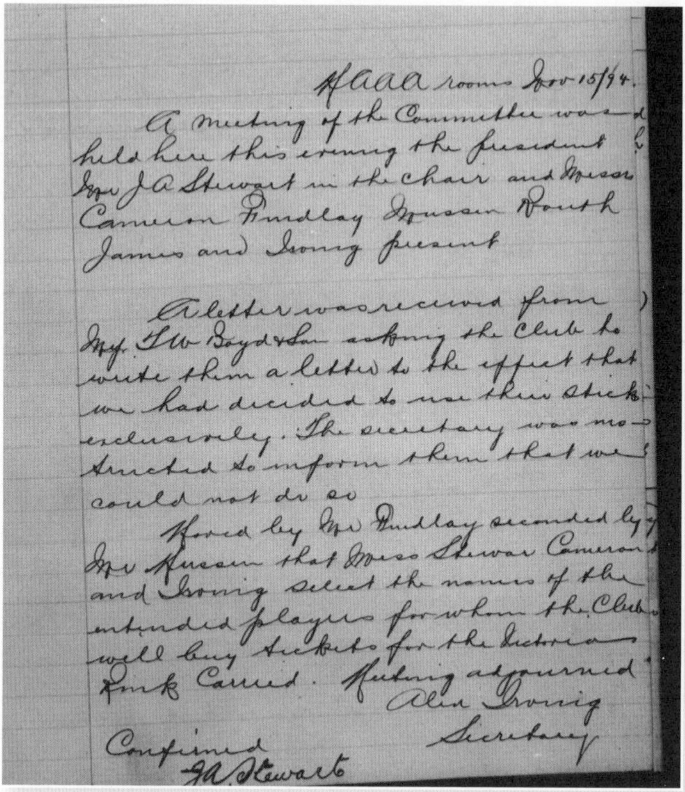

HAAA rooms Nov 15/94.

A meeting of the Committee was held here this evening the president Mr J A Stewart in the chair and Messrs Cameron Findlay Mussen Routh James and Irving present

A letter was received from Mess. T W Boyd & Son asking the Club to write them a letter to the effect that we had decided to use their sticks exclusively. The secretary was instructed to inform them that we could not do so

Moved by Mr Findlay seconded by Mr Mussen that Messrs Stewart Cameron and Irving select the names of the intended players for whom the Club will buy tickets for the Victoria Rink Carried. Meeting adjourned.

Alex Irving
Secretary

Confirmed
J A Stewart

Minutes requesting stick sponsorship

Treasurer Jack Findlay then proposed that the hockey club use its funds to purchase tickets for the players who were members of the club but had not the money to pay for ice time. Players needed a ticket to go into the arena to play or practice. Reluctantly, the board agreed.[275]

The first of December warned of the impending hockey season and impressed upon the first defending Stanley Cup champions how popular in the world they had become. The Hawthorne Skating Club had offered to merge with the champions, but then asked the club for financial assistance, as the Hawthorne Club could only offer players. The request was denied.[276]

Stewart's next hurdle became an international one. Students from Brown, Harvard and Yale universities had proposed a Canadian tour during the Christmas holidays.

The question: how much would the cup champions provide to cover expenses? The club agreed to $50, which coincidentally, was the original price of the Stanley Cup.[277] The American college students turned down the Montreal Hockey Club's proposal as not enough and instead accepted a challenge with the rival Montreal Victorias. The two teams agreed to play by American rules in the first half and by the rules that Stewart, Arnton and the others created in the second half.

The first half looked more like shinny or hurling, according to the *Montreal Gazette*, with five men to a side and without offsides, while using a lacrosse ball instead of a puck. "The ball is a great deal more erratic than the puck," the paper reported. "The Americans seemed adept at the use of the ball instead of the puck, but their strokes hadn't the sureness that is got from running flat pucks over flat surfaces, because the ball bounded." Despite tying the Victorias 1–1 in the first half and losing 4–1 in the second half, the Americans came away convinced the Montreal rules were the way to play this new game.[278]

The Americans lost 7–0 on New Year's Eve to a combined team of Toronto hockey players, and playing the Canadian style made the American team look slow.[279]

The first order of business in the new year was a request by the Winnipeg Victorias wishing to challenge the cup champions.

In January, the Winnipeg Victorias Hockey Club wrote and asked for an exhibition match, and inquired what kind of financial guarantee the club could give. Stewart and the board decided to give Winnipeg their entire share of the proceeds of the match.[280]

Normally in these kinds of exhibitions, the Winged Wheelers would give their intermediates a chance to play. But change was in the air for the hockey club. Stewart had retired, and Clare Mussen had been selected as his replacement at point. The always tough and hard-hitting Cameron was still the cover-point

More than two thousand showed up to the Victoria Arena to watch the revamped Winged Wheelers lose 5–1 to the western upstarts.

The Prairie boys were changing hockey's structure in a way that Stewart must have been silently proud of. The Victorias turned the game into a skating game, and then added the element of having a forward always offside, trying to pressure the Montreal defense as soon as the puck went into the Winged Wheelers' zone.

In one such moment, Winnipeg's Atty Howard was being checked by Mussen when Howard's skate came up and gave Mussen a nasty gash under his eye. Miraculously, Mussen did not lose his sight.

And while Stewart had his own issues in keeping the money away from the Montreal Hockey Club's players, his brother-in-law Bob Laing had problems with his Crystals team.

The Montreal Crystals had lost their first three games by a combined score of 25–4. The team was in trouble. While the Crystals had some up-and-coming junior and intermediate players, those young men were not ready to make the next jump. On February 2, the hapless Crystals traveled to Quebec, and not only pulled off an upset but pulled a uniform and a roster switch as well. Replacing the brown-and-white-clad Crystals were the Montreal Shamrocks, wearing their green sweaters with the winged feet. And the Shamrocks won 2–1.[281]

The Shamrocks were locked out of the AHAC, with the league stating no team could join the senior league until it had won the intermediate league. The Shamrocks had not done this. Instead, the Shamrocks tried to get in by amalgamating with the Crystals, and the Crystals' start made it easy for the executive to go for the plan, and elect new officers, all Shamrock men. The new executive fired the Crystal players and sent the Shamrock players to Quebec City.

Quebec protested the maneuver. Meanwhile the members of the Crystals who were not invited into the Shamrocks were determined to carry on with their old club, and on February 9, they showed up to play their home game against Ottawa. The problem was the Shamrocks showed up as well, so there were two Crystal teams waiting for the Ottawas.

In what could only happen in hockey, the two Crystal clubs bickered with the referee as to which team should face visiting Ottawa. Goodness knows what would have happened had the Ottawas appeared. But the Ottawas never came, having been unable to get down by train owing to that day's blizzard. Perhaps it's best to let the *Montreal Herald* tell the story:

> When the referee, Mike Grant, captain of the Victorias, put in an appearance at the Crystal Rink at the time announced for the commencement of the match, he was not unnaturally surprised to find that there were two Crystal teams anxious to compete for championship honors. The one team, which, for the sake of plainness, may be known as the Crystal-Shamrock team, was composed of White, goal; McDonell, point; Stephens, cover; Wall, Brown, Fairbairn and McQuisten, forwards. The other team, which might be called the Crystal-Crystals, was as follows: Lyons, goal; Ulley, cover; Boon, point; Hull, Murray, Jones and Laing, forwards.[282]
>
> Face to face with the difficulty of having to play two teams against a team that was not present, it may be unnecessary to state that Mr. Grant was somewhat at a loss, so he vamoosed the ranch in order to find Watson Jack, president of the Canadian Hockey Association.
>
> Upon Mr. Jack's arrival at the Crystal Rink, a number of different views asserted themselves. It is questionable, of course, whether he, as president, was wise in going to the rink at all, but still that does not dispute the fact he went. He was appealed to by both sides to decide whether the Shamrocks-Crystals or the Crystal-Crystals were the club to play the match, but this he could hardly do. There were questions and cross-questions between members of one club and the

> other. Mr. Polan and Mr. Willoughby both claimed to be president of the Crystal Hockey Club, but on what their claims were will come out in the very near future.
>
> After many heated statements the meeting broke up, but it is understood that Mr. Willoughby, of the Crystal-Crystals, placed in the hands of the association, along with other papers, a written statement that at a meeting of the Crystals held on Sunday, February 3, certain persons who played for the Crystals in Quebec on the 2nd were elected members of the Crystal Hockey Club—with the proviso that the minute should be back-dated to Friday, the 1st.[283]

A lively meeting took place that night at the Queen's Hotel in Montreal, which did not end until after four o'clock in the morning.

Blue laws did not interfere with lively meetings, apparently.

Joe Laing gave testimony that the old Crystal officers had never resigned, and therefore the amalgamation was illegal. They also submitted affidavits that the Shamrock players who formed the supposed Crystal team had not been elected until the Sunday following the Quebec match, although the minutes of the club show they had been elected the day before. Laing stated that it had been agreed at the Sunday meeting to backdate the minutes to Friday. The Crystals were fined seventy-five dollars, to defray half of the travel expenses and advertisements paid by the Shamrocks, and the matches were declared null and void.[284]

It was a decision that was as baffling as was the question of whether it was even legal considering it had been made on a Sunday. Wrote the *Montreal Gazette*, "The resolution that goes on record is about as miscellaneous a mixture as one could squeeze into four hours' deliberation, study it out four hours more, and then be almost four times as much in the dark as one was before he read it."[285]

While the Laings were battling their fellow Irishmen, the Jim Stewart-led Winged Wheelers were off to a great start, trying to capture their eighth straight league title. Montreal lost their opener at Quebec but won their next three games until they met the Winnipeg Victorias, who scored first and often, defeating Montreal 5–1.[286]

Montreal went on to defeat Quebec 6–3 on February 9, thus improving to 4–1 and looking like another championship run was at hand, although the 3–2 Victorias were gaining. Jimmy Stewart's brother-in-law had his own troubles with the Crystals, who had decided to combine with the Shamrocks after all. The finances of the independent clubs were starting to get serious, so Stewart and the Montreal Hockey Club decided to try to mend the relationship with the Montreal Amateur Athletic Association.

The club's February 12, 1895, meeting at the Montreal Amateur Athletic Association's boardroom had one sole purpose. With a full complement of fifteen members present, the hockey club wanted to join the MAAA as an affiliated club.[287]

The importance and timing of the affiliation was crucial to the development of hockey. The game had already spread to Winnipeg. Ottawa and Quebec were becoming competitive. Small clubs without financial backing could no longer become champions of Canada, as the cost of train travel and hotels was too prohibitive for all but the upper classes. The request was postponed, leaving the club's status uncertain.

After the request, the wings of the Winged Wheelers were clipped. On February 16, Montreal had traveled to Ottawa. A victory would make the Stanley Cup champions favorites to win its third straight cup. In front of more than two thousand paid witnesses, the visitors started off on fire. Archie Hodgson scored in the first thirty seconds when he was thirty feet offside. The Ottawa defensemen Weldy Young, Harvey Pulford and goaltender Fred Chittick made no attempt to stop Hodgson, but referee Robert Wall of the Shamrocks did not see the offsides and allowed the goal despite Ottawa's protests.

Six minutes later Havi Routh tallied as Montreal went up 2–0, and then eight minutes later kicked in another. The goal umpire admitted the shot was kicked in, but Wall allowed it, and Montreal looked like it was going to cruise to another victory and Stanley Cup, being up 3–0 fifteen minutes in.

With three minutes left in the half, Bert Russel tallied Ottawa's first. Just before halftime, Allan Cameron drew a penalty for fouling Russel. Montreal was still shorthanded when the second half opened, and immediately Routh and Ottawa's Chauncey Kirby drew trips to the penalty bench. This gave Ottawa a six-men-on-five advantage, but the Stanley Cup champions escaped the threat. There were only seven minutes left in the game when Kirby scored to bring the home team to within one, and the comeback was completed in the last two minutes of the game when Alf Smith tallied. Sudden death overtime loomed.

Montreal almost salvaged the victory when a loose puck in front of Chittick squirted behind him, but the Ottawa goalie recovered and knocked it aside. Twelve minutes into sudden death overtime, Russel skated the length of the ice to within a few feet of the Montreal goal and scored.

The hometown crowd went wild and swarmed the ice, lifting and carrying several of the Ottawa players into the dressing room.[288]

The train ride back and defeat were hard to take, but the Montreal Hockey Club was still in the driver's seat. Their next match would be against the Victorias on the 23rd, and that would be the game that could clinch the title for them.

Meanwhile, the MAAA responded to the hockey club's request for affiliation with its own request for a meeting, and Stewart, Findlay, Lowe and Alex Irving were selected to meet with the august body. The rest of the players would worry about facing the Victorias.[289]

Two days before the meeting the Montreal Hockey Club dropped a 4–2 decision to the Victorias, thus dropping to 4–3 on the season, while the Victorias climbed to 4–2. There was such excitement by the challengers that for the second game in a row, the Winged Wheelers watched as their opponents' fans streamed onto the ice and carried off the victors.[290]

If the Montreal Victorias won their last two games, they would be the new Stanley Cup champions. Montreal needed to beat the Crystals and wait for the Victorias to lose to the Crystals in the last game of the season to have any chance at retaining their trophy.

The results on and off the ice were not exactly what Stewart and his teammates sought.

The committees met and the four hockey men reported that they had a total membership of thirty-three, and that they were in a good financial situation, showing a $200 profit in 1893 and more than $400 in 1894. They further enticed their application by stating the game of hockey was gaining popularity in Montreal and that the club could probably bring another championship to the club.

William Maltby

AAA chairman Tom Paton, retired goaltender of the hockey club, pushed for the acceptance but met some objections from William Maltby, who, like Paton, was one of the original founders of the Amateur Athletic Association.

Maltby claimed the hockey club had nothing to offer the association since all the members of the club were already members of the association. Maltby said, "It was simply thirty-three of our own members coming forward and asking for a representation of three members on the board."

The MAAA board resolved on February 25 not to allow the Montreal Hockey Club to affiliate:

> The team members were already members of the AAA, and that the hockey club was already originated and fostered by the association, and up to some two years ago, was known as the MAAA Hockey Club. They have always worn the winged wheel of this association with our permission, and we have in our possession

> trophies won by their club, and also a photograph of their team in our room known as the MAAA Hockey Team Champions. About two years ago the hockey club seceded from the association and has since been known as the Montreal Hockey Club but is in reality a part of our association and we would be willing that this club come into the association as a connected club and have the privilege of a representative on the board of directors.[291]

Whatever small chance the hockey club had of winning its eighth straight championship dissipated March 2. More than 350 fans traveled to Ottawa to root on the Victorias. Jack Findlay, a Montreal Hockey Club member, would see firsthand if his club had any chance as he refereed. Six minutes in, Shirley Davidson lifted a shot that went through the flags. Only the goal umpire and the fans behind the Ottawa goal saw the score as play continued for about a minute afterward, but the goal counted, and the Vics went up 1–0. With a few minutes remaining in the half, Ottawa scored to tie the game. Kirby then gave Ottawa a 2–1 lead eight minutes into the second half, but the Victorias fought back. Graham Drinkwater scored about halfway through the half, and Bob MacDougall gave the Vics the lead with just a few minutes remaining. Ottawa fought hard to tie the score, but Bob Jones and the Vics' defense held off the home team.[292]

While the Victorias knocked off Ottawa, any hopes that Jimmy Stewart and the Montreal Hockey Club had of the season not falling apart completely would be against the combined Shamrock-Crystal combination, playing under the Crystal banner.

Through sixty minutes the valiant champions never trailed. However, every time Montreal scored, the Crystals fought back and tied it. Willie Fairbairn starred, scoring two goals in regulation, including the goal that tied the game after Montreal goalie Herb Collins was sent to the penalty box for roughing with the Crystals' Dave Brown. The teams were playing five a side at the time of the tieing goal.

With their legacy on the line, the Winged Wheelers made several attacks on the Crystal goal, but the Montreal players had lost heart, and the Crystals counter-attacked ferociously. Collins was called on to make several nice stops, but the defense could not clear the puck out of danger, the way Stewart used to before he went down with the injured shoulder. Fairbairn finally found a loose puck in a scrimmage in front of Collins and fired it home. For the third straight game, the Montrealers watched as the crowd stormed the ice and the winners were carried to the dressing room in celebration.[293]

The reign was over.

For the first time since 1887 there would be a new champion.

With the combination of the Shamrock and Crystal clubs, the Laing family exited the sport. Stewart's injury left him unable to compete, and yet the worst tragedy that befell the two men occurred less than two months later.

Joe Laing, at one time the champion oarsman of Canada, died in his Hibernia Road home on April 25. Laing was a member of the Odd Fellows, and they came out in force to his funeral.[294]

Jimmy Stewart was there to support his sister, Edith, who was Joe's widow, as well as Bob Laing and the rest of the family. The families had been very close since the Stewarts moved to Montreal in 1882.

It had been a rough four months of broken hearts.

When you're at the end of the road
And you lost all sense of control
And your thoughts have taken their toll
When your mind breaks the spirit of your soul
Your faith walks on broken glass
And the hangover doesn't pass
Nothing's ever built to last
You're in ruins

—"21 Guns" by Green Day

CHAPTER 19

USING THE TRAIN TO GROW THE GAME

Given the summer to contemplate, Jimmy Stewart had decided he was not going to play anymore, and he also decided to step down as Montreal Hockey Club president. Allan Cameron, who starred with the Crystals with Stewart and jumped to the AAA with him and accidentally collided with him during a game that ended Stewart's career, took over. One of Stewart's last acts was to have the new board look at whether the hockey club should play at the Crystal Rink or the Victoria. Stewart was so highly respected by the team members that he was not allowed to just fade away. When Stewart proposed that new President Cameron, new vice president Alex Irving and new secretary Andy MacKerrow be named the team's representatives to the league, Irving amended the motion and replaced himself with Stewart. The rest of the club approved—the former AHAC president was going to be a representative.[295]

Any hopes that the Montreal AAA would bounce back to their championship form was soon settled when the new Stanley Cup champions beat them 7–5 on opening night. The Winged Wheelers beat the Shamrocks 5–3 a week later, but they would proceed to lose the next four.

The season was in chaotic shambles, for both the MAAA and the league. On February 14, the Montreal Victorias lost the Stanley Cup in a one game challenge, 2-0, to the Winnipeg Victorias. The victory turned the Stanley Cup into national news in Canada.

On February 22, the Winged Wheelers was 2–5 after hosting and edging Quebec. With their season definitely ending without a championship and a Stanley Cup, Jimmy Stewart had three last items on which he and the hockey players agreed.

The Odd Fellows' view of taking care of the needy still resonated with Stewart, and despite the forgettable season, the hockey club could still do some good.

The first item was hockey's first formal old-timers game.

The storied Stanley Cup champions of the past would take on the present team in a March 3 exhibition, with all of the proceeds to be donated to the Surgical Instrument Department of the Montreal General Hospital Fair Fund.

Tom Paton came out of retirement to stand between the flags. Jimmy Stewart showed off his old-time lifting at point. Allan Cameron resumed his old cover-point position, although it is fairly safe to say he stayed clear of Stewart, unlike the last time they played together. Havi Routh, Alex Kingan, Alex Irving and Archie Hodgson were reunited in one final sendoff. Former treasurer Jack Findlay acted as referee. If there was any bad blood between the old and new players—and there is no indication that the hockey club was anything but united in its battles—it was left behind or forgotten.

But young men who continually practice, even those on a team that finished with two wins in eight games, are almost always going to beat former Stanley Cup champions who haven't practiced or played in at least a couple of years and who are in their thirties or forties.

But for one fun night the old Stanley Cup champions put on a show and gave the younger wearers of the blue and white a battle, although one wouldn't know from the youngsters' 5–1 victory.[296]

Another item Stewart proposed was an exhibition tour to the United States. When the college boys from Yale, Harvard, Columbia and Brown universities came the previous Christmas to play the exhibitions, they returned full of enthusiasm over the possibilities of the game when teamwork became involved. The results of spreading their stories – and the building of three ice arenas in the Eastern United States – led to eight clubs being formed in New York City, and college clubs being formed at Harvard, Yale, Columbia, Brown, Princeton and Johns Hopkins universities. The new St. Nicholas Skating Club rink at the corner of Sixty-Sixth Street and Columbus Avenue (the arena closed in 1962 to make way for the expansion of ABC television studios) was able to seat four thousand around a 180-by-80-foot rink, with the ice being made by an "enormous freezing apparatus."[297]

Hockey was not completely foreign in America. Although it had not caught on, except in some regional areas, one of those regional areas was in New York City, which happened to be the media capital of the United States. In 1896 Juliana Conover wrote a fictitious story that made *Harper's Round Table Magazine*'s front page, called "The Little Corporals," about a fourteen-year-old boy who moved from the United States to Germany and was asked by the school's principal to teach the German students how to play hockey.[298]

The Montreal Hockey Club and Montreal Shamrocks traveled to the States together to play three games in three cities in four days. The two squads even played a lacrosse game for good measure. The Shamrocks' Tom Wall took control of the two teams. Wall told the *Baltimore Sun*:

> We are making this trip with a view of furthering the introduction of hockey into the sports of the United States. In Canada it is the main one, and there is no reason why it should not be to winter sport what baseball is to summer pastimes. Certainly the men of these teams bear the same relation to hockey that the Orioles do to other baseball players.[299]

The newspapers did not know these two clubs finished a combined 3–13 in their league while the 1895 baseball Orioles finished first in the National League. Still if the newspapers could be impressed with these two clubs, hockey might be expanding even further.

The first match was played in the Ice Palace in Washington, DC. The Ice Palace was erected each winter inside the Convention Hall exhibit space at Fifth and L Streets NW, located just four blocks from the Washington Capitals current home ice at Capital One Arena.[300]

More than two thousand spectators filled the Convention Hall Ice Palace as the Shamrocks defeated the black-clad Montreals 3–1 in two 20-minute halves. From reports in the newspapers, however, it was hard to believe that these were two last-place teams.

"It seems to be true that Canadian babies are born with hockey sticks in their mouths," praised the *Washington Times.* "It appears to be perfectly easy for a Canadian to slip and slide around on ice and wield a shinny stick with dexterity. In fact, to see a Canadian skating, excites the impression that it was never intended for him to transport himself other than by steel runners."[301]

The Baltimore Hockey Trophy, 1897
Credit: Doug MacLellan/
Hockey Hall of Fame

With two days' rest and to see the sights, the players took a short train ride to Baltimore when the second game of their exhibition series took place. The winner would get the Baltimore Hockey Trophy.

The newly built North Avenue Rink would be the site for the next game. The players had a different challenge on this rink, with a sheet of ice that was 250 feet long and just 55 feet wide. The arena was located on North Avenue, between Charles Street and Lovegrove Alley, and extended north to Twentieth Street.

An interesting feature of Montreal winning the exhibition 7–6 was how the goals were scored. Wrote the *Baltimore Sun*:

> The puck was not carried directly in front of the goal, then pushed through, but the skaters would shoot from seemingly impossible positions, apparently taking no aim whatsoever. Every shot was lifted, which accounts for the large score, as the shot along the ice can be stopped with a skate or stick, but a lifted shot with the speed put into it by the Canadians is a hard customer to deal with . . . The lifting shots would occasionally go in among the rafters and banner decorations, and one shot demolished an electric light.[302]

The players could not possibly know this at the time, but perhaps the low ceiling would hinder the growth of hockey in Baltimore. The building owner would file for bankruptcy in 1899.

Two nights later, the two teams would face off under the bright lights of Manhattan. Before the trip it was agreed that the teams would compete for a trophy. With each side winning a match, the deciding competition would take place at the Ice Palace, at Lexington and 107th Avenues. About five thousand people showed up for the finale in East Harlem, and they were not disappointed when each team tallied once. The two teams agreed to stay over one more night and play off the tie.[303]

In the rematch it was agreed beforehand that the teams would play one twenty-minute half, and if still tied, a five-minute overtime period. Clarence McKerrow scored fourteen minutes in for Montreal, but Dave Wall tied the game three minutes later. After the twenty-minute period ended, the overtime started. Two minutes in, Wall tallied again to give the Shamrocks the win and the trophy. New Yorkers had seen sudden death hockey—and they were hooked![304]

The teams returned home to Montreal, but the Winged Wheelers were not finished yet. Before the trip the executive of the hockey club agreed to play the Montreal Victorias in an exhibition match, with the proceeds to benefit the fair fund for Montreal General Hospital. The game was scheduled for March 21, 1896.

The exhibition was fast but not necessarily up to championship caliber. The Vics scored a couple of goals before the half and tallied a third soon after the second half began. Clare Mussen scored twice to get the Montrealers close, but the Vics pulled away with a 5–2 victory.[305]

The hockey club kept their word, and their share of the proceeds was forwarded on to the hospital.[306]

CHAPTER 20

LEAVING THE PAST BEHIND

Jimmy Stewart could see where the game of hockey was headed during the summer of 1896. While the other hockey players played other sports, Stewart participated only in hockey. The game he had so loved and wanted to share was being popularly accepted. The British aristocrats accepted the Canadian sport, where the elite and the immigrant could compete against each other, all in the British tradition of sport.

By 1896 Stewart saw the unavoidable monetary aspects. The New York rink found it profitable to give the Canadian players a clean sheet of artificial ice while fans ponied up about two thousand dollars to watch a game between two last-place clubs whose players were just happy to play for free. And no one complained about coming back from a week-long trip to play another exhibition for the sole benefit of the hospital fund.

As one who felt strongly about giving back, Stewart came back and played one last game, with all proceeds going to help those who were abandoned like he could have been, if not for a caring grandmother, and for whom he repaid the favor by looking after his stepmother and half-sister after his father died in that horrible train accident.

But not everybody was James Stewart.

Some of the players looked for the money first and, especially in places that were receptive to *playing* hockey, did not necessarily agree with Stewart's view of the *culture* of sport.

The Winnipeg team that traveled 1,500 miles east to Ontario and Quebec to test their skills found out how lucrative getting a share of the gate could be. And the players brought that home with them.

"Hockey was viewed with some suspicion when first introduced into Winnipeg, and the players had to pay a good price for the privilege of securing a rink to hold their matches in, but it was not long before this state of affairs was changed, and the players were paid a good share of the door receipts."[307]

Many saw the money that could be made, and greed, one of man's inhumanity to other men, took over. For the son and grandson of proud Odd Fellows—the kind who sacrifice their own wishes to take care of the widows, educate the youth, advocate friendship, enact love and pursue truth—Jim Stewart's heartbreak must have been immeasurable.

By the time he was thirty-two, Jimmy lost his mother and his father, his best friend's brother married his sister, and his best friend's brother died. He spent four years as president of the first organized hockey league, and he resigned to spend four years winning league championships with the Montreal Hockey Club. But four years into that position, Stewart was first replaced on the ice and then later as club president.

He needed a change.

A new life. A place where his shadow could walk beside him. In peace.

And like his father before him who had left a relatively comfortable childhood in Northern Ireland for a new life in the British territory of Canada, the Canadian-born son was leaving his old life for a new life in the United States.

The Montreal Crystals, which he cofounded with his brother-in-law Bob Laing, floundered after Stewart joined the Montreal

Hockey Club, changing its name no fewer than three times in ten years.

The Montreal Hockey Club stumbled after Stewart's departure, finishing in first place only once, in 1902, and challenging for the Stanley Cup against the defending Winnipeg Victorias. By that time, the Winnipeg patrons were asked to pay $2 a seat (or about $60 in 2020) to see the Cup Final.[308] Game One was sold out in advance, less a few standing-room-only spots,[309] and the home team would defend the cup by taking the first game 1–0. Prior to Game Two, starting a superstition that would last decades, the Montrealers tore page thirteen out of their notebooks and bounced back decisively, winning 5–0 and evening the series in front of another sold-out crowd.[310] The Winged Wheelers jumped out to a 2–0 lead in the first half, but only after a Winnipeg goal was called back due to offsides. The Victorias scored ten minutes into the second half and pressured the Montreal defense for the last twenty minutes, but could not get the equalizer.[311] The Montreal Hockey Club won the Stanley Cup for what would be the last time. Before the Winged Wheelers could even defend its championship, every player but Archie Hooper deserted and jumped to a new team, the Montreal Wanderers.[312]

The Stanley Cup champions of 1902 had split in a political squabble, and the Wanderers were born out of the mergers of the Montreal Victoria Hockey Club and Montreal Hockey Club. Jack Arnton and Jimmy Stewart were together again. Except that both were now living in the United States. Hockey followed them on their personal journeys although both stayed away from the sport.

A former Winged Wheeler, James Norris, played only three games with the club before his father told him to grow up and get serious about work. Norris had to resign from the Montreal Athletic Association in 1898. At age twenty, Norris was sent to Chicago to work for the family's Norris Grain Company. Using trains to deliver wheat, "Big Jim" never lost his appetite for the sport—even playing in a Chicago league at the turn of the century—and eventually made enough money to purchase the

Chicago Shamrocks of the American Hockey Association. Within a couple of years of trying, he finally was able to purchase a National Hockey League team—the bankrupt Detroit Falcons, which he renamed the Red Wings in honor of the Montreal Winged Wheelers.[313] Today, that predecessor of the Red Wing logo still sits five stories up, on the face of the now-named Club Sportif Montreal Athletic Association, located on Peel Street in Montreal, just six blocks from where the Montreal Canadiens play.

Jimmy Stewart departed Montreal via train on February 10, 1901, moving to Sault Ste. Marie, Michigan, to start a new life as a bookkeeper for the Minneapolis, St. Paul and Sault Ste. Marie Railroad. Within just a few years, professional hockey made its first mark, with players departing Canada for first Pittsburgh and later northern Michigan when the International Hockey League was formed. That league lasted three years, ironically crippled by the train expenses of the distance between four clubs in Michigan's Upper Peninsula and the league's fifth in Pittsburgh.

Stewart was living in Sault Ste. Marie, Michigan, when the International Hockey League was formed. Stewart abandoned hockey when the players got paid, and the professional version of the sport he helped to create was following him on his career. The IHL was the first multi-city league to openly pay its players, and Sault Ste. Marie hosted two franchises—one on the Michigan side of the border and another on the Ontario side.

Thanks to the ease of train travel, originally designed to move product and natural resources from one part of the country to another, Canada was going to find out that its most important export was not maple syrup or timber, but hockey players.

And Americans were willing to pay big prices for them.

And the trains made it easy to get them.

What created the excitement in the United States was not the supply. The talent was no longer limited to Ottawa and Kingston. Toronto and the rest of Ontario and Manitoba were starting to develop high-caliber players. No, what drove professionalism was the demand that hockey enjoyed in Montreal. For the 1902–03 season, more than forty-three thousand people paid to attend senior hockey games in Montreal. More than twenty-five thousand were present at the arena for scheduled league matches, while nearly eighteen thousand saw the Montreal and Winnipeg Victorias struggle for the Stanley Cup.[314]

The Stanley Cup series referred to in the *Gazette* was an in-season challenge issued by Winnipeg and accepted by the trustees. The Winnipeg Victorias had lost to league champion Montreal the previous March in a three-game series in Winnipeg, and the western team wanted the trophy back. The series was played between January 29 and February 4. The best-of-three series became a four-game series when January 31st's Game Two had fifty-seven minutes of sudden death overtime played before the Westmount Police came in to close down the game because blue laws forbid playing on Sundays and the clock had struck midnight. The players continued anyway, and the police allowed the last three minutes of overtime to play out before clearing the arena. The game was delayed several times. Two of the most serious delays were caused by Jimmy Gardner breaking his clavicle and having to be replaced, and Tom Hodge fainting.[315]

After winning Game One and tying Game Two, Winnipeg pulled out Game Three before the Winged Wheelers retained the trophy by winning the final game. This team has been nicknamed the "Little Men of Iron," but with all the injuries they suffered this season, maybe "Brittle Men of Iron" might be more appropriate.

Besides Gardner's broken collarbone, almost every man on the team was sick during the season. The team had played thirteen games between January 3 and February 27. In an era when every player played sixty minutes and had to work, that was a lot of hockey for a body to absorb.

Said Montreal Hockey Club president Charles Chitty, "Although men may be called men of iron, they are not made of iron, and tired nature will give way. The whole thing in a nutshell is we have had too much hockey."[316]

Whatever was going on behind the scenes prior to Chitty's newspaper comment is unknown, but the players were not happy with being termed weak while the arena and hockey club were raking in the money.

Players were leaving Canada and playing professionally in the United States. Chitty and the Montreal AAA board fought hard to keep the players in line, but Dickie Boon, the team's captain, held a players-only meeting in October, and it was decided that if the board would not be player-friendly, it was time to start a new hockey club.[317]

The players gave the board one last chance. At the November 12, 1903, meeting, the players nominated former player Frank Bickerdike to be the team president. The other nominee was Harry Shaw, the long-time officer who first came on the board as secretary under Jimmy Stewart. Shaw won the election by vote.[318]

The players were not happy.

Every player except Archie Hooper resigned from the Winged Wheelers and created the Montreal Wanderers. Finding three other clubs that wanted to play in a league, the newly-named Wanderers started a league as well. The Montreal Hockey Club would never recover.

CHAPTER 21

THE DEATH OF TOM PATON (AND AMATEURISM)

Although Tom Paton had retired from hockey into a domestic life, athletics and organizing sport were never far from the household. For starters, Paton's brother-in-law was setting all kinds of records with the Montreal Victorias. As a center and rover, Russ Bowie starred as an eighteen-year-old with the Vics.

Ten days after Jimmy Stewart left Canada and his hockey past behind, Bowie gave one of the most prolific scoring displays ever seen. Bowie scored seven times, leading the Victorias to a 13–3 victory over the Montreal Hockey Club, in a game the *Montreal Gazette* called "as one-sided as a jug handle."[319]

The match was so bad for the team that Paton started and Stewart put his heart into, that the Montreal Hockey Club players and officials got into a heated exchange after practice and the team threatened to quit.[320]

Paton stayed away from hockey as well. He remained loyal to the AAA, bowling and curling being the two sports he favored as he aged. He couldn't openly root for his grown-up groomsman, but he certainly maintained a close relationship with him.

But Paton's spare time and energy were being spent with his wife and family. Lilly gave birth to a son, Willie, in 1894. The next year she gave birth to another son, Stewart. Just sixteen months later daughter Isabel followed. And in 1900 Thomas was born. Tragically, Thomas died eleven months later.

The Patons enjoyed their school days in the city, and the summers were spent out in Lakeside, a former community along the St. Lawrence River on the western end of the island of Montreal. Today Lakeside is known as part of Pointe-Claire, with parts stretching into Dorval. But in the early 1900s the area was cottage country, where the wealthy merchants went to get away from city life.

The hockey club that Paton had started and Jimmy Stewart turned into a champion, the Montreal Hockey Club, finally gave up competing with the professionals on November 17, 1908. But like everything involved with the politics of the AAA, the return to amateurism was complicated.

Paton's brother-in-law, Russ Bowie, was Canada's greatest hockey player at this point, and he and his teammates shared Paton's amateur ideals. The Montreal Victorias held their annual preseason meeting on November 12, 1908. At the meeting, concern was shared that each year more and more players were getting paid to play hockey and if amateurism was to be saved, the Victorias needed to make a stand.

The concerns the Vic players had was that professionalism tears friends and families apart; that while the Eastern Canada Hockey Association would let professionals and amateurs compete against each other, other sports leagues did not; interprovincial amateur football was the cleanest sport in Canada and successful; and it was felt that a large association that employed professionals would win hollow victories, as those victories did not give credit to the organizations they represented.[321]

Stanley Cup trustee Phil Ross was disgusted with what competition for the trophy he was in charge of had become. During the past decade—largely aided by the true but fantasy-esque tale of a team from the Yukon challenging for the Stanley Cup that generated headlines and gave celebrity to the trophy across the world—money and glory became the object for players, organizations and facilities. And the more money spent, the more money earned, and the more glory. At least that was the prevailing theory; the results didn't always pan out as hockey would find out.

As early as 1905, Ross expressed concerns that out-and-out amateurism – the kind that Jimmy Stewart walked away from – was as good as over.

Ross said, "Amateur sport means that a young fellow shall insist on taking exercise and playing games at purely his own expense. Then as soon as he becomes proficient in any sport, we commence to demand a lot of his time. We insist he shall play for his club in every contest that comes along, that he shall go travelling over the country for it, and that he shall train conscientiously, day in, day out, to keep himself fit for hard play.

"The better player he becomes the more we ask for his energy and pocket. We do all this in a country in which practically all of us have to earn our bread and butter, and while most of stick busily at earning our bread and butter we expect the young athlete who has got into senior company to give up several hours a day to keep himself fit to give us the greatest amount of satisfaction and entertainment in athletic sports. If he doesn't keep himself in the pink of condition we all slam him for his lack of local patriotism and gratitude for the applause we have bestowed upon him for playing for us for nothing."[322]

Ross then called to eliminate the hypocrisy of amateurism by legalizing professionalism, but finding a way to limit salaries so the weakest clubs can still compete.

Ross said, "I don't see what else can be done. Nor do I see much use in those of us who are not called to make any of the sacrifice hollering at the fellows who do make the sacrifice and want pay for it. What I begin to think is that whether an athlete is an amateur or professional is less importance than whether the whole structure of our athletic world is to continue such a heap of hypocrisy and lies as it is now."[323]

Within a few years, teams were paying mercenary hockey players as ringers just to play the important games, such as Stanley Cup matches. Ross sent a letter to every hockey association in Canada. Ross stated the trustees would not consider any players eligible for Stanley Cup games if the player played for more than one team during the season, whether in his association or any other. Ross complained that there was "promiscuous buying and selling of players accompanied by apparently dishonorable violations of contracts."

Ross continued with his strong words:

> There have been repeated cases where a club in one senior league would temporarily hire players from other clubs for their matches—a practice contemptibly unfair to the other clubs of its own league. Finally, there is seen in one of the leagues, the spectacle of a majority of one team, which has fallen behind in that league's series being hired toward the end of a season by another club for the purpose of pirating another championship which would not be won otherwise.
>
> The trustees of the Stanley Cup have never before, during the fifteen years of its existence, offered any opinions of their own regarding the constitutions, laws or proceedings of other hockey leagues, but the present condition of hockey points to the Stanley Cup becoming a gate-money asset to the club executive which is willing to gamble highest and most shamelessly in the purchase of players.[324]

In anticipation of the meeting and the regulations, Billy Findlay of the Montreal Hockey Club started to sign players prior to the meeting. The three players he signed eventually became Hall of Famers: Art Ross, Didier Pitre and Riley Hern.

The Montreal Wanderers, who were formed when Dickie Boon led a revolt of the entire squad of the Montreal Hockey Club, and the Montreal Shamrocks tried to force players to stay with their prior clubs by proposing a motion that players who played on the previous year's teams could not jump to another team. The hypocrisy of Boon and the Wanderers notwithstanding, the Montreal Hockey Club offered to allow a rule to be phased in but that it should not be presented at this meeting for the prior season's roster. The Winged Wheelers, who were now willing to pay some of their players, were trying to recover from a 1–9 season, and Ross, Pitre and Hern would go a long way toward making them more competitive.[325]

The lively meeting continued for forty-five minutes with the Shamrocks and Wanderers willing to allow the Winged Wheelers to keep Ross and Hern, but the Shamrocks wanted to keep Pitre.

After the vote went against Montreal 7–2, Billy Findlay immediately wrote his club's resignations, and the five other AAA representatives rose in unison to leave.

"I move that the resignation be left on the table," said one of the other delegates.

"You needn't leave it on the table," Findlay replied, "because we are going to attend another meeting tonight."

"Well sorry to see you go," said Quebec's Joe Power, the ECHA's new president.

"Good bye. Sorry," replied Findlay, and with that the six men donned their overcoats and walked out of the room.

The departure of the storied club, the Stanley Cup's first champion, stunned the meeting before D'Arcy McGee, Ottawa's representative, offered a quip to get the meeting back on track. "I guess we better adjourn before another club resigns," he said.[326]

Findlay wasn't bluffing.

The Montreal Athletic Amateur Association departed the professional hockey business completely and became completely amateur again, competing in the Interprovincial Hockey Union.

Montreal Hockey Club founder Tom Paton's friend Hugh Montagu Allan was now the honorary president of the entire AAA. Two months into the season Allan, whose father was a member of the original Odd Fellows, donated a trophy to be given to the top amateur team in Canada. In his letter to the league's president,

Allan, wrote, "This cup, I hope, eventually will become to the amateurs what the Stanley Cup now presents to the professionals, with the undesirable features eliminated."[327]

Nine days before Allan's gift, Tom Paton chaired a meeting of the St. Andrew's Society's charitable committee. Nothing unusual was published. The next day, Paton was scheduled to be at the Montreal Curling Club rink. Paton was club president, and the Montreal AAA Curling Club was competing for the MAAA Trophy against seven other rinks. Paton was still competing as one of the skips.

But while Paton's wife, Lilly, was at the Montreal Curling Club rink, Paton and an unnamed friend drove out to his Lakeside cottage. We don't know why Paton drove to his summer cottage in February, as the family would usually relocate from the city in June and then return in mid-September. The Lakeside (now absorbed into Pointe-Claire) cottage was only fourteen miles from home, and Paton was one of the first to own an automobile, but he was expected at the rink. Still, Lilly must have suspected something, for when her husband was not at the rink, she headed home.

Sometime around three in the afternoon, Paton suffered a heart attack. Medical assistance had been secured from nearby Pointe-Claire, but at a quarter to five, Tom Paton died.[328] He was so highly revered that the curling rink was closed and the tournament matches postponed. Wrote the *Montreal Gazette*:

> It is not given to everyone—it is given to very few—that when such tidings as reached the different curling clubs last night had been passed around, there should be a blanching of the faces of many old friends, and a disbelief for the moment that the news could be true. The different rinks became almost deserted, paying tribute to the memory of a well-loved friend.[329]

Paton's death was a shock to the athletic, business and social communities of English-speaking Montreal.

Paton had been one of the twelve incorporators of the Montreal Athletic Association, and the board of directors sent a heartfelt thanks to his widow. They also recorded the following in their minutes:

> [The board wants to] place on record their sense of the irreparable loss the Association has sustained by the demise of one who from it's [sic] inception, for which he was largely responsible, has ever been closely identified with it's [sic] interests, and whose many and varied services as active athlete, Officer, Director, resident and Counsellor, whose advice on all things affecting the welfare of this Association or sport in it's [sic] highest sense was ever sought, have materially aided to place this institution in it's [sic] present prominent position.
>
> They honestly hope that his splendid example of a noble hearted sportsman, whose memory was treasured by all those who know him, and whose name will go down as one of the finest types of Canada's athletes, will prove an incentive to the younger generation to set up the high principles by which his life was governed.[330]

Paton's death shocked Montreal. The St. Andrew's Club flew their flags at half-mast. Most of the curlers stayed home; some rinks reported that just three or four members engaged in scratch games, but it was only a mere pretense.

Amongst the athletes, however, Paton was not forgotten. Billy Aird, the former MAAA hockey player and Paton's long-time friend, received a cable from Glasgow, Scotland, where the Canadian curlers were playing an exhibition. The Canadian curlers expressed their heartfelt regret.

Paton's funeral was supposed to be private. But the list of mourners looks like the newspaper's index of the sporting news during the previous thirty years. Several of Paton's hockey teammates were in attendance. Russ Bowie was one of the pallbearers. Harry Shaw was there. So was Archie Hodgson. Sir Montagu Allan paid his respects. As did James Sutherland.

And coming in from Sault Ste. Marie, Michigan, was Jimmy Stewart.[331]

CHAPTER 22
BECOMING AMERICAN

I walk this empty street
On the boulevard of broken dreams
Where the city sleeps
And I'm the only one, and I walk alone
I walk alone,
I walk alone

Green Day's 2003 song, "Boulevard of Broken Dreams," could be the theme song for Jimmy Stewart's life. The sport of hockey languished as nothing more than a child's pastime until James Alexander Stewart channeled his passion and helped organized and structure a league, a championship and the playing rules. He was neither praised nor rewarded for his efforts, although the playing rules such as sudden death overtime, the size of the puck and goals, and even the competition for the Stanley Cup have lasted for more than one hundred thirty years.

By the end of the first decade of the twentieth century, Stewart traveled west, landing with the Grays Harbor and Puget Sound Railroad, living in Chehalis, Washington (about halfway between Portland and Seattle).[332] It may be hard to fathom, but the father's journey from Antrim, Northern Ireland, to Brockville, Ontario, was only one hundred eighty miles further than the son's journey from Montreal to Chehalis, Washington.

As if Stewart was the Pied Piper or Johnny Hockeyseed, hockey had expanded westward, thanks to a new generation of Montrealers who also departed the city. Frank and Lester Patrick, with financial assistance from their father, Joe, started the Pacific Coast Hockey Association in 1911. Within a few years, hockey expanded into Portland and Seattle. It appears that no one noticed the game's modernizer living amongst them, and everywhere Stewart turned, the game of hockey followed him. Stewart, for his part, faded into obscurity and concentrated on his railroad career. When the Seattle Metropolitans defeated the Montreal Canadiens in 1917 and captured the first Stanley Cup south of the 49th parallel, Stewart was nowhere to be found.

He never married, and lived as a boarder on Anderson Street. Stewart's past life was in the distance, and apparently not shared. On May 7, 1921, Stewart sailed aboard the SS *Princess Mary* to Ketchikan, Alaska, with a final destination of Skagway. He lived there for the summer and part of the winter, but in March 1922, Stewart moved back to Seattle and applied to become a United States citizen. His request was denied.

Stewart maintained his physique in his senior years. His blonde mustache had turned gray, and his forehead was a little higher on his head than when he was younger. Never having married, Stewart took in a young North Dakota-born cook named Don Ramsden to help pay the rent for their Belmont Avenue apartment.

By 1936, Stewart lived just five miles from the new arena for the National Hockey League's thirty-second franchise. As Seattle sports fans welcome their newest franchise, the Kraken, a lot has changed since James Stewart helped develop the rules of hockey as played since 1886.

Jimmy Stewart is not in the Hall of Fame. A photo of him playing for the Montreal Hockey Club is blown up and on permanent display, but Stewart resides on that photo anonymously. Stewart is not honored—nor has he been honored—by the sport at any level or in any regard. There is no tombstone marking his gravesite, located less than two and a half miles from Seattle-Tacoma International Airport. Likewise, Brockville residents do not even know their native son ever existed. There is no ice arena named in his honor. Anywhere. Or a trophy. He abandoned Canada, so perhaps it is fitting that he was never awarded an Order of Canada, although John Kenneth Galbraith and James Hillier were. Both were also born in Ontario before the establishment of Canadian citizenship and renounced their status as British subjects to become U.S. citizens.

Jimmy walked alone.

Whether it was his stubborn personality, his radically strict adherence to the British amateur code, his willingness to put the sport over his team until he didn't, or his willingness to support a farm system of talent to encourage those who weren't quite good enough to play at the highest level to still have motivation at the expense of the pockets of those who were at the top, it is lost in history what he did to upset his former Winged Wheeler teammates.

Consider this: James E. Norris, the future savior of the Detroit Falcons when they were in bankruptcy and the one who changed the team name to Red Wings, played three games for the senior Winged Wheelers in 1897. His father, cofounder and co-owner of Norris and Carruthers, decided that Jim Norris needed to help build the family's grain business in the US Midwest. So Jim Norris was kicked out of the house and sent off to Chicago, and he resigned from his membership with the Montreal Amateur Athletic Association. When he resigned, the club gave him a hardy farewell.

Jimmy Stewart foresaw the growth of hockey. He resigned as president of the Montreal Hockey Club on November 14, 1895, with his biggest failure apparently being the club's inability to win an eighth consecutive title. Stewart remained on the organization's committee, however, and made a number of resolutions to strengthen the club. His departure went unnoted in the hockey club's minutes.[333]

Frank, Lester and Joe Patrick started the Pacific Coast Hockey Association in 1911, and it wasn't long before Seattle received a franchise. Stewart was living in Seattle when the Seattle Metropolitans became the first American team to capture Lord Stanley's gift—a trophy that would have been long forgotten if not for Stewart's deft negotiations with Stanley Cup trustees Phil Ross and John Sweetland.

Major league hockey in Seattle lasted until the original Seattle Arena became more valuable as an inner-city parking lot. Seattle would flirt with professional minor league hockey for the next fifty years before becoming a junior hockey (ages sixteen to twenty, for the most part) landing ground for the past forty years, the metropolitan area supporting two clubs (Everett Silvertips and Seattle Thunderbirds) since 2003. Whether that continues with the new NHL Kraken remains to be seen.

As hockey tried to infiltrate the United States, many times succeeding but just as many times failing, Stewart did the same. He even traveled to Ketchikan, Alaska, on May 10, 1921.[334] Stewart lasted through just one dark winter in Ketchikan before he returned to Seattle in March 1922.[335]

Stewart lived a quiet, peaceful life in Seattle, although he did have a few friends. On August 16, 1938, the then seventy-four-year-old Stewart again applied to become an American citizen. He never married nor had children of his own, but did find three Americans to officially vouch for him. On September 27, 1943, the father of modern hockey's United States citizenship request was granted, just ten months after his most famous creation—sudden death overtime—was banned from the NHL regular season.[336]

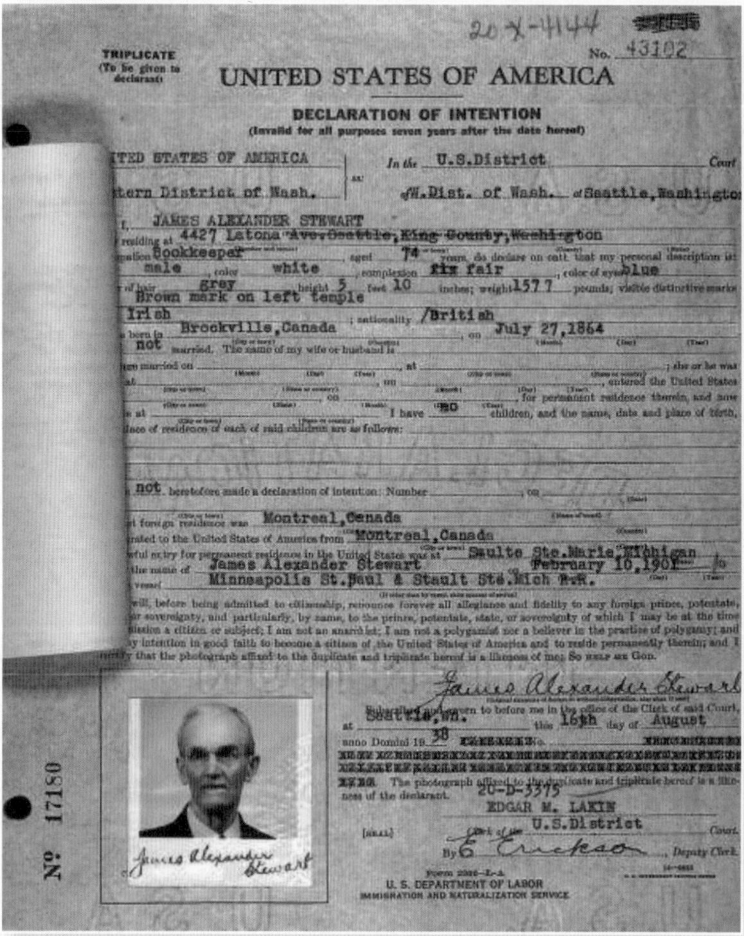
20-X-4144

TRIPLICATE
(To be given to declarant)

No. 43102

UNITED STATES OF AMERICA

DECLARATION OF INTENTION
(Invalid for all purposes seven years after the date hereof)

...TED STATES OF AMERICA ...tern District of Wash. } ss: In the U.S.District Court of W.Dist. of Wash. at Seattle,Washington

I, JAMES ALEXANDER STEWART
residing at 4427 Latona Ave.Seattle,King County,Washington
...pation Bookkeeper, aged 74 years, do declare on oath that my personal description is:
... male, color white, complexion fair, color of eyes blue
...of hair grey, height 5 feet 10 inches; weight 157 pounds; visible distinctive marks
Brown mark on left temple
Irish; nationality /British
...born in Brockville,Canada, on July 27,1864
... not married. The name of my wife or husband is
...re married on ..., at ...; she or he was
...at ..., on ..., entered the United States
... on ... for permanent residence therein, and now
...s at ... I have no children, and the name, date and place of birth,
...lace of residence of each of said children are as follows:

... not heretofore made a declaration of intention: Number ..., on ...

...t foreign residence was Montreal,Canada
...rated to the United States of America from Montreal,Canada
...wful entry for permanent residence in the United States was at Saulte Ste.Marie,Michigan
...the name of James Alexander Stewart, on February 10,1901
...vessel Minneapolis St.Paul & Stault Ste.Mich R.R.

...will, before being admitted to citizenship, renounce forever all allegiance and fidelity to any foreign prince, potentate, ...or sovereignty, and particularly, by name, to the prince, potentate, state, or sovereignty of which I may be at the time ...ission a citizen or subject; I am not an anarchist; I am not a polygamist nor a believer in the practice of polygamy; and ...y intention in good faith to become a citizen of the United States of America and to reside permanently therein; and I ...rtify that the photograph affixed to the duplicate and triplicate hereof is a likeness of me: So help me God.

James Alexander Stewart

Subscribed and sworn to before me in the office of the Clerk of said Court, at Seattle,Wn. this 16th day of August anno Domini 1938. ... The photograph affixed to the duplicate and triplicate hereof is a likeness of the declarant.

20-D-3375

EDGAR M. LAKIN
Clerk of the U.S.District Court.
[SEAL] By E. Erickson, Deputy Clerk.

Form 2203-L-A
U. S. DEPARTMENT OF LABOR
IMMIGRATION AND NATURALIZATION SERVICE

James Alexander Stewart

No 17180

Jimmy Stewart's immigration petition into the United States
Source: Washington, Petitions for Naturalization,
1860-1991, Petition 30810

Stanley Cup trustee Phil Ross stayed true to the sport, rolling with the changes, even though he did not necessarily approve of the manipulations that came in the chase for hockey's silver chalice. Despite financial setbacks from time to time, Ross settled down and married Mary in 1891—the same year he bought out his partner in the *Ottawa Journal*. Ross would stay a trustee of the Stanley Cup until 1949. Early during the cold morning on December 8, 1943, Ross's wife, the former Mary Littlejohn, died in Ottawa. Mary was also an immigrant, emigrating from her native Plymouth, North Carolina, to Toronto when she was a child.[337] Her death was noted in many Eastern Canadian newspapers.

Later that day on the other side of the continent, Jimmy Stewart woke up to another foggy late-fall Seattle morning. By the early afternoon the fog had burned off and the day was typical for December in the Emerald City—49 degrees Fahrenheit and humid. Later in the afternoon, Stewart took a walk. He strolled down the eleven steps leading from the front door of his two-story red brick apartment building. He turned right and headed down a gentle slope, by himself. He walked alone.

> *My shadow's the only one that walks beside me*
> *My shallow heart's the only thing that's beating*
> *Sometimes I wish someone out there will find me*
> *Till then I walk alone*

The former long-distance skater, who as a child skated back and forth across the St. Lawrence River and as a young man won the Carnival's skating exhibition in the one-mile and two-mile races managed to take fewer than three hundred steps that fateful afternoon. At the corner of Belmont and Pine Streets, the original Stanley Cup champion suffered a heart attack.

James Alexander Stewart, the man who introduced sudden death overtime to hockey, died suddenly. Despite his death occurring in broad daylight at a busy intersection, neither of the three Seattle newspapers noted the incident.[338]

The man who inserted the heart into hockey died when his own broken heart finally stopped beating. The Odd Fellows Hall was less than four blocks away from where Stewart died. Unlike what Stewart did for his father, mother, aunt and grandfather in Montreal and in Brockville, no one came for him.

Unnoticed, there was no celebration.

No fancy funeral like his friend Tom Paton.

Not a single flag flew at half-mast, not even in Brockville.

No obituary in any Canadian newspaper.

No funeral in the Forum such as Howie Morenz.

Like his departure from the Montreal A.A.A., Stewart's death wasn't even acknowledged.

He walked alone; he died alone.

An autopsy blamed arteriosclerotic heart disease—basically clogged arteries—due to senility, which in the 1940s was defined medically as "old age." [339]

The father of modern hockey is buried in Riverton Crest Cemetery in nearby Tukwila. The cemetery is unusual in that there are no boundaries separating the graves from the cars along the residential 140th Street. If not for the tombstones, one might confuse the burial grounds as a picturesque park. Stewart is buried here—officially in Section P, Lot 4, Space 28. There is no grave marker for the hockey pioneer, nor is there one for the people's whose final resting places are beside him, in front of him, or behind him.

Like he lived the last forty years of his life, he rests alone.

Surrounded, but unnoticed.

To find Stewart, you have to go into the cemetery and take the parallel paved path that is closest to 140th Street. The road turns to the left. Stay with the path a few steps. On the left is a giant tree, and to the right, in the second row of the deceased, is Stewart's unmarked grave, which rarely has been visited in more than seventy-five years.

Jimmy Stewart once became angry with his teammates over accepting free sticks in return for allowing the manufacturer to say they were the official provider. Seventy-eight years after his death, the owners of the National Hockey League's Seattle Kraken paid $650 million for the right to schedule games. Although an accountant by trade, those are numbers that would be out of Stewart's realm of comprehension.

With Seattle joining the NHL, the league now has thirty-two teams.

In Jimmy Stewart's day, at most there were four to eight top clubs.

In the world.

Jimmy Stewart was instrumental in helping the Montreal AAA stay competitive by starting an intermediate and junior hockey club. With professionals now ruling the hockey roost, the intermediate equivalent today would be the minor league system. While these numbers change annually, in 2020 there were thirty-one National Hockey League clubs, sixty-seven minor league clubs, sixty major junior clubs, and eighty-five university teams—and that's just in North America.

Stewart's rule book has evolved into the game being played worldwide today.

Although new to the National Hockey League, Seattle is now getting a second chance to win the Stanley Cup—the Metropolitans were the first US team to win the trophy by defeating the Montreal Canadiens in 1917. And in that same city, Stewart's apartment was converted into a transitional home to give thirty-one people a second chance in life. The low-priced units were for those who promise to live clean and sober, and were managed by the non-profit Pioneer Health Services. PHS manages more than eight hundred transitional homes in Washington State.[340]

The Capitol Hill home at 1733 Belmont was ironically named the Stewart House. But not after the Irish hockey Odd Fellow who called an apartment there home for ten years before dying, but for one of the Scottish founders of the organization.

Second chances.

Jimmy Stewart spent his life creating them.

First it was moving from Brockville to Montreal for his father, even though he was an adult, to help his dad transition to a new job as a train driver.

Then, just two years later, he stayed in Montreal helping his stepmother survive by supporting her and his half-sister in the aftermath of his father's death.

Jim Stewart's house on Belmont Street in Seattle, less than two miles away from where the Seattle Kraken play their games at Climate Pledge Arena.

A few years later, Stewart gave the disorganized game of hockey a new life by cocreating a rule book, organizing and running the first league, helping foster a relationship between the commoners and aristocracy, and running hockey's first dynastic organization.

Second chances.

After leaving Montreal, Jimmy Stewart moved first to northern Michigan before settling in Washington State. He watched the nascent sport of hockey grow, and little did the Seattle hockey fans of 1917 know one of their own was partially responsible for the Stanley Cup they had just won. And they wouldn't know—there's no record of him ever attending a game, even though twenty-three years earlier, he was the captain of the first Stanley Cup winner.

And for several years his former apartment was converted into a house for people who need a second chance.

For people who can't walk alone.

If Jim Stewart realized how important he was to the sport of hockey, he kept it to himself. The orphaned Odd Fellow who gave hockey its heart and soul finally had his own heart stopped.

And certainly no one from Montreal ever apologized, or thanked him.

In 1932 William Weldon recorded his reminiscences about that unique time in sporting history. The former manager of the Windsor Hotel and Montreal Amateur Athletic Association kept his thoughts private, but his son gave permission to share his father's words with Edgar Andrew Collard of the *Montreal Gazette.* The elder Weldon, whose financial battles with Stewart forced the hockey team to withdraw from the Montreal Amateur Athletic Association, recounted the history of the organization.

It was Weldon who first received the Stanley Cup with the order from Phil Ross to deliver the trophy.

At the end of Weldon's history comes his wistful thinking that maybe money ruined a good thing.

Weldon wrote:

> The Hockey Club was one of the bright spots in MAAA sports when hockey was played for the love of the game, but alas gone forever. When we look back at the long track record of players like Tom Paton, J. Stewart, Elliott, Cameron, MacNaughton, Hodgson, Barlow, Routh, Irvine, and others, we sigh for the days of real amateur sport, the game never having been the same since.[341]

By the time Weldon realized he was wrong, Stewart had long emigrated to Seattle, trying to become an American citizen. By the time Weldon's words became circulated, Stewart was long deceased.

Sometimes walking alone is the only way to take a walk.

CHAPTER 23
The Author s Final Thoughts

Sorry Cindarella, but sometimes there is no happy ending. Like the 1979 New York Rangers or the 2018 Vegas Golden Knights, a riveting rags-to-riches story usually ends short.

In researching and writing this book, I've stumbled across several moral dilemmas that I needed to address in my approach. The most important, of course, is what Jimmy Stewart would think of today's game and today's NHL and today's Seattle Kraken, and if he would approve of his story being told after so many decades of keeping it to himself, all the way to the grave.

I'm not sure.

There should be no doubt that once Jimmy Stewart moved away from Canada he left his memories in the past. He managed to come back for Tom Paton's funeral—perhaps he happened to be visiting his stepmother at the time or there may have been some other coincidence—and he definitely came back to bury her when she passed in 1917.

Although Canada's confederation occurred when he was three years old, Stewart did not refer to himself as Canadian on official papers. Although of Irish descent, he would claim he was a British subject, like most Canadians prior to the passage of the

Canadian Citizen Act of 1947. Stewart indicated as much on his immigration papers and to the United States Census takers.

And yet there is no question about the depth of his heart, how much he cared for his father and family. After Alex Stewart died in that horrible train accident—a hero whose painful death saved many lives—Jimmy Stewart stayed and helped his stepmother and half-sister while his brother departed for the Toronto area. He only felt free to leave after his brother returned to Montreal.

When Jimmy's sister Edi became a widow herself, Jimmy sacrificed his own personal desires to help take care of the women in a period of time where society was not kind to widows, leaving them to be caretakers or servants serving the P. D. Rosses and Tom Patons of Montreal society.

And yet Jimmy earned the respect of those in the upper classes.

Although he had an eleventh-grade education, he also earned the respect of the college boys. He was not universally liked, but he was respected, and without his guidance we probably would not have the NHL today.

His teammates and opponents alike were mainly single men who were not raising families and kept active as a lifestyle. Most of the players came from money, or were clerks. And almost all of the players competed in multiple sports. Hockey was a sport to play when it was too icy for lacrosse, or rugby, or golf, or any of a number of other sports. For example, Stewart's teammate, Archie MacNaughton, kept himself active all year long. In 1886, MacNaughton played for the Montreal Lacrosse Club when the team won the Canadian title by winning ten of twelve matches. He was a star forward with the Montreal Hockey Club, the first champion of the Amateur Hockey Association of Canada. He captured individual Canadian titles in speed skating and snowshoeing, being one of the stars of the Tuque Bleue. He also was the lightweight boxing champion of Canada and the sprinting champion of Quebec.

Jim Stewart gave his heart to hockey, and while he was playing, only to hockey.

Hockey followed him around as if he were Johnny Appleseed. First to Northern Michigan and then to the Pacific Ocean. I'm sure it dawned on Jimmy that train travel that made it easy for him to have a career also gave the opportunity for those willing to sacrifice a chance for a better life. And as James Creighton brought his childhood game to Montreal from Nova Scotia, the others brought the more formalized game of hockey, with rules, and skates, and sticks, to wherever the train tracks were laid.

For the last forty-plus years of his life, Jim Stewart stayed silent on the sport he had nurtured. He was nowhere to be seen in the International Hockey League in 1904-07, when the two Sault Ste. Maries each had teams. Nor was he involved in the Patricks' Pacific Coast Hockey Association, and when Frank and Lester Patrick were on the selection board of the Hockey Hall of Fame, Jim Stewart's name never came up. It's highly likely that the two Patrick brothers, who grew up in Montreal, were too young to understand the roles played by hockey's first ten-year player.

But if he were looking down and seeing how the NHL in particular and the hockey world in general run the sport today, I suspect Jimmy would have a different opinion. Admittedly conjecture on my part from what I learned, but I suspect he would be like every other curmudgeon and complain about the "outrageous" salaries, now paid in numbers that were incomprehensible to the retired bookkeeper. There's still too much stickwork, and he seems to be a play-without-a-helmet kind of guy. I don't think he could even begin to fathom that in August 2019 the Arizona State University hockey team would travel to Beijing, China, (by plane, not train) and beat the Kunlun Red Star of the Kontinental Hockey League to claim the Fu Xing Cup. Arizona? Hockey? In August? In China? Nope. The Fu Xing Cup? Gentlemen don't speak that way. That was never in the master plan.

But Jimmy Stewart would also see hockey's heart—the Hockey Fights Cancer program, how the NHL reacted to the

Humboldt Broncos 2017 bus accident; he would see the joy as today's players joke about the unfortunate Denny Pratt tragedy and recite other lines from the forty-year-old movie *Slap Shot*; he would certainly approve of the efforts of opposing players who stop being enemies and become caring human beings whenever a true tragedy affects one of their own; he'd certainly marvel at and appreciate the offensive skills of players such as Connor McDavid, but also the unappreciated defensive skills of players such as Brett Pesce and Jared Spurgeon; Jimmy Stewart would laugh at and with the rest of his teammates about the locker room tomfoolery; and I think he'd shed a tear to see the usually unnoticed efforts by many hockey players who try to make the world a better place by donating their time, energy and money to their favorite causes.

Overall, I believe Jimmy Stewart would approve.

If he'd care to tune into a Stanley Cup Final game, he'd see the passion that hockey players from all over the world play with, whether they are from Sweden or Switzerland or Canada or the United States.

Jimmy Stewart fought Phil Ross and the elites for respect. And in giving the Montreal Hockey Club respect, the Stanley Cup trustees and caretakers have been respected many times exponentially. That's a daily lesson for us all.

I hope if Jimmy Stewart looked down and saw the fight between Arvidsson and Hagelin and Josi and Hornqvist, he saw the heart and passion these men play with for a trophy that became popular thanks to a humble immigrant's beginnings to being the most respected and hardest to win trophy in sports.

I hope Jimmy Stewart feels he no longer walks alone.

ENDNOTES

INTRODUCTION

[1] Kitchen, Paul. *Win, Tie, or Wrangle.* Manotick, Ontario: Penumba Press. 2008. P. 67-8.

CHAPTER 1: A HOCKEY FIGHT

[2] Attendance figures came from Wikipedia https://en.wikipedia.org/ wiki/ Stanley_Cup_Finals_television_ratings for the United States. The Canada ratings came from: Shoalts, David. "NHL ratings boost gives Rogers Media something to smile about." *The Globe and Mail.* June 14, 2017. For the Chinese ratings, see: McGran, Kevin. "Stanley Cup fever translates well in China." *The Toronto Star.* June 1, 2017.

[3] For an amazing historical account of everything relating to the early evolution of hockey, please read *On the Origins of Hockey* by Jean-Patrice Martel, Carl Giden and Patrick Houda.

[4] The Irish played hurley, with the most famous early account occurring in the 12th Century epic *Tain Bo Cuailgne*. To the north, the Scottish played shinty. The differences between the two games were minimal.

The winters in what is now the United Kingdom were not as long or drawn out as they are in Canada. However, it still gets cold and the rivers and lakes do freeze over, and young English, Irish and Scottish children started bringing shinty and hurley onto the ice. Some adventurous youths even started wearing ice skates.

In England, the sport of choice was bandy, and when the young British subjects started wearing ice skates, the game became known as hockey-on-the-ice.

The informal game of hockey called shinny in Canada is derived from these four games. Add in North America's long, cold winters and Canada was inevitably an incubator for a winter sport.

Emmanuel Orlick wrote a series of articles for the *Montreal Gazette*, postulating hockey began in Montreal. Orlick was protesting James Sutherland's Canadian Amateur Hockey Association's report that stated hockey began in Kingston, a claim long since disproven.

In the Sept. 15, 1943, edition of the *Montreal Gazette*, Orlick wrote, "If the CAHA [Canadian Amateur Hockey Association] investigators were looking for the origin of shinny or any of their sister games I have no quarrel with them, but why try to mislead the public and themselves by labelling it hockey. In Hockey, where this game is called Hurley, it is traceable back to 1272 BC."

Three days later in the same publication, the McGill University professor quoted his campus newspaper, the *University Gazette*, that claimed on Dec. 1, 1877, that hockey is different because the stick used was different and the block of wood was the propellent instead of a ball.

Assume for a moment that Orlick's belief is correct. Any sport with a puck or block and a different kind of stick would be classified hockey. This cannot be an acceptable definition. Even the Society of International Hockey Researchers agreed that in order to define what *is* hockey, you have to define what hockey is.

In 2002 six extremely well-researched, well-educated and well-intentioned SIHR members compromised with this definition:

"The wording we have agreed upon, borrowed or adapted from, in particular, the Houghton Mifflin and Funk and Wagnalls definitions, contains six defining characteristics: ice rink, two contesting teams, players on skates, use of curved sticks, small propellant, objective of scoring on opposite goals. Thus, **hockey** *is a game played on an ice rink in which two opposing teams of skaters, using curved sticks, try to drive a small disc, ball or block into or through the opposite goals*." (See the Society of International Hockey Researchers website.)

When I individually met all six members of the committee, they all agreed the definition was a compromise as a way to validate or debunk the claims being published that Nova Scotia was hockey's birthplace. All six agreed the definition was missing something, but none knew exactly *what*. After years of contemplation and research, I think I have stumbled on the words that were missing: *organized with consistent rules from year-to-year.*

To develop hockey from a game to an organized sport requires one more requirement: continuity. None of the early attempts to organize were consistent from year to year, decade to decade.

DATELINE: CAMBRIDGESHIRE, ENGLAND, 1763

The child's game of bandy or hockey-on-the-ice got a little more serious when the bored boys of this English village practiced their speed skating by trying to slap a bung across a few acres of frozen water. The *bottle stopper* was a primitive name for what would eventually be called a *hockey puck*, and the stick used to whack the bung would be called a *hockey stick*. Compared to today's NHL, the game was not particularly fast, as a player would skate as long and hard as he could, until one of his thirty opponents would catch up, where the player with the bung would try to shoot toward the opponent's goal, which may have been about ten yards across.

5 "The World of Sport." *The Montreal Herald.* Jan. 7, 1887. P. 8

6 Bogert, Beverley. "Ice Hockey." *Outing Magazine.* V. 21. P. 252.

7 https://www.humanities.mcmaster.ca/~beowulf/main.

8 Gilbert, John. "Saints Fall to Houston in Shoot-Out." *The Minneapolis Star-Tribune.* Oct. 3, 1972. P. 1C, 4C. See also, Gilbert, John. "WHA Experiments with Penalty Shots as Tie Breakers." *The Minneapolis Star-Tribune.* Oct. 7, 1972. P. 1B and 3B.

9 Bogert, Beverley. "Ice Hockey." *Outing Magazine.* V. 21. P. 254-6.

CHAPTER 2: BROCKVILLE AND THE ODD FELLOWS

10 Lockwood, Glenn J. *The History of Brockville.* Brockville, Ont.: Henderson Printing Company. 2006.

11 "The Brockville Skating Rink." *British Central Canadian.* Nov. 25, 1863. A blog by Doug Grant called "Brockville History Timeline" published the newspaper story and source. The website, as accessed in Nov. 2019, is brockvillehistoryhandbook.wordpress.com.

12 *Sépultures non catholiques de la région de Montréal, 1767–1899.* Bibliothèque et Archives Nationales du Québec (BAnQ). http://www.banq.qc.ca/archives/genealogie_histoire_familiale/: accessed 24 Aug. 2014.

13 Stillson, Henry L. *The Official History and Literature of Odd Fellowship.* Boston: The Fraternity Publishing Company, 1896. P. 65-66

14 *Ibid,* p. 423-6.

15 Woodyatt, James; Campbell, C. T.; and King, J. B. "History of Odd-Fellowship in Canada Under the Old Regime." 1879: Brantford, Ont.: Expositor Steam Printing House. P. 72.

16 *Ibid,* pp. 72-3.

17 Stillson, Henry L. *The Official History and Literature of Odd Fellowship.* P. 65-66. Boston: The Fraternity Publishing Company, 1896., p. 447-9.

18 Duffy, Ewan. "Ireland's Railway Archaeology." http://industrialheritageireland.info/ railwayarchaeology/

19 Bogart, Dan; Shaw-Taylor, Leigh; and You, Xuesheng. "The development of the railway network in Britain." https://pdfs.semanticscholar.org/beca/ae2e1cf76dca3ecc5a252d529e583806ecec.pdf.

20 See http://www.thecanadianencyclopedia.ca/en/article/railway-history

21 See http://www.uppercanadavillage.com/1860s-life transportation

[22] Akenson, Donald Harman. *The Irish in Ontario, Second Edition: A Study in Rural History*. 1999: McGill-Queens's Press. P. 241

[23] See http://www.askaboutireland.ie/reading-room/digital-book-collection/digital-books-by-subject/statistical-surveys-of-ir/antrim/ and the website AskAboutIreland.ie, a collaboration of Ireland's museums and libraries.

[24] Phoenix, Eamon. "Irish Famine: How Ulster Was Devastated by Its Impact." BBC. Sept. 26, 2015.

[25] To convert into 2019 dollars, the railroads were paying an equivalent of $26.49, compared to farming, which paid $19.13 to $22.08 per day. A United States dollar conversion tool was used because a reliable Canadian historical tool could not be located. Still, in the context of the times, a reader should be able to ascertain the huge opportunity immigrants such as Alex Stewart saw in jumping to the railroad industry in the late 1850s.

[26] Ottawa, Canada, Marriages, 1826–1937, for Leeds and Greenville, p. 94.

[27] Hruby, Patrick. "The Olympics Show Why College Sports Should Give Up on Amateurism." *The Atlantic*. July 25, 2012.

[28] *Ibid.*

CHAPTER 3: THE ORIGINS OF HOCKEY

[29] Gladwell, Malcolm. *Outliers: The Story of Success*. New York: Little Brown and Co. 2008.

[30] Palmer, Bryan D., "Nine Hour Movement." In *The Canadian Encyclopedia*. Historica Canada. Article published Feb. 07, 2006; Last Edited Apr. 12, 2018. https://www.thecanadianencyclopedia.ca/en/article/nine-hour-movement.

[31] "Victoria Rink." *The Montreal Gazette*. Mar. 3, 1875. For further reading, please see Vigneault, Michel. "Big Bang Theory, Missing Link, or What Is Hockey?" Toronto: The Society for International Hockey Research. *The Hockey Research Journal*. Volume XVIII, p. 19-26.

[32] On Mar. 3, 1875, the game at the new Victoria Rink in Montreal was the first game of organized hockey. This match was organized by a twenty-five-year-old engineer named James Creighton, who also kept busy in his spare time by judging skating contests at the Victoria Rink. He decided to reach into his Nova Scotia childhood and bring the outdoor countryside game indoors.

Creighton organized the game, found eighteen men to participate, arranged with the rink to schedule a time to play, and publicized the event in a couple local newspapers. The game Creighton learned in Nova Scotia and presented in Montreal was basically the same as having been played in England as early as 1763.

But we disagree that this was organized hockey's birth date. It's true there was a game scheduled and played on this date, and a 2–1 score was indicated in the *Montreal Gazette*, but the players participated in street clothes. A uniform would come two weeks later. This game meets the SIHR definition requirements, but there was nothing permanent that developed from this game.

33 So little in fact that Creighton and his nine men per side moved on, with just a few games per year, mostly as mid-winter training for lacrosse players.

Creighton never took credit for inventing hockey. His list of accomplishments in life was quite extensive—so much so that calling him the father of hockey is a misnomer. If he is the father of hockey, he is at best a deadbeat dad who was there in the beginning and stayed a few years. But labelling Creighton a deadbeat dad is slanderous and unfair. In fairness Creighton was a contributor, and in his own words, he never claimed to be more than that.

34 Fitsell, J. W. "CREIGHTON, JAMES GEORGE AYLWIN," in *Dictionary of Canadian Biography*, Vol. 15, University of Toronto/Université Laval, 2003–, accessed Oct. 22, 2019, http://www.biographi.ca/en/bio/creighton_james_ george_aylwin_15E.html.

35 The four hockey books Bill Fitsell has authored are: *Hockey's Captains, Colonels & Kings* (1987), *Hockey's Hub: Three Centuries of Hockey in Kingston* (2003), *How Hockey Happened: A Pictoral History of the Origin's of Canada's National Winter Game* (2007), and *Captain James T. Sutherland: The Grand Old Man of Hockey & The Battle for the Original Hockey Hall of Fame.* (2012).

36 Gnaedinger, F. G. "About the Origin of Hockey." Montreal Gazette. Jan. 21, 1941. P. 14.

37 *Ibid.*

38 "Victoria Skating Rink." *The Montreal Herald and Daily Commercial Gazette.* Feb. 3, 1876. P. 3.

39 "Grand Skating Tournament." *The Montreal Herald and Daily Commerical Gazette.* Feb. 5, 1876. P. 3.

40 "The Hockey Match." *The Montreal Herald and Daily Commercial Gazette.* Feb. 7, 1876. P. 3.

41 Information noted from looking up the members of the McGill Hockey Club as published in the *McGill Reporter*, Jan. 31, 2014. The article, written by hockey historian Earl Zukerman, referenced the Feb. 1, 1877, *McGill University Gazette*. The players were then researched using the 1881 and/or 1871 Canadian Censuses to determine parentage and lifestyle.

42 "Sports and Pastimes. Hockey." *The Montreal Gazette.* Nov. 15, 1881. P. 4.

43 "Hockey Club." *The McGill University Gazette.* Apr. 1, 1883. P. 4.

44 Kitchen, Paul. *Win, Tie or Wrangle.* Manotick, Ontario: Penumbra Press, 2008. P. 14-15.

45 "Hockey. Quebec vs. Montreal." *The Quebec Morning Chronicle.* Jan. 24, 1881. P. 1.

46 Gerald J. J. Tulchinsky, "CANTIN, AUGUSTIN," in *Dictionary of Canadian Biography*, Vol. 12, University of Toronto/Université Laval, 2003–, accessed Aug. 1, 2019, http://www.biographi.ca/en/bio/cantin_augustin_12E.html.

47 Edgar Andrew Collard, "ROSS, PHILIP SIMPSON," in *Dictionary of Canadian Biography*, Vol. 13, University of Toronto/Université Laval, 2003–, accessed Aug. 1, 2019, http://www.biographi.ca/en/bio/ross_philip_simpson_13E. html.

CHAPTER 4: AN IMMIGRANT'S DEATH

48 Metcalfe, Alan. "The Evolution of Organized Physical Recreation in Montreal, 1840–1895." Histoire Sociale—Social History. P. 150.

49 *Ibid.*

50 Washington Petitions for Naturalization, 1860–1991. Pėtition 43102.

51 *Montreal Gazette.* "The Races at the Victoria Rink." Jan 24, 1883. P. 7.

52 "The Skating Races." *Montreal Gazette.* Jan 26, 1883. P. 8.

53 Skating. *Montreal Gazette.* Feb 20, 1883. P. 8.

54 "Snowshoeing." *Montreal Gazette.* Nov 28, 1883. P. 8.

55 Snowshoeing is still practiced as a hiking-type activity in many regions of North America where snowfall is sustained over a period of months every year. For more information on snowshoeing, see http://snowshoes.com/learn.

56 Bishop's Winter Carnival Illustrated. Montreal: G. Bishop. Feb. 1884. P. 10.

57 "The St. Charles Annual Races." *Montreal Gazette.* Mar. 17, 1884. P. 8.

58 "Skating. Speed Skating in Montreal." *Montreal Gazette.* Jan 14, 1884. P. 8.

59 A tender, or coal-car, was a special rail vehicle used by a steam locomotive containing its fuel and water. Steam locomotives consume large quantities of water compared to the quantity of fuel, so their tenders are necessary to keep them running over long distances.

60 "The Pointe-Claire Accident." *The Montreal Daily Witness.* Oct. 24, 1884. P. 6.

61 A *semaphore* is the telegraphy system conveying information at a distance by means of visual signals with handheld flags, rods, etc. When the semaphore is up, opposing trains can see traffic is either coming toward them or on their tracks. When the semaphore is down, it appears that the tracks are clear.

62 "The Railway Collision." *The Montreal Daily Witness.* Oct. 25, 1884. Page 2.

63 "Honoring the Dead." *The Montreal Daily Witness.* Oct. 25, 1884. Page 6.

CHAPTER 5: A SON HONORS HIS FATHER

64 The Montreal Winter Carnival. Montreal: J. H. Gould & Company. 1884. Found at https://static.torontopubliclibrary.ca/da/pdfs/37131055474217d.pdf

65 "The Montreal Carnival from Harper's Bazaar Mar. 8, 1884." *Victoriana Magazine.* Accessed at http://www.victoriana.com/history/montrealcarnival.htm.

66 Bogert, Beverley. "Ice Hockey." *Outing Magazine.* V. 21. P. 252.

67 *Ibid,* p. 253

CHAPTER 6: THE RICH KID'S INFLUENCE

68 "Sale of Pork at Auction in Montreal." *The Chicago Tribune.* Jul. 31, 1863. P. 4.

69 *Ottawa Daily Citizen.* Sept. 9, 1864. P. 2.

70 Canada. *Ottawa Daily Citizen.* Nov 27, 1868. P. 3.

71 "Death of Mr. John J. Arnton." *The Montreal Gazette.* Nov. 14, 1894. P. 2, and "Bank of Montreal." *The Montreal Gazette.* June 5, 1894. P. 6.

72 1871 Canada Census. Province of Quebec, District No. 106 Montreal West, Sub District No. 8 St. Antoine Ward, p. 18.

73 An amalgamation of articles from "The Children's Carnival." *Montreal Gazette.* Jan. 28, 1878. P. 2. and "Victoria Skating Rink. The Juvenile Carnival." *Montreal Daily Witness.* Jan. 28, 1878. P. 4.

74 "The Carnival." *Montreal Daily Witness.* Mar. 6, 1878. P. 2.

75 "Hockey." *Montreal Gazette.* Jan. 24, 1881. P. 5.

CHAPTER 7: FORMING THE CRYSTALS

76 "Seekonk Scullers." *The Boston Globe.* June 14, 1880. P. 1.

77 "Sporting Events." *The Boston Globe.* June 15, 1880. P. 1.

78 "Holmes Captures the Amateur Championship Prize." *The Boston Globe.* June 16, 1880. P. 1.

79 "On The Water." *The Washington Evening Critic.* Sept. 8, 1881. P. 4.

80 "The Regatta Over." *The Washington Evening Star.* Sept. 10, 1881, p. 4.

81 "Returned Home." *The Montreal Gazette.* Sept. 14, 1881. P. 5.

82 "C.A.A.O. Regatta." *The Montreal Gazette.* Aug. 8, 1887. P. 5, 8.

83 "Tenth Annual Regatta of the National Association of Oarsmen." *The Detroit Free Press.* Aug. 9, 1882. P. 6.

84 "Holmes, of Pawtucket, Proves Himself the Fastest Senior Sculler." *The Detroit Free Press.* Aug. 10, 1882. P. 1.

85 *Ibid.*

86 "Aquatic. A Chat with a Champion." *The New Orleans Times-Democrat.* Mar. 23, 1883. P. 2.

87 "Oarsmen on the Charles." *The Boston Globe.* June 19, 1883. P. 1.

88 "The Newark Regatta." *The Montreal Gazette.* Aug. 9, 1883. P. 8.

89 "Rowing on the Passaic." *The New York Tribune.* Aug. 9, 1883, p. 8.

90 "Is Laing an Amateur?" *The Montreal Gazette.* Aug. 20, 1883. P. 8.

91 *Ibid.*

92 Hockey. *The Montreal Gazette.* Nov. 21, 1882. P. 8.

93 Hockey. *The Montreal Gazette.* Nov. 28, 1882. P. 8.

94 One of the problems when trying to transport back to time and place is sometimes location names change. Joseph and Robert Laing opened up their tobacco shop at 70 St. Joseph in 1883. In Lovell's 1883–84 city directory, the name Laing was misspelled as Lang, and that is the spelling the *Montreal Gazette* used although Joe Laing was already fairly famous in Canada for his rowing exploits. In 1884 the City of Montreal changed the name of the street from St. Joseph to Notre Dame West, and the 1883–84 Lovell's City Directory clearly notes that the street name has changed (page 28) and the street address is listed as 70 Notre Dame West (page 119). In 1884, the City of Montreal got rid of the east and west appendages and renumbered the street so the address changed to 1904 Notre Dame. In the 1884–85 Lovell's City Directory, the spelling of Laing name was also corrected (page 164). The tobacco shop did not move in those three years. As of 2019 a lamp antique store has been in its location for the last several years.

95 Hockey. *The Montreal Gazette.* Jan. 3, 1884. P. 8.

96 "Sporting News. Hockey" *The McGill University Gazette.* Feb. 1, 1884. P. 8.

97 "Victoria vs. Crystal." *The Montreal Gazette.* Jan. 29, 1884. P. 8.

98 "The Winter Carnival." *The Montreal Daily Witness.* Feb 2, 1884. P. 5.

99 "The Carnival." *The Montreal Gazette.* Feb. 5, 1884. P. 5.

100 "The Hockey Matches. Wanderers vs. Crystals." *The Montreal Gazette.* Feb. 6, 1884. P. 7.

101 "The Carnival." *The Montreal Gazette.* Feb. 7, 1884. P. 5.

102 "The Carnival." *The Montreal Gazette.* Feb. 8, 1884. P. 5.

103 "Hockey Match." *The Montreal Gazette.* Feb. 9, 1884. P. 5. Weather data located on p. 3.

104 "The Hockey Matches." *The Montreal Gazette.* Feb. 11, 1884. P. 5.

105 "Hockey Matches This Morning." *The Montreal Daily Witness.* Feb. 11, 1884. P. 4.

106 "Sporting Notes." *Ottawa Daily Citizen.* Feb. 12, 1884. P. 1.

CHAPTER 8: THE BIRTH OF THE MONTREAL AAA

[107] MacDonald, Duncan A. L. "Turning Back Hockey's Pages." *The Montreal Gazette.* Jan. 8, 1935. P. 12.

[108] "Ten Quick Facts on . . . The South African War." Published by Veterans Affairs Canada. https://www.veterans.gc.ca/eng/remembrance/information-for/educators/quick-facts/south-african-war.

[109] The Detroit Red Wings claim their logo was based upon the shield of the Montreal Amateur Athletic Association, whose headquarters are located just a half-mile away from the Bell Centre.

[110] In 1966 when the Montreal Metro was completed Burnside was renamed as part of de Maisonneuve.

[111] The Constitution of the Montreal Amateur Athletic Association, as found in the official minutes of the MAAA Montreal Amateur Athletic Association, MG 28, I 351, Vol. 1 File 1, Minute Book No. 1, June 1881–Jan. 1886. P. 9-15.

[112] Edward A. Whitehead, Angus Grant, Nicholas Hughes, William Maltby, Archibald Stevenson, Robert McGibbon, Hugh Becket, McGill Stewart, Samuel Baylis, Tom Paton, James Whyte, and George Starke, June 20, 1881, from the minutes of the Montreal AAA Montreal Amateur Athletic Association, MG 28, I 351, Vol. 1 File 1, Minute Book No. 1, June 1881–Jan. 1886. Page 1.

[113] Hedley, James (ed.) *Canada and Her Commerce.* Montreal: Sabiston Litho & Pub. Co. 1894.

[114] *Ibid.*

[115] "The Lacrosse Dispute." *The Montreal Gazette.* Nov. 5, 1884. P. 8.

[116] "Lacrosse." *The Montreal Gazette.* Nov. 6, 1884. P. 8.

[117] Montreal Amateur Athletic Association, MG 28, I 351, Vol. 1 File 1, Minute Book No. 1, June 1881–Jan. 1886. Page 268.

[118] "Formation of the Montreal Hockey Club." *The Montreal Gazette.* Nov. 29, 1884. P. 8.

[119] Hockey. *The Montreal Gazette*. Jan. 21, 1881. P. 1.

[120] The Constitution of the Montreal Hockey Association, as found in the official minutes of the MAAA, Vol. 6, p. 22.

[121] "Memories of a Great Winter Carnival at Montreal in '87." *The Ottawa Citizen.* Mar. 18, 1939. p. 2.

CHAPTER 9: THE CARNIVAL YEARS

[122] "The Hockey Tournament." *The Montreal Gazette*. Jan. 28, 1885. P. 5.

[123] "The Hockey Tournament." *The Montreal Gazette*. Jan. 28, 1885. P. 8.

[124] "The Hockey Tournament." *The Montreal Gazette*. Jan. 29, 1885. P. 5.

[125] "The Hockey Tournament." *The Montreal Gazette.* Jan. 31, 1885. P. 5.

[126] A combination of three articles: "The Hockey Players." *The Montreal Daily Witness*. Jan. 31, 1885. P. 6; "The Hockey Tournament." *The Montreal Gazette.* Feb. 2, 1885. P. 5; and "The Montreal Hockey Tournament." *The Ottawa Daily Citizen.* Feb. 3, 1885. P. 2. The Citizen article quotes a story from the *Montreal Star.*

[127] "The Hockey Players." *The Montreal Daily Witness.* Feb. 2, 1885. P. 2.

[128] "Hockey. Victoria vs. MAAA." *The Montreal Gazette.* Feb. 7, 1885. P. 8.

[129] "Hockey. St. James vs. Metropolitan Clubs." *The Montreal Gazette.* Mar. 12, 1885. P. 8.

[130] "Sir Edward Clouston, Leading Banker, Dead." *The Ottawa Citizen.* Nov. 25, 1912. P. 13.

[131] "Out-door Sports." *The Montreal Witness.* Dec. 14, 1885. P. 4. In the Dec. 15, 1885, *Montreal Gazette,* the game was listed as a scratch match because only a few members of the Montreal Hockey Club showed, despite the rink purchasing a number of pewter trophies for the winner.

[132] Guyot, F. "A Brief History of the Small Pox Epidemic Outbreak From 1871 to 1880 and the Late Outbreak of 1885." Page 10. http://eco.canadiana.ca/view/ oocihm.05135

[133] Bliss, Michael. *Plague: A Story of Smallpox in Montreal.* HarperCollins. 1992. Excerpt published in *The Monreal Gazette*. Oct. 13, 1991. P. E-5.

[134] Marsh, James H., "The 1885 Montreal Smallpox Epidemic." In *The Canadian Encyclopedia*. Historica Canada. Article published Apr. 02, 2013; Last Edited Jan. 25, 2019. https://www.thecanadianencyclopedia.ca/en/article/ plague-the-red-death-strikes-montreal-feature.

[135] Myall, James. "Fear, Prejudice and Vaccinations." *Bangor Daily News* blog. May 1, 2019.

CHAPTER 10: FINDING A CAUSE, WRITING THE RULES

[136] In the early days of sport, a *goal* was considered a *game*. The term *game* was used for a point in several British-based sports, and is still used today in tennis.

[137] Bogert, Beverley. "Ice Hockey." *Outing Magazine.* V. 21. P. 253-4.

[138] "The Rinks." *The Montreal Gazette.* Mar. 19, 1879. P. 4.

[139] "Our City Government." *The Montreal Gazette.* Dec. 28, 1878. P. 4.

[140] An interesting aside, Woods would be the only person in our story, besides Phil Ross, still interested in hockey when it turned professional. A travelling salesman for Hodgson, Sumner and Company, he did so well in Ottawa that he eventually settled there and started the Woods Manufacturing Company. His company had offices in every major Canadian city, and Woods' goal was to supply everything needed by prospectors, lumbermen and surveyors,

from underwear to snowshoes. Woods became renown for supplying Richard Byrd's 1928 Antarctic campaign and Francis Younghusband's sponsored 1921 attempt at climbing Mt. Everest. At the time of his death in 1930, Woods was a director for the Ottawa Auditorium, home of the Ottawa Senators. Source: *The Ottawa Journal.* Dec. 20, 1930. P. 7.

141 "Hockey. New Rules for the Regulation of the Game." *Montreal Gazette.* Jan. 8, 1886. Page 8.

142 "Hockey." *The Montreal Daily Herald.* Jan. 8, 1886. P. 1.

143 "Hockey. New Rules for the Regulation of the Game." *Montreal Gazette.* Jan. 8, 1886. Page 8. All rules in block quotes may be referred to this endnote.

144 NHL Official Rules. 2018–19. As published by the National Hockey League, 2018. All references to NHL current rules may be referenced to this endnote. For recommended further reading: Fyffe, Iain: *On His Own Side of the Puck* (2014).

145 Fitsell, J. W. "Hockey Captains, Colonels and Kings." 1987: Ontario: Boston Mills Press. p. 34.

146 Bogert, Beverley. "Ice Hockey." *Outing Magazine.* V. 21. P. 253.

147 *Ibid,* p. 253.

148 Fitsell, J. W. "Hockey Captains, Colonels and Kings." 1987: Ontario: Boston Mills Press. p. 34..

149 Bogert, Beverley. "Ice Hockey." *Outing Magazine.* V. 21. P. 253.

150 "Note and Comment." *The Montreal Gazette.* Jan. 6, 1886. P. 8.

CHAPTER 11: THE FIRST SEASON

151 "Opening of the Great Hockey Tournament." *Montreal Daily Herald.* Jan. 16, 1886. Page 1.

152 *Ibid.*

153 *Montreal Gazette.* Sports and Pastimes. Note and Comment. Jan. 25, 1886. Page 8.

154 *Montreal Gazette.* Hockey. A Manly Letter. The Referee Speaks Out—A Sensible Opinion. Jan. 28, 1886. Page 8.

155 *Ibid.*

156 *Ibid.*

157 Hockey. "MAAA vs. Crystal Rink." *The Montreal Gazette.* Feb. 23, 1886. P. 8.

158 Ice polo was a game similar to hockey. Seven players were on a team, although some leagues allowed six by mutual agreement. Onside play was not enforced. A short stick, similar to a field hockey stick today, was used. Although different rules were used, hockey skills translated well. Ottawa goalie William O'Dell, for one, moved to St. Paul, Minnesota, and tended goal for the local ice polo team.

[159] "The Snow Shoe Club Concert." *The Burlington (Vt.) Free Press and Times*. Feb. 26, 1886. P. 8.

[160] "Our Laurels Won." *The Burlington Free Press and Times*. Feb. 27, 1886. P. 8.

[161] "Hockey. Crystals vs. MAAA." *Montreal Gazette*. Mar. 6, 1886. P. 8.

[162] "The End of the Great Hockey Tournament." *The Montreal Herald and Daily Commercial Gazette*. Mar. 6, 1886. P. 5.

[163] "Hockey. Quebec vs. Crystal—Match for the Championship." *The Montreal Gazette*. Mar. 20, 1886. P. 8.

CHAPTER 12: BRANDING

[164] "Hockey. Formation of a Dominion Association." *Montreal Gazette*. Dec. 9, 1886. P. 8.

[165] *Ibid.*

[166] *Ibid.*

[167] *Ibid.*

[168] "Hockey in Ontario." *The Dominion Illustrated Monthly*. Mar. 1893. pp. 99-100.

[169] *Ibid.*

[170] *Ibid.*

[171] Ontario Hockey Association. *The Montreal Gazette*. Dec 3, 1891. Page 8.

[172] Montreal Amateur Athletic Association, Minute Book No. 2, Jan. 1886–Dec. 1888. Page 107, 109.

[173] "Hockey. A Rough Match." *The Montreal Gazette*. Jan. 15, 1887. P. 8.

[174] "Hockey. A Good Game." *The Montreal Gazette*. Jan. 22, 1887. P. 8.

[175] "The Skating Rinks." *The Montreal Gazette*. Feb. 8, 1887. P. 8.

[176] "Hockey. The First Match." *The Montreal Gazette*. Feb. 22, 1887. P. 8.

[177] "Hockey. Still Champions." *The Montreal Gazette*. Feb. 25, 1887. P. 8.

[178] Andy Shearer was the father of Norma and Douglas, the first siblings to win Academy Awards. Norma won best actress for *The Divorcee*, while Douglas won seven Oscars for his pioneering sound technology. In *The Film Encyclopedia*, Ephraim Katz (2001, New York: HarperCollins, p. 1247) states that "during his more than 40 years with MGM (Douglas) contributed more than any other man in Hollywood to the perfection of motion picture sound."

[179] "Hockey. The Crystals Win." *The Montreal Gazette*. Mar. 12, 1887. P. 8.

[180] Kitchen, Paul. "Win, Tie, Or Wrangle." Manotick, Ontario: Penumba Press. 2008. P. 15-16.

CHAPTER 13: THE EMERGENCY BIRTH OF THE PLAYOFFS

[181] "Hockey. Canadian Hockey Association." *The Montreal Gazette.* Nov 10, 1887. Page 8.

[182] *Ibid.*

[183] "Hockey. The Series Dates." *The Montreal Gazette.* Dec 14, 1887. Page 8. A series schedule, which is in common use today, is when it is agreed that each team plays its opponents a set number of times. In this case, it was agreed to play each opponent once at "home" and once "away."

[184] "Hockey. The Championship Series." *The Montreal Gazette.* Mar. 14, 1888. P. 8.

[185] "The Hockey Championships." *The Montreal Gazette.* Mar. 16, 1888. P. 8.

CHAPTER 14: LORD AND LADY STANLEY ATTEND THE CARNIVAL

[186] "Shooting at the Carnival." *The Montreal Gazette.* Jan. 7, 1889. P. 8.

[187] "Hockey. Montreal vs. Crystal." *The Montreal Gazette.* Jan. 19, 1889. P. 8.

[188] The legal pass in hockey was the equivalent of a lateral on a kickoff return for American football. The player receiving the pass or lateral must be behind the player sending the pass. In hockey, play was stopped but there was no penalty.

[189] "The Champions at Hockey." *The Montreal Gazette.* Feb. 4, 1889. P. 8.

[190] "Montreal's Carnival." *The Boston Daily Globe.* Feb. 5, 1889. Page 8.

[191] "The Ice Palace." *The Montreal Gazette.* Feb. 5, 1889. P. 8.

[192] "Carnival! Opening of the Castle." *The Montreal Witness.* Feb. 5, 1889. P. 8.

[193] A bully predates the faceoff. The puck was placed on the middle of the ice, and each player tapped the ice then his opponent's stick. After the third tap, the puck was free to whomever could take it.

[194] "Hockey. A Grand Game at the Victoria Rink." *The Montreal Gazette.* Feb. 5, 1889. P. 8.

[195] "The Coming Winter Game (By One Who Plays It)." *The Pall Mall Gazette* (London, Eng.). Oct. 4, 1889. P. 3.

[196] "Hockey. A Grand Game at the Victoria Rink." *The Montreal Gazette.* Feb. 5, 1889. P. 8.

[197] "Skating Hockey. A Rattling Game in the Victoria." *The Montreal Witness.* Feb. 5, 1889. P. 4.

[198] *Ottawa Journal.* Aug. 28, 1889. P. 4.

CHAPTER 15: THE SAME, OLD, BORING CHAMPIONS

[199] "Two Very Speedy Skaters." *The Montreal Gazette.* Feb. 19, 1889. P. 8.

[200] "Hockey. The Halifax Club Coming." *The Montreal Gazette.* Feb. 23, 1889. P. 8.

[201] "Haligonians at Hockey." *The Montreal Gazette.* Feb. 26, 1889. P. 8.

[202] "Chebuctos vs. Crystals." *The Montreal Gazette.* Feb. 28, 1889. P. 8.

[203] "The MAAA Champions." *The Montreal Gazette*. Mar. 2, 1889. P. 8.

[204] "Hockey." *The Montreal Gazette.* Mar. 13, 1889. P. 8.

[205] The Canadian Hockey Convention. *The Montreal Gazette*. Nov. 23, 1889. Page 8.

[206] "Montreal Defeats Quebec." *The Montreal Gazette.* Jan. 8, 1890. P. 8.

[207] "Hockey. Montreal vs. Victorias at the Dominion Rink." *The Montreal Gazette.* Feb. 19, 1890. P. 8.

[208] *Ibid.*

[209] "Hockey. The Champions Defeat the Dominions after a Stubborn Game." *The Montreal Herald.* Feb. 26, 1890. P. 8

[210] "Hockey. Montreal vs. Dominion." *The Montreal Gazette*. Feb. 26, 1890. P. 8.

CHAPTER 16: THE NOT REALLY NEEDED STANLEY CUP

[211] Quebec Vital and Church Records (Drouin Collection), p. 20.

[212] "The Ottawas Champions. Montreal Hockey Team Defeated by Four Goals to Three." *The Montreal Gazette.* Jan. 9, 1892. P. 8.

[213] There were no goal nets in those days. Like lacrosse, two six-foot flag poles, six feet apart, marked the goals.

[214] "We Are the People, Now. The Ottawa Men Get Some New Ideas About Hockey." *The Montreal Gazette*. Mar. 8, 1892. P. 8.

[215] *Passenger Lists of Vessels Arriving at New York, New York, 1820–1897.* Microfilm Publication M237, 675 rolls. NAI: 6256867. Records of the US Customs Service, Record Group 36. National Archives at Washington, DC. Year: 1904; Arrival: New York, New York; Microfilm Serial: T715, 1897–1957; Microfilm Roll: Roll 0522; Line: 1; Page Number: 1.

[216] "The Hockey Champions." *The Ottawa Journal.* May 20, 1892. P. 4.

[217] "Lord Stanley Promises to Give a Championship Cup." *The Montreal Gazette.* Mar. 19, 1892. P. 8.

[218] Letter from Philip S. Ross to Philip D. Ross, Dec. 18, 1897. Located in the P. D. Ross files at the Canadian National Archives.

[219] Letter from C. C. Ross to Philip D. Ross. Located in the P. D. Ross files at the Canadian National Archives. Billy and Willie were the same person, just referred differently by the parents.

[220] Schedule For the Season. *Ottawa Daily Citizen.* Dec. 16, 1892. P. 5.

[221] *Ibid.*

[222] "Hockey: Ottawa Has A League." *The Montreal Gazette.* Dec. 19, 1892. p. 2.

[223] "Hockey Men Are Ready." *The Montreal Gazette.* Nov 5, 1892. P. 8.

[224] "Sporting Miscellany." *The Detroit Free Press.* Feb. 5, 1893. P. 6.

[225] "It Was Fast Hockey." *The Ottawa Journal.* Feb. 14, 1893. P. 4.

[226] Cricket greaves were a piece of armor to protect the shins. These were made of a harder material than the shin pads the other players wore.

[227] A legitimite criticism of using newspapers as source material is validated with this statement. Several sources must be used to try to figure out what actually happened when the people who witnessed left no other records. Why this sentence? The article for the game in the *Ottawa Daily Citizen* on Mar. 4, 1893, simply stated this: "A despatch (sic) from Montreal states the hockey match that was to have taken place between the Montreal and Crystals was forfeited to the Montrealers." The match was actually played.

[228] "Montreal vs. Crystals." *The Montreal Gazette.* Mar. 4, 1893. P. 8.

[229] "Those Hockey Protests." *The Montreal Gazette*. Mar. 13, 1893. P. 2.

[230] *Ibid.*

[231] *Ibid.*

[232] "Playing with the Puck." *The Montreal Gazette.* Mar. 11, 1893. P. 8.

[233] "Protests Are Thrown Out." *The Montreal Gazette.* Mar. 14, 1893. P. 8.

[234] Diary of Philip Ross. Located in Canadian National Archives. Philip Dansken Ross fonds MG30-98. Container 3.

CHAPTER 17: THE POWER STRUGGLE

[235] Bogert, Beverley. "Ice Hockey." *Outing Magazine.* V. 21. p. 254-6.

[236] Rogers, Charles Gordon. "A Hockey Song." The Dominion Illustrated Monthly. Vol. 2, No. 2 (Mar. 1893), p. 109.

[237] Montreal Amateur Athletic Association, MG 28, I 351, Vol. 1 File 4, Minute Book No. 4, Sept. 1891–Oct. 1893. Page 305-307.

[238] "The Stanley Cup." *The Ottawa Journal.* May 1, 1893. P. 5.

[239] Montreal Amateur Athletic Association, MG 28, I 351, Vol. 1 File 4, Minute Book No. 4, Sept. 1891–Oct. 1893. Page 311-312.

[240] Montreal Amateur Athletic Association, MG 28, I 351, Vol. 1 File 4, Minute Book No. 4, Sept. 1891–Oct. 1893. Page 315-6.

[241] Ancestry family tree website, accessed Nov. 1, 2019. https://www. ancestry. com/family-tree/person/tree/54411452/person/27100462986/story.

[242] Montreal Amateur Athletic Association, MG 28, I 351, Vol. 2 File 1, Minute Book No. 5, Oct. 1893–May 1897. Pages 30-1.

[243] Montreal Amateur Athletic Association, MG 28, I 351, Vol. 6 File 1, Montreal Hockey Club Minute Book, Nov. 1893–Nov. 1901. Pages 3-6.

[244] Montreal Amateur Athletic Association, MG 28, I 351, Vol. 2 File 1, Minute Book No. 5, Oct. 1893–May 1897. Pages 32-3.

[245] "The Stanley Cup." *The Ottawa Journal.* May 1, 1893. P. 5.

[246] Montreal Amateur Athletic Association, MG 28, I 351, Vol. 6 File 1, Montreal Hockey Club Minute Book, Nov. 1893–Nov. 1901. Page 2.

[247] Montreal Amateur Athletic Association, MG 28, I 351, Vol. 2 File 1, Minute Book No. 5, Oct. 1893–May 1897. Page 33-4.

[248] Montreal Amateur Athletic Association, MG 28, I 351, Vol. 6 File 1, Montreal Hockey Club Minute Book, Nov. 1893–Nov. 1901. Page 7.

[249] Montreal Amateur Athletic Association, MG 28, I 351, Vol. 2 File 1, Minute Book No. 5, Oct. 1893–May 1897. Pages 36-7.

[250] "Hockey Association Meeting." *The Quebec Daily Telegraph.* Dec. 14, 1893. P. 3.

[251] Montreal Amateur Athletic Association, MG 28, I 351, Vol. 6 File 1, Montreal Hockey Club Minute Book, Nov. 1893–Nov. 1901. Page 11.

[252] "Montreal Defeats Quebec." *The Montreal Gazette.* Jan. 6, 1894. P. 6.

[253] Montreal Amateur Athletic Association, MG 28, I 351, Vol. 6 File 1, Montreal Hockey Club Minute Book, Nov. 1893–Nov. 1901. Page 11-2.

[254] "Ottawa Hockey Men on Top." *The Montreal Gazette.* Jan. 29, 1894. P. 5.

[255] "The Montrealers Turned Down." *The Ottawa Evening Journal.* Jan. 29, 1894. P. 5.

[256] So far as we can tell, this was the first career-ending injury in hockey history.

[257] "Ottawas Colors Lowered." *The Ottawa Daily Citizen.* Feb. 26, 1894. P. 5

[258] Montreal Amateur Athletic Association, MG 28, I 351, Vol. 6 File 1, Montreal Hockey Club Minute Book, Nov. 1893–Nov. 1901. Page 13.

[259] Montreal Amateur Athletic Association, MG 28, I 351, Vol. 2 File 1, Minute Book No. 5, Oct. 1893–May 1897. Page 77.

[260] "Trouble for Hockeyists." *The Montreal Gazette.* Mar. 12, 1894. P. 8.

[261] "Montrealers Victorious." *The Montreal Gazette.* Mar. 19, 1894. P. 8.

[262] See "The Hockey Cup Goes to Montreal." *The Ottawa Journal.* Mar 24, 1894. P. 1. and "Montreal The Champion." *The Montreal Gazette.* P. 8.

[263] Montreal Amateur Athletic Association, MG 28, I 351, Vol. 6 File 1, Montreal Hockey Club Minute Book, Nov. 1893–Nov. 1901. Page 15-6.

[264] Montreal Amateur Athletic Association, MG 28, I 351, Vol. 6 File 1, Montreal Hockey Club Minute Book, Nov. 1893–Nov. 1901. Page 17.

CHAPTER 18: FIGHTING

[265] Montreal Amateur Athletic Association, MG 28, I 351, Vol. 2 File 1, Minute Book No. 5, Oct. 1893–May 1897. Page 105.

266 Montreal Amateur Athletic Association, MG 28, I 351, Vol. 6 File 1, Montreal Hockey Club Minute Book, Nov. 1893–Nov. 1901. Page 17.

267 Montreal Amateur Athletic Association, MG 28, I 351, Vol. 2 File 1, Minute Book No. 5, Oct. 1893–May 1897. Page 105-6.

268 Montreal Amateur Athletic Association, MG 28, I 351, Vol. 2 File 1, Minute Book No. 5, Oct. 1893–May 1897. Page 111.

269 Montreal Amateur Athletic Association, MG 28, I 351, Vol. 6 File 1, Montreal Hockey Club Minute Book, Nov. 1893–Nov. 1901. Page 18-20.

270 Montreal Amateur Athletic Association, MG 28, I 351, Vol. 2 File 1, Minute Book No. 5, Oct. 1893–May 1897. Page 125-6.

271 Montreal Amateur Athletic Association, MG 28, I 351, Vol. 2 File 1, Minute Book No. 5, Oct. 1893–May 1897. Page 131.

272 Montreal Amateur Athletic Association, MG 28, I 351, Vol. 6 File 1, Montreal Hockey Club Minute Book, Nov. 1893–Nov. 1901. Page 21.

273 "Shamrock Hockey Club Formed." *The Ottawa Journal.* Nov. 17, 1894. P. 1.

274 "The Quebecs Sustained." *The Ottawa Daily Citizen.* Feb. 11, 1895. P. 5.

275 Montreal Amateur Athletic Association, MG 28, I 351, Vol. 6 File 1, Montreal Hockey Club Minute Book, Nov. 1893–Nov. 1901. Page 25.

276 Montreal Amateur Athletic Association, MG 28, I 351, Vol. 6 File 1, Montreal Hockey Club Minute Book, Nov. 1893–Nov. 1901. Page 27.

277 Montreal Amateur Athletic Association, MG 28, I 351, Vol. 6 File 1, Montreal Hockey Club Minute Book, Nov. 1893–Nov. 1901. Page 26.

278 "Something about Hockey." *The Montreal Gazette.* Dec. 29, 1894. P. 8.

279 "Hockey. The Americans Defeated." *The Montreal Gazette.* Jan. 1, 1895. P. 8.

280 Montreal Amateur Athletic Association, MG 28, I 351, Vol. 6 File 1, Montreal Hockey Club Minute Book, Nov. 1893–Nov. 1901. Page 28.

281 "Crystals Defeat Quebec." *The Montreal Gazette.* Feb. 4, 1895. P. 5.

282 The full names of the Crystal-Shamrock team were: James White, goal; James McDonnell, point; Frank Stephens, cover; Bob Wall, Dave Brown, Willie Fairbairn and Stewart MacQuisten, forwards. The full names of the Crystal-Crystals were: Herb Lyons, goal; Charles Ulley, cover; George Boon, point; William Murray and Walter Laing, forwards. The first names of Crystal-Crystals forwards Hull and Jones are unknown.

283 "The Quebecs Sustained." *The Ottawa Daily Citizen.* Feb. 11, 1895. P. 5.

284 "Crystal-Shamrock Mix." *The Ottawa Journal.* Feb. 11, 1895. P. 1. Full details are the meeting are presented in "That Muddle in Hockey." *The Montreal Gazette.* Feb. 11, 1895. P. 5. Some notes in this section are combined from the two sources. First names were researched from the Montreal City Directory as both sources misidentified some of the participants, as well as the Society for International Hockey Research database and the 1891 and 1901 Canadian censuses.

[285] "That Muddle in Hockey." *The Montreal Gazette.* Feb. 11, 1895. P. 5. It's a long article, nearly half of the page. This section comes from near the end of the article, third column.

[286] "Hockey. Won by Winnipeg's Victorias." *The Montreal Gazette.* Feb. 5, 1895. P. 8.

[287] Montreal Amateur Athletic Association, MG 28, I 351, Vol. 6 File 1, Montreal Hockey Club Minute Book, Nov. 1893–Nov. 1901. Page 33.

[288] "Things Are Changed." *The Ottawa Evening Journal.* Feb. 18, 1895. P. 5.

[289] Montreal Amateur Athletic Association, MG 28, I 351, Vol. 6 File 1, Montreal Hockey Club Minute Book, Nov. 1893–Nov. 1901. Page 35.

[290] "The Victors Victorious." *The Montreal Gazette.* Feb. 25, 1895. P. 6.

[291] Minute Book No. 5, Montrel Amateur Athletic Association, MG 28, I 351, Vol. 2, File 1. Pages 247-8.

[292] "Victoria Defeat Ottawa." *The Montreal Gazette.* Mar. 4, 1895. P. 6.

[293] "Hockey Men Kept Busy." *The Montreal Gazette.* Mar. 4, 1895. P. 6.

[294] "Funeral of 'Joe' Laing." *The Montreal Gazette.* Apr. 29, 1895. P. 3.

CHAPTER 19: USING THE TRAIN TO GROW THE GAME

[295] Montreal Amateur Athletic Association, MG 28, I 351, Vol. 6 File 1, Montreal Hockey Club Minute Book, Nov. 1893–Nov. 1901. Pages 39-41.

[296] "Past and Present. The Present Team Beat the Past Champions." *The Montreal Gazette.* Mar. 4, 1896. Page. 2.

[297] "Hockey. The Canadian Game Likely to Boom in New York." *The Montreal Gazette*. Jan. 7, 1896. P. 5. Article originally appeared in *New York World.*

[298] In case the reader is interested, here is where the story can be found. Conover, Juliana. "The Little Corporals." *Harper's Round Table.* Feb 18, 1896. Vol. XVII, No. 851.

[299] "Canadian Hockey Players." *The Baltimore Sun.* Mar. 9, 1896. P. 6.

[300] Kelly, John. "We May Be Champions Now, But Hockey Got Off to a Rough Start in Washington." *The Washington Post.* June 11, 2018.

[301] "Game of Hockey Giants." *Washington [DC] Times.* Mar. 8, 1896. P. 7.

[302] "Wonderful Hockey Play." *The Baltimore Sun.* Mar 10, 1896. P. 6.

[303] "A Tie Game at Hockey." *The New York Times.* Mar. 11, 1896. P. 6.

[304] "Hockey." *The New York Sun.* Mar. 12, 1896. P. 4.

[305] "The Victorias Defeat the Montrealers Five to Two." *The Montreal Gazette.* Mar 23, 1896. P. 6.

[306] Montreal Amateur Athletic Association, MG 28, I 351, Vol. 6 File 1, Montreal Hockey Club Minute Book, Nov. 1893–Nov. 1901. Page 49.

CHAPTER 20: LEAVING THE PAST BEHIND

[307] "Hockey in the Canadian North-West." *The Canadian Magazine*. Jan. 1896. P. 242-7.

[308] Advertisement in *The Winnipeg Tribune.* Mar. 12, 1902. P. 5.

[309] "All Is Ready for Tonight." *The Winnipeg Tribune.* Mar. 13, 1902. P. 1.

[310] "Montreal Won on Saturday." *The Winnipeg Tribune.* Mar. 17, 1902. P. 5.

[311] "Well, the Cup Is Going East." *The Winnipeg Tribune.* Mar. 18, 1902. P. 3.

[312] MacDonald, D. A. L. "Turning Back Hockey's Pages." *The Montreal Gazette.* Jan. 22, 1935. P. 12.

[313] For details on how Norris came to own the Detroit Red Wings, please see my earlier book, *Deceptions and Doublecross: How the NHL Conquered Hockey*. There is some question whether the historical legend of the Red Wings is truth or myth. Norris never bothered changing the name of the Shamrocks, his earlier hockey club. And with Norris Grain shipping regularly to Minneapolis, it would be no surprise to know that Norris knew about Red Wing, Minnesota, a wheat-growing town about fifty-five miles southeast along the Mississippi River. The Detroit Red Wing logo looks fairly similar to the Red Wing Shoe Company as well as the Red Wing Stoneware and Pottery logos, both of which long predate the hockey club, with a Cadillac tire placed in front. And perhaps as a jab at Chicago Blackhawks founder Frederic McLaughlin, with whom Norris battled when he owned the Shamrocks, the town of Red Wing was named after the nineteenth-century Dakota Chief Red Wing, who was an ally of British solidiers during the War of 1812. The Blackhawks were named after a military unit that McLaughlin claimed to have commanded during World War I, which in turn took its name from the Sauk Nation chief. The Dakotas and Sauk often squabbled.

[314] "Many Saw Games." *The Montreal Gazette.* Mar. 2, 1903. P. 2. The actual numbers: 1902 League: 26,126. 1903: 25,315. One game in 1903 was not played. Stanley Cup matches, 1903: Game One—3,637; Game Two—4,820; Game Three—5,127; Game Four—4,282.

[315] "Is Not Finished." *The Montreal Gazette.* Feb. 2, 1903. P. 2.

[316] "Have Had Too Much Hockey." *The Ottawa Journal.* Feb. 27, 1903. P. 10.

[317] "Hockey Change Promised." *The Ottawa Journal.* Oct. 28, 1903. P. 1

[318] Montreal Amateur Athletic Association, MG 28, I 351, Vol. 6 File 2, Montreal Hockey Club Minute Book, Nov. 1901–Nov. 1906. Image 596.

[319] "Vics Were Strong and Won Out With an Odd Number." *The Montreal Gazette.* Feb. 21, 1901. P. 2.

[320] "Trouble in Montreal Hockey." *The Ottawa Journal.* Feb. 22, 1901. P. 9.

CHAPTER 21: THE DEATH OF TOM PATON

[321] "Victoria Well Off." *The Montreal Gazette.* Nov. 13, 1908. P. 2

[322] Ross, P. D. "Says Semi-Professionalism is Only Solution of Difficulty, *The Winnipeg Tribune.* Dec. 18, 1905. P. 8.

[323] *Ibid.*

[324] "Montreal Resigns." *The Montreal Gazette.* Nov. 16, 1908. P. 2.

[325] Zweig, Eric. *Art Ross*. Toronto: Dundurn. 2015. P. 84-86.

[326] "Montreal Resigns." *The Montreal Gazette.* Nov. 16, 1908. P. 2.

[327] "Cup for Amateurs." *The Montreal Gazette.* Feb. 20, 1909. P. 2.

[328] "Mr. T. L. Paton Dead." *The Montreal Gazette.* Feb. 11, 1909. P. 9.

[329] "With the Curlers." *The Montreal Gazette.* Feb. 11, 1909. P. 2.

[330] Montreal Amateur Athletic Association, MG 28, I 351, Vol. 2 File 4, Montreal Hockey Club Minute Book 8, Sept. 1907–Jan. 1910. Page 277.

[331] "Obituary Record." *The Montreal Gazette.* Feb. 13, 1909. P. 6.

[332] Year: *1910*; Census Place: *Elma, Chehalis, Washington*; Roll: *T624_1654*; Page: *8B*; Enumeration District: *0035*; FHL microfilm: *1375667*

CHAPTER 22: BECOMING AMERICAN

[333] Montreal Amateur Athletic Association, MG 28, I 351, Vol. 6 File 1, Montreal Hockey Club Minute Book, Nov. 1893 to Nov. 1901. Page 39.

[334] The National Archives at Washington, DC; Washington, DC; *Passenger & Crew Lists of Vessels Arriving at Ketchikan, Alaska.*; Record Group Title: *Records of the Immigration and Naturalization Service, 1787–2004*; Record Group Number: *85.*

[335] The National Archives at Seattle; Seattle, Washington; ARC Title: *Petitions for Naturalization, 1890–1991*; NAI Number: *592779*; Record Group Title: *Records of District Courts of the United States, 1685-2009*; Record Group Number: *21*

[336] Washington Petitions for Naturalization, 1860–1991, 3604-P-30810.

[337] "Passing Regretted of Ms. P. D. Ross." *The Ottawa Citizen.* Dec. 8, 1943. P. 1.

[338] Newspapers searched included the *Seattle Post-Intelligencer*, *Seattle Times* and *Seattle Star.*

[339] Death certificate of James A. Stewart, issued by the Washington State Department of Health. State File No. 5673. Registrar's Number: 5822.

[340] "Capitol Hill's transitional homes offer second chances." Capitol Hill Seattle Blog. Posted July 17, 2012. https://www.capitolhillseattle.com/2012/07 / capitol-hills-transitional-homes-offer-second-chances/.

CHAPTER 23: THE AUTHOR'S FINAL THOUGHTS

No project like this is a solo project, but this doesn't even start without the blessings of my wife, Annette, and family, for allowing me to spend several thousand hours researching and writing during the past twenty years.

Thanks are in order to the following who helped guide me on the path:

Philip Holzman, D'Arcy Jenish, James Milks, Paul Patskou, Kevin Shea, Todd Denault, Andrew Ross, Michel Vigneault, Jean-Patrice Martel, Iain Fyffe, Dan Mason, Craig Bowlsby, Jeff Obermeyer, Lenard Kotylo.

The cover photo comes courtesy of the website HockeyGods.com, who found it in the public domain from the Canadian National Archives.

Craig Campbell at the Doc Seaman Resource Centre of the Hockey Hall of Fame, for his assistance in pointing out various publications and scrapbooks. Also for help in providing photos of the people's trophy, aka the Stanley Cup

Special thanks to Eric Zweig, the most knowledgeable hockey historian I know. Eric agreed to review my text – which as a general rule, he doesn't like to do – agreed to send me a few paragraphs of his impressions, and sent me five pages of notes.

I owe a debt of gratitude to Prof. Stephen Hardy, who took an academic approach in reviewing my work and research prior to publication. It's not every day that a non-graduate student can get some outstanding feedback prior to publication, so I feel blessed and grateful for Prof. Hardy's efforts and suggestions – most of which I took and implemented.

Thanks to Bill Fitsell, for sharing his lifetime work and card catalogue of everything hockey.

Lorna Johnston of the Brockville Historical Museum, for her time and assistance, as well as the staff at the Brockville Public Library and the Brockville Public Cemetery.

The staff of Riverton Crest Cemetary in Tukwila for escorting my son and I to Jimmy Stewart's final resting place so we can pay our respects.

Odd Fellows Laurel Delony (Grand Lodge of Washington) and John Nichols (Grand Lodge of Ontario) for doing the monotonous work of researching their archives.

The fabulous editing job was done by Stacey K., known as Grammargal at Fiverr. The wonderful cover was done by Rose Miller, and the colorization of the cover photo was done by Gabriel, known as nemoxx on Fiverr.

The Society for International Hockey Researchers have a dedicated group of hockey lovers who have stepped in where organizations such as the NHL, the NHLPA and the various alumni associations have failed to promote and record the sport's long history. If you are interested in contributing, please Google them and join. I've been proud of my association with SIHR for nearly twenty years

And James Stewart, thank you for your gift and courage. The "other" Jimmy Stewart might have given us the enduring movie *It's a Wonderful Life*, but you gave us something better to look forward to each Christmas – a wonderful game.

The late comedian George Carlin once explained hockey as three simultaneous events happening all at one: "ice skating, playing with a puck, and beating the shit out of somebody." Thanks to Jimmy Stewart, Carlin was not wrong.

INDEX

An italicized page number indicates a photo.